608

THATCHER'S KINGDOM

THATCHER'S KINGDOM

A View of Britain in the Eighties

MARGARET JONES

Collins

*To Britain, a country with which, despite
many ups and downs, I have an enduring
love affair*

Acknowledgments and thanks are due to the *Sydney Morning Herald* for permission to use material which originally appeared in the *Herald*.

© Margaret Jones, 1984

First published in 1984 by William Collins Pty Ltd, Sydney
Typeset by Setrite Typesetters, Hong Kong
Printed by Dominion Press, Hedges & Bell, Victoria
Design by Deborah Johnston

National Library of Australia
Cataloguing-in-Publication data

Jones, Margaret.
    Thatcher's Kingdom.

    Includes index.
    ISBN 0 00 217301 8.

    1. Great Britain — Social life and customs —
    1945-   I. Title.

941.085'8

CONTENTS

CHAPTER ONE

THE THREE REVOLUTIONS

I first came to Britain in 1956: a dangerous year for the world, the year of Suez and of the Hungarian rising. It was also the year in which the British social revolution, quietly fermented over the years by working-class novelists and playwrights, came to a head and exploded in the public's face. A new piece of social terminology—Angry Young Man—came into the language, and retired colonels in Cheltenham went barking mad at this furious working-class assault on privilege.

This was the first of the three social revolutions I was to witness over the next twenty-five years.

But in the grey spring of 1956, to a young Australian arriving in Britain, the traditional values seemed to be holding fast. In those now ancient days, before cheap air fares, most new arrivals travelled by ship, and the length of the voyage gently cushioned the culture shock. And in those days I also entered as of right, for my passport bore the magic words 'British citizen'. Today I must have a work permit to come into the country, and I must report yearly to the Home Office in its hellish anterooms at Croydon, waiting endlessly on hard benches with rows of patient Indians and Hong Kong Chinese. (Not all Austra-

1

lians have got used to this changed state of affairs. A middle-aged acquaintance of mine was asked by a very young immigration officer at Heathrow how long he intended to stay in Britain. He replied 'None of your business, sonny,' and, taking back his passport, walked unchecked through the barrier.)

In 1956, Britain looked prosperous enough. The shortages of the immediate postwar years had become a bad memory, and the welfare state, only a decade old, had the bloom of idealism still clinging to it.

The parks were full of daffodils, and Earls Court was full of young colonials coughing their lungs out in the filthy smogs which still occasionally smothered London. The Clean Air Act had not yet taken effect, and the glowing Portland stone of churches and monuments lurked unsuspected under the rich black patina of centuries of muck.

Old traditions held the nation in their grip. Women wore twin sets and pearls, there was still a Season, and homburgs and bowlers were standard sightings on the City-bound Tube. The *Times* had classified ads on its front page, and it recorded each year the appearance of the first cuckoo. In the personal column, anonymous supplicants gave thanks to St Jude for his intervention with the Almighty, and there were annual tributes to Richard III, 'king and martyr, foully slain at Bosworth Field'.

Struggling to make a living as a freelance, I wrote a lyrical piece for the *Times*. It was called 'The Stranger's Eye' and itemized the small delights of London—among them, the practice of serving tea at afternoon theatre performances, with trays brought to one's seat by waitresses in black dresses and frilly aprons.

That was my downfall. When I went back to suggest another piece, I was told that I was not sufficiently assimilated into the English scene to become a *Times* contributor.

What was my offence? I asked nervously.

It was those damned waitresses and their pots of tea.

'*Times* readers do not have tea brought to their seats in

the theatre,' the *Times* lady said severely. 'That is a very lower middle-class thing to do. *Times* readers drink a gin-and-tonic in the bar at interval.' So came my first initiation into English class rituals.

The *Times* undoubtedly wouldn't have approved of Lyons Corner Houses either, but they were a godsend for those of us who were young and poor and too unsophisticated to discover obscure trattorias in Soho. Stuffing ourselves with stodgy English food to the strains of a Palm Court orchestra made us forget the mournful rain, the freezing bathrooms and the shilling-in-the-slot gas fires.

Lyons had their own rules, which were just as rigid as the *Times'* code of conduct. We were having dinner one night at a Corner House near Piccadilly Circus when the Scottish waitress suddenly snatched the menu away and substituted another. Fearful, we looked at the prices—only to find that they were lower. 'Och, I'm sorry, luv,' the waitress said. 'I gave you the one with the high prices. We keep it specially for the whoors.'

Out in the street, the tarts paraded, and joking Cockneys presided over stalls of whelks and jellied eels. There were a number of black faces about, but they mainly seemed to belong to jolly bus conductors, and no one took much notice. Enoch Powell's vision of the Tiber foaming with much blood was still in the future.

On the surface, then, it was very much as I expected; but there were a few jarring shocks. In 1956 I took part in my first political demonstration. It was a traumatic experience for someone coming from a country where street protest had not been seen since World War I. Children of the Sixties and Seventies, who drank protest in with their mothers' milk, would find it hard to understand how heady and how frightening it felt, as part of a huge crowd howling for blood.

In this case, the blood was Anthony Eden's, and the demonstration was the massive anti-Suez protest which helped to cut short his political career.

That Sunday afternoon I learned another useful lesson: that passion and violence stirred behind the bland and often impassive British mask.

I was swept along to Downing Street by an enormous mass of bodies and a great, baying noise, half-alarming, half-intoxicating, which resolved itself into a chant of 'Eden must go! Eden must go!' I found myself shouting like the rest; and confronting—for the first but not the last time—the famous line of tall British bobbies who moved remorselessly forward, arms linked. Those were the days before riot shields, plastic baton rounds and tear gas, but the head-down charge of the implacable blue line was effective enough.

Later, they brought in police horses and things got rougher. I was backed into a doorway by a mounted policeman and trapped there, while strings of foam from the horse's mouth dripped onto my face. Like the rest of the demonstrators, I ended the day running for my life up Whitehall while the horses charged.

For me, it was a new and very unexpected view of Britain. In the summer of 1982, reporting the Falklands war, I remembered the turbulent days of the anti-Suez protests, and speculated on why there was no comparable public outcry against the sending of a war armada to the South Atlantic.

Another very significant event in 1956 passed at first almost unnoticed. John Osborne's *Look Back in Anger* was produced by the newly-formed English Stage Company at the Royal Court and was largely ignored by the critics; but it gained notoriety by word of mouth and quickly became a public scandal.

Looking back, it is astonishing how outraged the Establishment then became over a play which did nothing but express the feelings of young working-class people, who banged on the doors of privilege with their redbrick diplomas only to find that the gates often remained implacably closed.

Osborne's Jimmy Porter was the first anti-hero, the first Angry Young Man. His ferocious dissatisfaction with the system, expressed in an unstoppable tirade, made him the voice of a whole generation. It was a voice which was to become increasingly heard, and it was announcing, though nobody then knew it, the amazing Sixties.

* * * * * *

I left Britain in 1961 and came back again in 1967. The country seemed almost unrecognizable. I had been working in North America for two years, as a correspondent in New York and in Washington, and the contrast was totally bewildering.

The United States was caught up in the late Sixties in two great traumas: the civil rights struggle, and the growing popular revolt against the Vietnam war. Life was real, life was earnest. Haircuts were short-back-and-sides. Lyndon Johnson, the doomed president, was in the White House, and on the college campuses and in the black ghettoes, rebellion was growing.

I could hardly believe it when I arrived in London and found the whole nation—or so it seemed—decked out for a hairy fancy-dress party. The Swinging Sixties had arrived, Carnaby Street and the King's Road dictated fashion, and men had rediscovered the lost delights of showy plumage.

In the street fashion show, boys in velvet, curls down to their shoulders, went by with girls who, by contrast, looked like young warriors in their brief mini-skirts and knee-high boots. 'The last days of the Roman Empire,' an old man standing beside me murmured ominously, and a good many American commentators wrote stern pieces about Britain sinking giggling beneath a sea of hedonism.

The Union Jack, once the symbol of British might, was used satirically as a design motif on everything: mugs, shopping bags, chamber pots, alarm clocks, tee-shirts.

As Britain was not involved, there were only glancing

references to the Vietnam war. As a one-person protest I bought (inevitably in Carnaby Street) a shopping bag emblazoned with the Viet Cong flag; and I gave a pint of blood for North Vietnam to a Quaker group which ran an unhygienic, do-it-yourself blood collection service in the basement of a church hall.

Slogans were 'Forget Oxfam—feed Twiggy', 'Ban the bra', and 'Scrap Polaris'. With the Beatles and the Rolling Stones, Britain had already given the world a new popular culture; and in 1967, three Liverpool poets, Adrian Henri, Roger McGough and Brian Patten, brought out a book of poems, *The Mersey Sound*, which was to become a publishing phenomenon.

It became the best selling anthology of modern British poetry ever published, and sold more than 300,000 copies. Allen Ginsberg, the most famous of the American beat poets, told the world: 'Liverpool is at the present moment the centre of consciousness of the human universe.'

Nearly twenty year later, British popular culture of the Sixties still grips the public imagination. In 1983, there was standing room only at Sothebys when Beatles and Rolling Stones memorabilia were auctioned. A Los Angeles buyer paid £8,800 for John Lennon's piano, a Japanese department store bought some hand-written Beatles' lyrics for £6,000, and Merseyside County Council spent scarce ratepayers' funds on a picture of Paul McCartney and one of his children. Now the city of Liverpool runs special tours for visitors to Beatles' sacred sites, and in May 1984 the world's first Beatles Museum was officially opened.

In London, in 1967, the Clean Air Act had done its work. Whole groups of buildings, notably the splendid complex round Trafalgar Square, had been cleaned and brought back to the state their architects intended, so that London glowed almost like an Italianate city whenever the sun shone.

When I had left Washington, Americans had commiserated with me in that earnest American way at going to live in a country that was no longer a Great Power. (This was at a time when the full atrociousness of Vietnam had not yet sunk in, and when the United States was taking its world responsibilities very seriously.)

But I found Swinging London ravishing, with its cheeky street fashions, its sparkling buildings, and its mysteriously improved weather—the infamous smogs now only a bad memory.

It took a while to realize that, as in 1956, other forces were bubbling away below the surface—particularly on the campuses of the new universities, where lecturers in sociology and political science were inciting the young to question all Establishment values. This radicalism, having been branded deep into student consciousness then, is still having its effects in British politics today.

There were some open signs of revolution: sit-ins at the London School of Economics, and a massive and violent anti-American demonstration outside the American Embassy in Grosvenor Square. Even so, the ferment of the late Sixties in Britain was mild compared to the upheavals on American campuses, or to the worker-student riots in France. In 1968, we watched with fascination on television the bloody running war between police and students on the streets of Paris. The French take naturally to the barricades; the British seem better at one-off demonstrations.

Looking back, the most revolutionary change in Britain in the Sixties was the rise of street culture. Two decades later, the highest accolade is still 'street credible' and even in fashion, the great couture houses have never regained their dominance. In 1983, half-shaven punk hairstyles with a cockatoo crest on top began on the streets and ended up, in a prettified form, on the covers of *Vogue* and *Tatler*.

* * * * * *

I spent most of the Seventies in China and in Australia, and did not come back to Britain until the summer of 1980, in time to watch the early days of the Thatcherite revolution.

Once again, I seemed to have come to a totally different country from the Britain of the Fifties and Sixties. The national catchcry was that the country was going down the drain; and the British themselves said it so often that the rest of the world had come to believe it.

Certainly London seemed much dirtier, more crowded and more rundown—though, by contrast, big provincial cities like Manchester and Glasgow had cleaned themselves up amazingly. They were no longer the dark, satanic hangovers from the Industrial Revolution which I remembered from the Fifties.

London had acquired some unfamiliar features, notably the tall, snowy Arab sheiks who stalked gravely through the parks, their bodyguards a pace behind, while their black-crow women picnicked in giggling groups on the grass. (Selfridges, these days, is always full of Arab women, veiled to the eyeballs, but converging on the underwear racks with a fanaticism which shows that things may be very different underneath the dusty black.)

For old times' sake, I took a tourist bus round London, and found that the sights were much as they always had been—with one notable exception. The bus guides now point out with pride the burnt-out shell of the Iranian Embassy in Prince's Gate. It remains to this day a testimony to the skilled ruthlessness of the SAS, who demonstrated when they lifted the siege in 1980 that their motto, 'Who dares, wins', means exactly what it says, though 'Don't count the cost' might be also applicable.

It was still too early for the country to realize it; but the breaking of the siege was also a signal given by the new Prime Minister, Margaret Thatcher, that in matters of life and death she is a pragmatist. The Provisional IRA should have taken note. Then ten young men need not have died later, in a useless hunger strike in the Maze Prison in Belfast. (Many people in Britain would have undoubtedly liked a repeat performance by the SAS in 1984, at the

Libyan People's Bureau in St. James's Square, but this time Thatcher diplomatically held her hand.)

In 1980, the rapid slide into mass unemployment had begun. But it seemed to me that if the country was going down the drain, then it was doing it with great richness and style. The arts were as flourishing as ever, the immigrant population had grown large enough to produce a noticeable cultural diversity, and (whatever the colonels and their ladies in Cheltenham might think) it seemed a splendid thing to see mosques in the Gorbals and Regent's Park, and to buy soul food, to hear reggae pulsating in the streets, or to watch Rastafarians shaking their dreadlocks before pictures of Emperor Haile Selassie at the Notting Hill Carnival.

In 1980, I went to the first of the party political conferences which were to dominate the autumn for me for the next three years. I also saw for the first time in close-up the Prime Minister in action.

Mrs Thatcher, little more than a year in office, was still flexing her muscles. The profound changes which she was striving to bring about in Britain were only vaguely understood by most of the electorate. But the Thatcherite revolution was taking shape, and it is still unfolding.

CHAPTER TWO

DOWN THE DRAIN

Is Britain really going down the drain?

As 1980 slid into 1981, it was possible to think so. The country, which had seen the full might of the Industrial Revolution and built with ruthless energy one of the world's greatest empires, was now finding itself in deep economic decline. In the tables published by the Organisation for Economic Cooperation and Development, Britain was shamed by the remorselessly downward trend of its employment and productivity figures. Its performance was not much better than that of the traditionally 'poor' countries like Italy and Belgium, and it began to be derisively known as the sick man of Europe, a role once filled by Turkey.

Anyone living in Britain during the early Eighties could hardly fail to take fright at what was happening to the country, as the bottom dropped out of the economy. The prosperous south-east was the least affected, but even in London, there were scenes which those who had lived through the Great Depression must have recognized with something like despair.

Coming home from the theatre, or from dinner in the West End, we of the well-fed middle classes were jolted out

10

of complacency by the sight of long lines of men and women bedded down for the night outside the Embankment Tube Station. It had been a dossers' refuge in the Thirties, and fifty years later the pattern was being repeated. The homeless lay side by side in orderly rows on the hard pavement, as though in some sort of bizarre British queue. Some made coverlets of newspapers or sheets of cardboards, others had assembled makeshift beds and rain shelters. A few lay reading by the light of street lamps with an air of raffish intellectualism; most turned hopelessly on their sides, covering their faces with their folded arms.

The police left the pavement dossers alone. But after complaints by righteous commuters, they started to clear them out of the shiny new subways leading to the Charing Cross mainline station, where they had found shelter in increasing numbers. I saw a young policeman, embarrassed but determined, rousing sleeping men—some old and frail—and pushing them out into the freezing night. It was not a comfortable experience.

Even in the elegant side streets of the West End, it became a common thing to see men sleeping in cardboard cartons purloined from dress shops. They curled up in uncomfortable foetal positions, waiting for the opening of employment agencies which recruited casual dishwashers and kitchen hands for the West End hotels. George Orwell, who himself worked as a *plongeur* in the Thirties, would have recognized the scene instantly.

There have always been buskers and a few professional beggars in London. But increasingly, people who were not professional mendicants were walking up to strangers in the streets and asking for money for food. At the big railway stations, men who looked as if they might have been skilled tradesmen not so long ago became touts, plunging into the traffic to snatch up taxis for old and over-laden travellers.

The British, who deep down have never become emotionally reconciled to being part of Europe, whatever they may see as the practical advantages of belonging to the EEC, squirmed when the European Community sent inspection teams to the worst hit industrial areas to see if they could be made salvageable by EEC funding.

The great industrial cities were themselves in decline. Glasgow, for example, which had a population of 1.2 million after World War I, had less than 800,000 people in the early Eighties. Its giant industries, like shipbuilding and iron and steel, were in ruins; and the city fathers now had unlikely hopes of developing a tourist industry, believing that the charms of haggis and kilts would lure American visitors. In one area of the once mighty Strathclyde region, male unemployment was between 60 and 70 per cent. The walls of the city were scrawled with the graffiti of despair: 'No dope, no hope', and 'Fuck the polis'. As a sign that bigotry was as alive here as in Northern Ireland, King William of Orange rode his white horse through the murals on gable ends.

No one could avoid the reality of what was happening. The use of visuals by television commentators brought the economic situation home with the force of a blow. At the end of each week, the nation's screens showed jobs lost and jobs gained in all the industrial sectors of Britain, with flashing lights on maps (green for gained, red or yellow— the much greater number—for lost) pinpointing the acuteness of the recession.

Night after night, the television screens also showed distraught factory managers standing in the ruins of once-profitable enterprises, stumbling, half-stunned, through a recital of what had happened to them. And, of course, for every factory that went down, a cluster of small suppliers went down too.

Whole areas, whole towns, started to look like industrial deserts. Managements walked out of factories and left them standing, and municipal councils had to spend ratepayers' funds knocking them down when they became rat-infested firetraps.

In Glasgow I was shown the site of the huge Singer sewing machinery factory, wiped out with the loss of 10,000 jobs. 'A century of work blasted away in a single year', our guide said despairingly.

As the recession deepened, emigration fever took hold of the country. Because of the world slump, most countries mercilessly squeezed their immigration quotas, but in the early Eighties, whenever Australia House arranged an information day in the provinces, the queues of the hopeful —and of the hopeless—stretched for blocks on end.

When I talked to families who had been selected to go to the most-desired countries, they always gave the same reason for making the move: there is no future here for us or for our children.

Ironically, migration contributes to the British malaise. Unlike the United States in the last century, the better-off nations are no longer willing to generously open their doors to the poor and the near-helpless. Instead, they quite deliberately skim off the cream of the workforce, the skilled men and women who already have jobs in Britain but who want to emigrate to improve their lifestyle. Those left behind are the unskilled and the unambitious, the dropouts from the technological age, who are most likely to end in the dole queues.

The Thatcher Government knew, of course, that the monetarist policies which it was determinedly following would be certain to result in great job losses. But it considered that this was a reasonable price to pay for the curing of the 'British disease', and for the emergence of a slimmer, sleeker, healthier British industry. Once this was done, the monetarists said, the unemployment situation would right itself.

Inflation was seen as the number one enemy. 'Bringing down the rate of inflation can only be done by restricting the money supply, and doing that inevitably causes difficulties for business and rising unemployment,' said Nicholas Ridley, one of the government's economic spokesmen, in January 1981. 'The high level of unemployment is evidence of the progress we are making.'

Thatcher and her advisers genuinely believed that they were in the lead as radical economic reformers. 'Britain is conducting an economic experiment on behalf of the whole western world,' a Treasury official told me confidently soon after I arrived in London.

But no one expected the massive scale of the losses, and the consequent high cost of financing the dole queues. Part of the economic master plan was the use of revenues from the lucrative North Sea oil fields for the stimulation of new industries, particularly in the high-tech area. In fact, these revenues have, in the early Eighties, been increasingly diverted to the social security sector. Keeping the dole payments up for the nation's three million unemployed was in 1983 running at £5 billion a year.

In late 1983, overall unemployment was steady at 13 per cent of the workforce. But in parts of the country it was much higher: 16 per cent in the Midlands, 20 per cent in parts of Scotland, 21 per cent in Northern Ireland.

The rate of increase in the unemployment figures was terrifyingly rapid. When the Thatcher Government came into office in 1979, the figure was 1.3 million, at that time considered very high. (The Tories campaigned in the 1979 election on the slogan 'Labour Isn't Working', with posters showing dole queues stretching into the distance. Later it was revealed that the 'jobless' in them were actually Young Conservatives, who had donated their acting services free to the Cause.)

Within three years, two million people were added to the dole queues. In 1982, 12,000 companies went into liquidation in England and Wales—the highest level ever recorded —and in that year personal bankruptcies rose by 60 per cent since the day the Thatcher Government had taken office.

It all looked like Apocalypse Tomorrow, and the Labour Party was torn between jubilation at being presented with what seemed at that time a certain election winner, and anger at what was happening to the country. The Thatcher Government had, the Labour leadership said, plucked the industrial heartland out of Britain.

The terrible summer of 1981, when London, Liverpool and Manchester exploded in a series of riots (which were in part racial, but mainly the result of festering resentment over inner-city conditions), confirmed some of the warnings that Britain was on the brink of disaster.

Novels and plays started being written giving visions of a future where street violence might become the British way of life. Even the Queen's press secretary, Michael Shea, wrote a novel called *Tomorrow's Men*, perhaps as a reaction from the stifling need for tact in his daily life. I have often wondered what the Palace thought of the Shea version of things to come, when law and order had broken down in Britain and the cities were ruled by quasi-military gangs of the far Left and far Right.

Occasionally, upon seeing a gang of skinheads on the streets with their shaven heads and half-mast trousers and lace-up leather boots, or the young toughs who favour army disposal camouflage uniforms and cartridge belts, it seems remotely possible. (It is interesting that in these latter days, violence and patriotism seem to go hand in hand. I have seen skinheads in Union Jack tee-shirts and red, white and blue braces; and few people are as patriotic as the National Front.)

If the riots of '81 were a fair sample, British cities certainly have the potential for further explosions. But by the end of 1983, when I left Britain, it looked as though the original outrage over the size of the dole queues had settled down into a sullen resignation.

In the summer of 1981, the first People's March for Jobs would its way from Liverpool to London. It was fed, sheltered and cheered on by communities all along the route, and it was greeted by an emotional crowd of 100,000 when it reached London. It was an echo, however, faint, of the Jarrow hunger marches of the Thirties. And to people like me, who stood in Trafalgar Square to see the marchers arrive, it seemed impossible that the government should survive many more such massive demonstrations.

But by 1983, when the march was repeated, the ghosts of Jarrow—the ragged, hungry men and women of the Depression—had long since left its fringes. Now it was purely a media event, a compact little group of 500 marchers, all stylishly uniformed in yellow oilskins and matching hats, looking as if they had been outfitted in the King's Road. The television cameras dutifully recorded the march, but there was no real heart left in it.

Britain seems to have accepted large-scale unemployment as a fact of life, and books with titles like *The Survivors' Guide to Unemployment and Redundancy* have started to appear on library shelves.

There was, however, a mild uproar in 1983 when the satirical cartoon book *101 Uses for the Unemployed* came on the market. A successor to *101 Uses for a Dead Cat*, it made bitter fun of the jobless, and suggested that they could be used as building blocks, bicycle stands, pincushions, punchbags, food for pets or for third world countries, as human cannon balls or as substitutes for foxes in hunting countries. It has been attacked as cruel and heartless, but it is also seen, with its violent arsehole humour, as satire in the tradition of Voltaire or Swift.

In the summer of 1981, I wrote a piece—at the time of the wedding of the Prince and Princess of Wales—on the decline of Britain, and it is interesting to look back and see how many of the prophecies have been fulfilled.

At the time, the monetarist school was forecasting that the following year, the Thatcher prescription for a restyled Britain would be showing noticeable results. Two well-known experts of this school, Alan Budd and Bill Robertson, said that within a year or so inflation would have dropped to 8.9 per cent compared with 22 per cent in 1980, that output would be up by 1.8 per cent, and that unemployment would be static at 2.7 million.

As it turned out, the monetarists were wrong on everything but inflation, which has been the Thatcher Government's big success story. By the middle of 1983, inflation was down below four per cent (though it has since risen again) but unemployment soared to a high of 3.2 million before it steadied and started to ease off a little. The economy remained in deep recession, and the Treasury had to wait until 1983 before it could talk about an upturn and could forecast a modest growth rate of 2.5 per cent in 1984.

On the other hand, the Keynesians, mainly centred round Cambridge University, have proved over-pessimistic. The director of the Department of Applied Economics at Cambridge, Wynne Godley, said when I was writing my piece that the prospects for the Eighties were 'absolutely frightful'. 'I can only describe it in apocalyptic terms,' he said. 'It is a prospect so dreadful I cannot really believe there won't at some stage be a sort of political revolution which will demand a basic change of policy.'

But far from demanding a change of policy, the British electorate in 1983 voted back Mrs Thatcher and her monetarist dogmas, even though she made it plain to the voters that all she was offering them was the same bitter mixture as before.

Among the reasons was the one which I have already advanced—that Britain has, in fact, become reconciled to life on the dole. Another is the fact, overlooked to its cost by the Left, that though 13 per cent of the electorate was out of work in 1983, the year of the general election, yet the remaining 87 per cent was doing rather nicely.

Between 1982 and 1983, average earnings rose twice as fast as inflation. People with jobs were significantly better off in real terms than they were three years before, when pay rises were three times as high, but were constantly being outstripped by inflation.

Because of the lower inflation rate, wage demands dropped to a reasonable level and there were fewer confrontations between the unions and the government. In 1982–83, the average level of settlement was 6.5 per cent, compared to the astronomical claims of up to 30 per cent in the past. (It should be noted, however, that wage rationality was at worker rather than management level. The former boss of British Leyland, Sir Michael Edwardes, arranged a 38 per cent pay rise for himself when workers were being offered 3.8 per cent. In 1982, the managing director of ICL, Robert Wilmot, took a pay rise of 100 per cent while his workforce received nine per cent. Sir Lawrie Barratt of Barratt Developments received a 39 per cent rise while his workers received seven per cent. The Thatcher ideal cut-off rate of five per cent of salary increases does not apply in the nation's boardrooms.)

Officially, of course, the Thatcher Government does not have a prices and incomes policy except in the public sector (where it has fought, not always successfully, to keep pay rises to the absolutely minimum). In fact, it is mainly low productivity and the spectre of the dole queue that have brought down wage increases to their present low level.

But whatever the reason, it is true that with much lower rates of inflation, the British worker now has more money in his or her pay packet, and is not—so far at least—in the mood for change. A few months after the general election, the Labour Party sank to its second lowest popularity level since World War II, and it was not until the leadership changed later during the year that it looked like having a chance of challenging Thatcher.

Whether, however, the Prime Minister would have survived if the Falklands war had not happened is a point that historians will argue over for years.

The Falklands touched upon Britain's most vulnerable nerve—the fact that it is no longer regarded by the rest of the world as a first-class power. The nation as a whole is still suffering from post-empire blues.

The Prime Minister was able to rally the nation behind her during the South Atlantic crisis of 1982 because of one simple fact: sending a task force to 'biff the Argies' gave Britain, for a short but glorious time, the aroma of past glories. Due to the brilliant stage management of the Ministry of Defence, the war even seemed (until it was too late to do anything about it) to be almost bloodless, and it would be hypocritical to suggest that most of the country didn't thoroughly enjoy it.

It was a stroke of genius (though dictated by necessity) that the chosen instrument of vengeance on the Argentinians should be the Royal Navy—Britain's pride, once the mighty ruler of the seven seas.

Even those who objected vehemently to the waste of lives and money in trying to preserve as British a piece of windswept, treeless territory that nobody even wanted were hypnotized by the sight of the great ships sailing majestically out of Portsmouth. (A poll taken at the time showed that 60 per cent of those questioned thought the Falklands were islands off Scotland.)

Cheering crowds lined the docksides, armadas of small boats escorted the war fleet out of harbour, and excited girls tore off their shirts and bared their breasts at the departing troops, repeating the ancient rituals of women inciting their men to bloodlust on the eve of battle.

Whole gatherings of people all over the country burst spontaneously into 'Land of Hope and Glory', and 'Rule Britannia', with a fervour that no one could have expected to see in this generation.

Millions of television viewers saw fresh-faced young squaddies, who had not heard of Goose Green or Bluff Cove (where they were to meet their deaths), packing the bars of the task force ships and singing: 'We're all going to the Mal-al-vinas, We goin' to kill ourselves an Argie or two...'

The Prime Minister herself was clearly high on adrenalin and emotion. 'Rejoice, rejoice,' she cried in Downing Street when news of the recapture of South Georgia came through. And in a throwaway remark which she was to be

19

made to repent later, she said at a political meeting that it was 'thrilling' to deal with such great matters after the dull business of struggling with unemployment and the economy.

For a time, in fact, the Falklands adventure persuaded the British that the country was *not* going down the drain, and whether that was true or not, there is no doubt that the events of the summer of 1982 did improve Britain's standing in the world. It was a country once again to be taken seriously, with a Prime Minister who not only was a warrior figure, but a very successful warrior at that. The world laughed at the spectacle of gold-braided, macho Argentian generals retreating before the wrath of the blonde Britannia.

Thanks to the Falklands, Britain felt it could hold up its head again and stop apologizing. Obviously there are those who dissented from this point of view and found the cost in British and Argentinian lives unacceptable. The dissenters may even have been in the majority; but if so, either they were a silent majority or their voices were not heard above the jubilant singing of 'Land of Hope and Glory'.

* * * * * *

The most important economic factor in keeping both the Thatcher Government and Britain afloat in the early Eighties has been North Sea oil. Without it, it is conceivable that the economic collapse would have been much more severe.

The offshore oil industry employs 100,000 people. It has given Britain its only Eighties boom town, the Scottish city of Aberdeen. Offshore oil and gas reserves in the United Kingdom continental shelf are estimated to be worth £400 billion, and have made Britain self-sufficient in energy.

In September 1983 the Prime Minister inaugurated Britain's huge Magnus oilfield, built one hundred miles north of the Shetlands at a cost of £1.3 billion. The Magnus platform is the biggest single piece steel structure in the world, three times as high as the tower of Big Ben, and built to withstand 100-foot waves and 100 miles per hour winds.

By a complicated piece of technological magic, Mrs Thatcher pressed a button in London and unveiled a plaque at the rig 700 miles away.

It was the sort of occasion that the Prime Minister loves. She jubilantly described the building of the Magnus rig as an achievement comparable with the Great Wall of China.

It clearly reinforced her apparently unshakeable faith in the future of Britain—a nation, she said, which is in the forefront of computer information, control and communications technology. 'We've got something to celebrate,' Thatcher said.

CHAPTER THREE

THE THATCHER FACTOR

Margaret Hilda Thatcher, born on 13 October 1925 above a grocer's shop in Grantham, Lincolnshire, Prime Minister of the United Kingdom since May 1979, is a political phenomenon, easily the most interesting western politician of the Eighties.

She is also a paradox. The first scientist ever to become a British Prime Minister, she is intent on pushing the nation forward into an era of technological change, and has no patience with the lumbering, dinosaur industries which created Britain's wealth in the last century. She would like to see Britain catch and surpass even Japan in such new fields as micro-electronics.

At the same time, she is a political counter-revolutionary, with a profound dislike for trade unions and socialism, and a frequently expressed wish for a return to what she regards as the moral absolutes of the Victorian era. According to her enemies she wants to dismantle the welfare state and reintroduce self-help policies for the major part of the population, leaving only a safety net to catch the poor and the feckless.

She has been called the New Britannia, the Iron Lady, the last of the Eminent Victorians. She herself undoubtedly believes that she is the chosen instrument of Britain's economic salvation—the Prime Minister who, with good luck and good management, will go down in history as having averted Britain's decline.

Sometimes she puts this vision of herself in homely language, describing herself as the nurse who must force the patient to take bitter medicine for his own good, or urge a reluctant bed case to get on his feet and stop malingering.

Sometimes she has loftier aspirations. As she entered Number 10 Downing Street after the election of 1979, she quoted no less eminent an inspirational source than St Francis of Assisi:

Where there is discord, may we bring harmony,
Where there is error, may we bring truth.
Where there is doubt, may we bring faith.
Where there is despair, may we bring hope.

She is the despair of the cartoonists. They can do nothing much with her regular features and impeccable grooming. So they portray her in character roles.

In 1983, she figured three times in a retrospective exhibition of the work of Britain's most savage political cartoonist, Gerald Scarfe. At the time, I wrote for the *Sydney Morning Herald*:

Scarfe shows her first in 1975 (when she became leader of the Tory Party) as an ornamental and nervous lady dog winning first prize at Cruft's. That cartoon is labelled Top Bitch and is frankly derisive.

By 1982, things have changed. Here Mrs Thatcher, all beaky nose and bared teeth, has become the figurehead of a battleship advancing on the Argies. The satire is savage, but at least the lady is taken seriously.

But the highpoint of the exhibition, in more ways than one, is Scarfe's of Thatcher in 1983. Now the Prime Minister has become too large to be confined on the flat dimension of paper. She towers over everything, a cartoon sculpture two metres high, executed in shining steel.

Britannia in armour, equipped for war with trident and

shield, she stands on a stone base labelled The Tomb of the Unemployed. From her breasts, murderous steel spearheads jut out, ready to impale her enemies. The intention is to pillory the Prime Minister, but it is difficult not to sense awe and even a trace of admiration.

After five years of government, Mrs Thatcher strikes fear, tinged with respect, in her opponents—not to mention her own followers.

'The best man in her Cabinet,' President Reagan once said admiringly, thus infuriating (not for the first time) feminists everywhere.

'Maggie's got guts!' a heckler shouted at the new Leader of the Labour Party, Neil Kinnock, at a meeting in 1983. 'It's a pity other people had to leave theirs on the ground at Goose Green to prove it,' Kinnock shouted back.

Margaret Thatcher has become such a dominating figure as a Prime Minister that some of the earlier views of her personality acquire a fascination all of their own. The political commentator Brian Walden quotes 'an old Tory friend from the shires,' prudently unnamed, as describing Mrs Thatcher, when she was elected as Leader of the Conservative Party, as 'a good-looking woman without doubt, but as common as dirt'.

Earlier, in 1969, when she became shadow Education Secretary, a journalist on the *Sunday Telegraph* wrote: 'Mrs Thatcher is a very pretty woman in a soft suburban way, with a nice mouth and nice teeth and large round dolly eyes, like a candy box tied off with two shiny bows of blue ribbon.'

A *Daily Telegraph* parliamentary writer was even more dismissive in the early Sixties: 'To [Mrs Thatcher's] intellectual and forensic abilities she added yesterday a new frock.'

Her admirers, on the other hand, tend to go over the top. A resolution put forward at the 1982 Conservative Party conference by the Manchester delegation said:

This conference is proud to tell the world that Britain has the best, most hardworking Prime Minister and political leader on earth. Mrs Thatcher is full of backbone and guts, a real Tory, and the best thing since sliced bread.

Paul Johnson, former socialist and former editor of the *New Statesman* now turned into an outrageously right-wing conservative, was one of the Prime Minister's greatest admirers—though, as we shall see later, he now has doubts. He said in an interview:

She is talked about as the Iron Lady, as though she is cruel, not interested in individual feelings. Of all the Prime Ministers I have known, she is far and away the most tender-hearted.
Margaret Thatcher has strong and deep emotions and principles. She is the first Christian Prime Minister since Gladstone.

Johnson said at that time that he expected Thatcher to be in office for 13 or 14 years in all, as after that a Prime Minister's ability declines sharply. The job was just too taxing.

Though it's true that in Margaret Thatcher's case, she does have two advantages. She did start quite young. She does possess the most remarkable physical stamina of any politician I've come across.
It may be that women are better equipped by nature than men to become prime ministers. They go through the absolutely shattering experience of childbirth.

Mrs Thatcher has clearly come a long way since the days when after winning the seat of Finchley for the Tories she was described as, among other things, 'an attractive mother of twins'. (It being then the fashion, as it still is today in more reactionary quarters, to describe women in terms of their childbearing function.)
Actually, Margaret Thatcher did not expect to become Prime Minister. She has been quoted more than once in her

political career as saying that her earlier main ambition, though she was not an economist, was to become Chancellor of the Exchequer. This is hardly surprising in view of her preoccupation with curing the nation's economic ills. She also said in an interview in 1974, only five years before she went to Downing Street, that she did not expect to see a woman Prime Minister in Britain in her time.

Her total commitment to politics dates from her childhood in Grantham. It is probably true to say that the fact she is now in Downing Street is due to her father, the redoubtable Alfred Roberts—the keeper of the corner grocer's store which, in the Eighties, has been turned into a restaurant. The shop area itself has been restored to its 1930s state as a sort of Thatcher mini-museum.

If Alfred Roberts had been born a few decades later, he would probably have gone to grammar school, then on to university like his daughter Margaret. He would also almost certainly have gone into national politics instead of stopping as he did at local government level and indulging his oratorical tastes as a lay preacher.

For a future politician he was an ideal father. He involved his daughter in the political process from her early childhood. At the age of ten, Margaret Roberts took part in her first general election, running as a messenger between the polling stations and the Party committee rooms. It was 1935, and her father was supporting the National Government candidate. From then on, she was incurably addicted.

According to Nicholas Wapshott and George Brock, who brought out the first serious (that is, non-adulatory) biography of the Prime Minister in 1983, the other strong influence on Thatcher in her most impressionable years was her grandmother, Phoebe Stephenson, 'a fiercely Victorian woman with strict morals and a habit of delivering homilies'. She exerted a deliberalizing influence on the household and this rigidity was reinforced by the family's devout Methodism. The only social life that Margaret and her sister Muriel had was bound up with the Church, and Thatcher has said that she never went to a dance in her life until she went up to Oxford.

The strands which were to knit her political life together were therefore clearly evident in her childhood: the obsessive interest in politics (implanted by her father), the Victorian ideas of social morality (inculcated by her grandmother), and the general tendency for upward striving in a family which had already elevated itself from the working class into the lower middle class. (Margaret Thatcher was to take it a class higher.)

At school, Thatcher was ambitious, hardworking and very serious, winning scholarships to grammar school and to Oxford. The satirists have amused themselves with spoof 'diaries' of her schooldays, in which she is portrayed as a prig and a swot. The fact is, though, that just as she is not a natural subject for cartoonists, she is also not a natural subject for satire. The funniest send-up of life at Number 10, the 'Dear Bill' letters in *Private Eye*, centres on Denis Thatcher and not his wife.

Apart from her father, Denis Thatcher has probably been the most important influence in Thatcher's life. By marrying an older man (he is ten years her senior) whose business interests had already made him reasonably affluent (though not embarrassingly rich) she was freed, right from the beginning, from the sort of economic bondage that she would have encountered in another sort of union.

She worked as a chemist for some years after Oxford. But when she married in 1951, she abandoned that career and studied for the bar. She qualified as a barrister in 1954, and specialized in the tax field until politics absorbed all her energies. In between time, with her usual competence, she produced twins, a boy and a girl, thus dispensing with the need for further childbearing.

Denis Thatcher, however, has provided his wife with a good deal more than financial security. He has advised and supported her emotionally right throughout her political career, and on the whole has been a remarkable success as a Prime Minister's husband.

There have been a number of attempts to use Denis Thatcher's business interests to discredit the Prime Minister, including suggestions that he was involved in the now famous 'Oman affair' of 1984 with his son Mark. But though the companies with which he is involved may raise some eyebrows, the most serious charge proved against him so far is that he has used Number 10 Downing Street notepaper to write his own business letters.

In the election of June 1983, I went out on the campaign trail with the Thatchers, and it was surprising how many times the excited cry that went up from the crowds was not 'There's Maggie!' but 'There's Denis!'

When Margaret Thatcher went to Downing Street, Denis Thatcher made a promise, probably as much to himself as to the country at large. 'I intend to be the most shadowy husband of all time,' he said.

In fact, Denis has had little chance of becoming too shadowy. For one thing, he had already achieved a kind of immortality by becoming the first husband of a Prime Minister in modern history. (Perhaps they ordered things differently in earlier matriarchal societies. In our own time, the other women Prime Ministers—Mrs Gandhi, Mrs Bandaranaike, Mrs Meir—have lost or mislaid their husbands along the way.)

If Denis Thatcher had been sent over to Downing Street by central casting for the role of PM's Consort, nobody would have believed it. He was an ex-oil company executive very much used to running his own show, a profane, impatient, golf-playing man who liked to drink with his own cronies and who seemed totally unsuited to walking behind his wife with his hands clasped behind his back.

But what everybody forgot was that he was also a veteran of years of Party dinners, Party socials, Party bazaars, Party conference cocktail parties, at which he has always stood gallantly by his wife's side.

What has really endeared Denis Thatcher to the nation,

however, is that the satirists who are largely baffled by his wife find him an irresistible target.

As well as the real-life Denis, a whole mythology has grown up round his *doppelganger*, the Denis who writes a letter to his friend Bill Deedes, the editor of the *Daily Telegraph*, in every issue of *Private Eye*. The 'Dear Bill' letters have been collected in a book which has sold 65,000 copies in paperback (a miracle in these hard times for the publishing industry) and Denis Thatcher himself has become the star of the West End success 'Anyone for Denis?' which ran until it was killed off by the Falklands war.

The *doppelganger* Denis was actually the creation of two *Private Eye* satirists, Richard Ingrams and John Wells. The latter played the title role in 'Anyone for Denis?' with the actress Angela Thorne as The Boss.

Ingrams and Wells may have originally intended the 'Dear Bill' letters as a cruel send-up of life *chez* Thatcher, but the *Private Eye* Denis rapidly became a cult figure.

'Dear Bill' was a logical follow-on to Mrs Wilson's Diary, which the *Eye* ran when Harold Wilson was Prime Minister, and which also turned into a West End farce, with the usual ingredients of dropped trousers and explosions in the kitchen.

Downing Street is said to be not altogether amused by the way the *Eye* letters have caught Denis Thatcher's speech patterns, with their frequent references to wogs, nigs nogs, union leaders with smelly socks and ponces wearing brothel-creepers. 'Dead accurate', someone very close to Number 10 once said to me. Carol Thatcher has also testified that the 'Dear Bill' letters give a picture of her father which is by no means untrue.

Both Margaret and Denis Thatcher bore up creditably when 'Anyone for Denis?' opened at the Whitehall Theatre. They went along to a special Sunday evening performance, with tickets at £50 a head to benefit charities nominated by the Prime Minister. The cast were invited back to supper at Number 10 afterwards.

It was an evening which strained Margaret Thatcher's tolerance to the utmost. She herself, played by Angela Thorne as bossy and immaculately coiffed, came out of it triumphantly, but to see her husband portrayed as a tipsy buffoon must have been painful to her. The elegant satirical 'Dear Bill' letters had been broadened into vulgarity. Nevertheless, the public loved it, and it was filmed for television, making Denis Thatcher a household word if he was not already one.

About the time of 'Anyone for Denis?' one of Denis Thatcher's friends described him as 'an old-fashioned gentleman, kind and courteous to ladies, a man's man, enjoys his pint, calls a spade a spade, and uses four letter words where necessary.'

Apart from one indiscretion over sporting links with South Africa, which he supports, he has remained mute on public issues, and he strolls along behind the Prime Minister on official occasions to the manner born. (Male correspondents have often said what a rotten job this must be, and so it is. Women have done it from time immemorial.)

Physically, he protects his wife in crowds, and has been known to tell her bluntly to go to bed when, over-fatigued and over-stimulated, she cannot make the decision for herself to end the evening.

In 'Dear Bill', the fictional Denis comments on a picture of ex-President Jimmy Carter and his wife hand in hand that 'there is something bloody rum about a bloke of Carter's age going round holding hands with his wife in public.' A quick flip through the picture file will produce evidence to contradict this. Denis and Margaret hold hands quite a lot.

They also live in surprisingly modest domesticity at Number 10, in what the Prime Minister (relating back to her own childhood days) half-mockingly describes as 'the flat above the shop'.

She hasn't bothered much about redecorating. An

acquaintance who has seen the private quarters describes it: 'Like a motel suite, my dear. Acres of Dralon.' There is no live-in domestic staff, and Mrs Thatcher, according to her biographers, cooks her husband a hot breakfast every morning, though she herself eats only grapefruit, toast or an apple.

The idea of the Prime Minister of the United Kingdom bent over a hot stove in a meagre London kitchen is bizarre by world standards, but it fits in with the deliberately cosy British image. Visiting presidents and heads of state sweep up to Number 10 Downing Street in bullet-proof motor-cades and with motor cycle escorts and secret service men guarding them. But when they leave, the Prime Minister of the day still comes out alone on the footpath to see them off, like a suburban hostess farewelling her guests.

Whatever security arrangements there may be inside, one solitary policeman still stands guard outside Number 10. He knocks on the door to admit visitors, for there is no exterior door knob. Until the threat from the IRA became too serious, the access to Downing Street was unrestricted; and tourists, ordinary Londoners, and harmless eccentrics could gather unhindered outside the Prime Minister's house. There used to be quite often a vigil in aid of some lunatic cause or another being staged there, but nowadays the public gets no nearer than the barricades where Downing Street debouches into Whitehall.

*　*　*　*　*　*

One of the main ingredients in Margaret Thatcher's politi-cal success has always been her enormous reserve of physical energy. She needs less sleep than most people, and can manage indefinitely on four or five hours a night. Over-work does not affect her health, and she is a walking advertisement for the apparent virtues of long hours, late nights, lack of exercise, and a scrappy diet.

She appears to dislike holidays. To her ministers' des-

31

pair, she keeps her own vacation down to two weeks a year, which she usually spends at a castle in Switzerland. Asked once what she did to relax, she said doubtfully: 'Now and then one goes for a walk.' But it was clear that relaxation was not a subject to which she gave a great deal of thought.

She has the great gift of being able to keep her enamelled bloom intact, no matter how long she has been on her feet. I once saw her performing on the campaign trail in heavy rain, only half-sheltered by an umbrella, and she still emerged looking dry and immaculate, while the rest of us were miserable and bedraggled.

She has no mercy on the soft, easy-living sybarites of the House of Commons. In a profile of Thatcher, the Observer quoted one of her ministers:

> It's one a.m. and you've had a hell of a day, so you're tottering down a Commons corridor with a whole bottle of claret swilling around inside you wondering when on earth you can go to bed, when you see this vision in blue drifting along looking as if she has just emerged from the beauty parlour. 'Ah!' she says, 'How are you dear? Now tell me what you think about these new statistics; and what do you propose to do about them?' It is absolutely terrifying.

Those close to her are half proud of and also half alarmed by her toughness. 'We have been speculating about what would happen if She fell under a bus,' one of her junior ministers said to me over dinner. 'That is, always supposing the bus did not come off second best—which seems more likely.'

Her extraordinary good health has held up right throughout her career. Her only known recent setbacks have been a problem with varicose veins, and a detached retina in 1983. She had an operation to deal with this, but with her usual refusal to accept incapacity she was back at work within a matter of days. At an age when most people have long since become reconciled to the idea of spectacles, she only started to occasionally use them at fifty-seven.

She has come to subscribe to the idea of herself as Superwoman. When she went on her first European tour after an eye operation, she was asked if such a trip, only weeks after surgery, was not too much: 'It may be too much for a normal person who has had an operation,' she said, 'but, after all, it is me we are talking about.'

Her appearance seems unaffected by the burden of office. Even during the worst days of the Falklands fighting, she showed little sign of strain. Many leaders of nations appear to age rapidly, as is shown by the 'before' and 'after' pictures of Jimmy Carter; while even Ronald Reagan's carefully embalmed look seems sometimes to be falling apart. But power obviously acts on Thatcher like an intoxicant. She is permanently high on it.

She has also dealt very competently with the problems which seemed implicit in being Britain's first woman Prime Minister. She has done so largely by ignoring them.

When she first moved into Number 10, there were some bitchy male attempts to denigrate her with references to the shrillness of her voice, or to the way in which she carried her handbag, or even (incredibly enough) to the fact that she might be menopausal.

All this is now far in the past, as are the days when Thatcher occasionally allowed herself to be photographed washing up in a frilly apron. (Nowadays, she is more likely to be pictured firing a weapon, haranguing potential customers on the virtues of British-made arms, or wearing a combat jacket in Ulster.)

She has disappointed the feminists. Some of them hoped, against all odds, to find in her a Sister. She is in her own way a very liberated woman, but she is not a Sister.

She has also disappointed the large number of women voters who supported her in 1979 because they believed a woman Prime Minister would 'look after women's interests', or 'make things better for women'. Thatcher's interest in specifically female issues is minimal, and it probably always has been so despite all her chat to interviewers about good housekeeping.

So many women were vocal about being let down by the first Thatcher government that it was expected they would contribute to a big swing against it in the 1983 election. When it came to the crunch, however, this did not happen.

Feminists tend to clench their teeth and murmur, 'Well, she's not really a woman, she's turned herself into a man.' But whatever women may think of Thatcher, it is still hard not to feel a tiny flash of satisfaction at the spectacle of the Prime Minister putting down her male colleagues in public. The man who would attempt to sexually harass Thatcher, in any sense of the term, has yet to be born.

There is also, of course, the theory that men actually enjoy being bossed about by Thatcher—that she represents to the middle and upper-class sector of the nation at least the stern nanny, the school matron, the all-powerful headmistress, even the strict disciplinarian of erotic fantasies.

The editor of the *Daily Telegraph*, William Deedes, the crony to whom Denis Thatcher allegedly writes his 'Dear Bill' letters, made a very interesting summing up of the Prime Minister's femininity:

> Like many of her kind, she declines to submit to rules which men like to make for themselves about everything from snooker to politics. Old school ties, male codes of loyalty, Buggins' turn and all the rest, are simply not in her book. If she dislikes a senior civil servant, the fact that he is a friend of a brother-in-law and was at Eton with him doesn't count. He is superseded. This is the woman who tore up the male rule book.

'Not temperamentally suited to Whitehall clubbability,' the authors Nicholas Wapshott and George Brock said about her. Interestingly enough, though, she has her portrait hung as Prime Minister in the Carlton Club, that bastion of male privilege.

But the longer she stays in office, the fact that Thatcher

is a woman becomes less and less relevant. And women politicians of the future should praise her at least for bringing this miracle about.

* * * * * *

Politics in Thatcher's Britain tend to be heavily influenced by the Prime Minister's own two main preoccupations. One is her inflexible determination to turn Britain round, to cure the British malaise, to restore the nation to what she considers is its rightful place as a world power, both in the political and economic spheres. The other is her ambition to recreate in the Britain of the Eighties what she sees as the Golden Age of Victorian England.

In the Victorian era, she told an incredulous House of Commons in 1983, there was 'acceptance of personal responsibility, freedom of choice, and indeed, the British Empire, which took both freedom and the rule of law to countries which would never have known them otherwise.'

This second theme was only introduced in the last months of her first term of office. The curing of Britain's economic ills is a much more long-running theme, one which goes back well into her earlier political history.

Whatever the side-effects have been, it is hard not to have some sympathy with Thatcher's original vision. The British have always taken an odd sort of pride on their ability to muddle through. They think themselves superior in their easy-going approach to life to the efficient, regimented Germans, to the intellectual French, or to the over-excitable Mediterranean nations. This attitude makes Britain one of the most attractive places in the world to live; but it has not, for many years now, done much for productivity or for industrial growth.

When I came back to Britain in 1980, the slide was very noticeable. 'Muddling through' had turned into inefficiency on a terrifying scale. Everything took longer, was done more reluctantly and was less well done. Even small services were not as good as they used to be. In the area of London in which I lived, the only way of getting morning papers delivered in time to read them at breakfast was to take your business to an Indian newsagent whose children were still willing to get up early. Sunday papers, delivered as late as eleven a.m. in central London, seemed an alarming sign of the British malaise.

In the great industrial areas, there was overmanning and low productivity. The unions were strangling themselves with ludicrous demarcation practices, and discrediting themselves with wild cat strikes. Britain was subsidizing at a crippling rate, through the EEC, the selfish or inefficient farmers of other Community countries, even though agriculture was one area in which it was itself highly productive.

The political catchword in the Sixties had been consensus, with mild-mannered socialists and gentlemanly Tories ruling the country in turn. (It has been fascinating, in the Eighties, to hear speakers from the Labour benches harking back to the days of Prime Ministers like Harold Macmillan and Alec Douglas-Home with great nostalgia.)

Then all that ended. Along came a hard right, radical Tory Prime Minister who didn't believe in consensus at all. 'For me, consensus,' Thatcher said (she was in Melbourne at the time), 'seems to be the process of abandoning all beliefs, principles, values and policies. So it is something in which no one believes, and to which no one objects.'

She has also been more ruthless than other Prime Ministers, chopping off heads whenever she has considered it useful to do so. (In 1983, against all precedent, she sacked her Foreign Secretary, Francis Pym, once considered to be her rival for the leadership of the party.) She has also shown herself ready to accept personal unpopularity while she is in the process of pushing through policies which she believes to be good for the nation. Whatever she is, she is not an expedient politician.

At the Party conference in 1980, when the effects of

36

monetarism on Britain were beginning to be seen, she stood on the platform of the conference hall in Brighton, and hurled defiance at her critics. People were, she said, very fond of talking about economic U-turns. '*You* turn if you want to,' she told the Party faithful. 'The lady's *not* for turning!'

The phrase, which has since been much quoted, was not her own, but the brainwave of her 'theatrical' speech writer, the dramatist Ronald Millar; but she delivered it with the bravura of the actress she increasingly resembles. (Unlike any politician I have ever seen, she actually bows from the waist, stage fashion, to acknowledge applause.)

Thatcher's ideas for restructuring the British economy are in part based on the theories of the monetarist economists Milton Friedman and F. A. Hayek, both of whom she met in the late Seventies, and in part on the preaching of one of the most remarkable and original politicians of our time, Enoch Powell.

Powell, whose great virtue is both to think and say the unthinkable, was preaching monetarism of a sort as early as 1957; and Thatcher's biographers, Wapshott and Brock, have pointed out that in 1968, long before the world had heard of Friedmanite doctrines, Thatcher herself was urging cuts in public spending and self-discipline by governments.

Her recipe for turning round the economy was also more simply expressed, in her early years as Prime Minister, along the lines of the principles of good housekeeping: the nation must not spend more than it earns.

She was fond of quoting homely examples, saying once in an interview:

I would like us to become the savers' party. Good Lord, my grandmother, who was the wife of a railway guard, had saved £600 when she died in 1935. That generation did. My father earned 14 shillings as a manager of someone else's grocery shop, of which 12 shillings went to digs, one shilling went to

37

saving, and one was for spending. Now *they* saved. And, my goodness, government after government plundered their savings by what they called reflation. £100 in 1935 is worth only £8.70 now.

Thatcher thus came into office with the conviction that inflation was the enemy, and that the way to control inflation was through control of the money supply.

She had every cause for alarm, for in the first twelve months of her government, inflation rose to 22 per cent. The Prime Minister started talking angrily about 'suitcase money' and reminding the nation about what had happened in Germany after World War I, when inflation got out of control.

In those early days, though, she was having difficulty selling monetarism to her Cabinet, some members of which remained obstinately Keynesian in their economic outlook.

It was at this time that the terms 'Wets' and 'Dries' came into everyday use. ('Wets' originated with the contemptuous comment 'He's wet!' scrawled by Thatcher herself across a submission by an unhappy official.)

The 'Wets' believed that the cost to the nation of controlling the money supply and of savagely cutting back public-sector spending would be too high. The 'Dries' or Thatcherites accepted that the cost had to be paid. It was assumed that British industry would accept the harsh realities of the Eighties and trim and streamline itself so that it could survive. Companies that either could not or would not adapt themselves would obviously go to the wall. (Nobody in Thatcher's Cabinet at that stage could have guessed how high the number of bankruptcies would turn out to be.)

In 1980, the Tory MP for Reigate, George Gardiner, put the government's point of view at a Conservative Party meeting:

The inflation virus racing through our system is so strong it is bound to be a painful business killing it. Yet kill it we must. So

we are in for a very rough two years. Firms unable to adapt
will go bankrupt, and the unemployment figures will top two
million.

Well, everybody knows what happened next. British
industry became not only lean but positively cadaverous,
the dole queues reached an all-time high (in actual
numbers) of more than three million, and Mr Gardiner's
'very rough two years' stretched into three and then into
four, with few tangible signs of economic rebirth.

There were also some odd early side-effects of the
government's economic policies. The pound sterling
became exceptionally 'hard' and was the wonder of the
currency markets. North Sea oil and high interest rates, at
one time up to 17 per cent, sent the pound soaring; and it
reached in the summer of 1980 the totally unrealistic level
of 2.40 against the US dollar.

The high pound made it easier for the British to buy
expensive imported goods and take holidays abroad; but it
also hit the export trade very hard, because British goods
started pricing themselves out of world markets. Tourists
stayed away from Britain in great numbers, and even
Americans could be heard complaining loudly on buses
about the cost of spending a holiday in London. (When I
arrived in London in 1980 I paid more for a single room in
a second-rate London hotel than I did in the Waldorf-
Astoria Towers in New York.)

Even the Arabs fled London temporarily, taking their
property deals and their patronage of medical clinics to
'cheap' cities like New York or Paris or Rome. For a while,
the swish of a burnous or the discreet lifting of a veil was a
rare sight on London streets.

But all this was marginal to Thatcher's main objective to
bring down inflation. In this she succeeded beyond the
government's hopes, keeping her pledge to the nation that
Britain would not become a country of 'suitcase money'.

The government has also been able to claim some success

in turning round the state-owned, loss-making giants—notably British Leyland and British Steel—which have, over the years, ingested billions of taxpayers' money. They might not be profitable, but sections of them are within sight of breaking even. When that happens, Thatcher intends to sell them off.

Their higher productivity, though the government is unlikely to admit this, has been largely achieved by making tens of thousands of workers redundant, and by putting the fear of God into the rest. Trade union militancy has greatly weakened in the Thatcher years, and even the National Union of Mineworkers, traditionally one of the most powerful and aggressive unions in Britain, has failed to give its leadership unqualified support when strikes have been called.

The miners brought down the government of Edward Heath in 1974, and the present NUM president-for-life, Arthur Scargill, boasted when he took office that he would do the same for Thatcher. But he was to learn, in the prolonged and bitter coal strike of 1984, that not all his members were ready to follow him to the barricades.

The long-term effect of Thatcherism on the British economy has yet to be seen. It appears that the worst of the British recession is over, but the efficacy or otherwise of the Prime Minister's bitter medicine probably cannot be measured until the world recession ends.

Only then will it be known whether the patient will bounce up, lean, trim and fighting fit, or whether the purgation is likely to prove fatal. So far she has produced no economic miracles.

* * * * * *

Thatcher's preoccupation with the Victorian era is even more interesting than her experiments with monetarism. It may have had its origins in her father's household which, as we have seen, was dominated for the first ten years of her life by her Victorian grandmother. Margaret Roberts and her sister Muriel were brought up on maxims like 'Cleanliness is next to godliness,' and 'If a thing is worth doing it is worth doing well.'

Thatcher's view of Victorian England is a curious one. She seems to see it enveloped in a golden glow, as though great poverty had not co-existed with great wealth, and as if the 'freedom of choice' she speaks of to the House of Commons had not been largely confined to the upper and middle classes. It was not, in her vision, a Dickensian world of wretchedness and child labour and reeking slums; rather it was a cosy era, rich in virtuous benefactors, who built hospitals and workhouses for the undeserving poor.

She does indeed believe implicitly in the Victorian qualities of self-help and 'getting on'. Why should she not? She herself is the living exemplar of them.

But it seems difficult for her to accept that in every society there are millions of people who are never likely to rise above subsistence level, or that poverty can be an inherited disease.

This blind spot was very clearly illustrated by a throwaway remark she made once about the lengthening dole queues. Unemployment should not be such a serious problem, she said. The solution was for workers to collect their redundancy money and start small businesses of their own. The derision this statement attracted seemed to surprise her.

It was largely to ensure that the indignities of the Victorian era would never be repeated that the welfare state was created. In Britain today, people do not die for lack of urgent medical treatment. Couples who have been married for fifty years are not separated and forced into single-sex workhouses, and marches for jobs are at least no longer hunger marches.

Thatcher and her ministers have said repeatedly that they do not intend to dismantle the welfare state, but there are equally strong signs that at least partial destructuring is the

the Prime Minister's long-term ambition.

Her ideas about personal responsibility, like her monetarist theories, go back to the period before she became Prime Minister, or even Leader of her Party. In a lecture she gave at Blackpool during the Party conference of 1968, she made this clear.

> I believe that the great mistake of the last few years has been for the government to provide or to legislate for almost anything. Part of this policy has its roots in the plans for reconstruction in the postwar period when governments assumed all kinds of new obligations. The policies may have been warranted at the time, but they have gone far further than was warranted or is advisable...
>
> There is nothing wrong with people wanting larger incomes. It would seem a worthy objective for men and women to wish to raise the standard of living for their families and to give them greater opportunities than they themselves had. I wish more people would do it. *We should then have fewer saying 'the state should do it.'*

After Thatcher had become Prime Minister, the first indication that she intended to put her ideas about self-help into practical form came with her strong encouragement of private medicine, and with suggestions that Britain might do better to return to a two-tier system of medical care. Under the first Thatcher government, the vestigial private sector did indeed start to grow again, and private health insurance schemes reported booming business.

By 1983, the government was giving notice of cuts in spending on the National Health Service as well as of its intention to privatize such hospital services as cleaning and laundry.

It was also in 1983 that the 'Victorian' theme actually surfaced. Thatcher first made reference to the Victorian virtues of self-help, good works, and empire-building in an interview. She then defended them, as we have seen, in the House of Commons.

In the beginning it was thought to be something of a

joke, and the cartoonists gleefully dressed Thatcher in the weeds of the widow of Windsor—a role to which her profile seemed unexpectedly suited.

Confirmation that the Prime Minister was not joking, however, came in a series of documents drawn up by a secret policy-making unit established by Thatcher and leaked to the *Guardian*. No one denied that they were genuine, though Downing Street hastily said that the contents of the documents were suggestions and not firm proposals.

The program for social engineering contained in them, however, is radical (or reactionary) by the standards of the Eighties. The main suggestions were:

- Actively encouraging women to stay at home and look after children instead of going out to work.
- Putting the care of the old, disabled, and even unemployed school leavers back onto the family.
- Helping parents to set up their own schools.
- Providing backing for schools with 'a clear moral base,' such as religious schools. Vouchers would also be given to parents towards the cost of their children's education, to allow them to take them out of the State school system and send them to private schools.
- Training of children in the management of pocket money, and guidance in setting up savings accounts.
- Changing the culture, so that business and wealth creation were accepted as desirable and laudable aims in life.

(In a very significant aside, Thatcher once said: 'No one would remember the good Samaritan if he had only had good intentions. He had money as well.')

The leaked documents, even if only 'suggestions', outraged the Labour Party, which is, in theory at least, dedicated to ending both private medicine and private education in Britain.

In the House of Commons, Labour MPs described the

plans as being 'as Victorian as Dickensian poverty'. The then Labour spokesman on social security, Brynmor John, spoke of the Cabinet team which drew up the documents as 'a gaggle of sociological Dr Strangeloves who plan to engineer Britain into a sub-Orwellian world of handouts and private charity'.

The Left organized 'Victorian workshops' with the aim of showing the darker side of Victorian Britain to the nation.

In September 1983, the *Guardian*, which had earlier in the year published the 'leaked' documents on personal responsibility, ran a postscript to the affair by printing some extracts from a paper given at the annual conference of the British Society for Population Studies by Professor Michael Anderson of Edinburgh University.

Thatcher does not usually read newspapers, preferring to rely on digests prepared for her by her press secretary. If she did, Professor Anderson's account of life in the Victorian era would probably surprise her.

Victorian Britain was not a stable society, he said, with families remaining in the same community for most of their lives. It was an era of considerable movement, where more than half the adult population ended their lives in different areas to those in which they were born. Community life is far more stable in the present century.

High mortality rates (especially for women) broke up marriages more often in Victorian times than divorce does in the Eighties.

The level of sexual morality was not nearly as high as is usually imagined, with the illegitimate birth-rate more or less matching that of the high point of the Sixties. In the early 19th century, 60 per cent of all women conceived their first child out of wedlock.

In the Victorian era, families were even keener to get rid of their aged relatives than they are today. Professor Anderson told his audience:

Right back into the early 19th century and beyond, it is clear the aged normally depended on poor relief for their support, and that large numbers were in institutional care...

Overall, the evidence would strongly suggest that the aged were only likely to live with and be supported by relatives where they had property which gave them power over their relatives' future living standards, where they could be useful (for example, in child care), or where their support was heavily subsidized by charity or by poor relief.

This is a somewhat different picture of Victorian values to the Thatcherite one.

* * * * * *

One other thing needs to be said about Thatcher as a politician, and that is that there are actually two different Thatchers. One is merging into the other as time goes on, and she feels her powers more, but the other was very visible in her first term of office.

This is the Thatcher who appears on television, consciously softening her image on the suggestion of her advisers, who fear that she comes on too strong, being wise and womanly and above all, compassionate. This is the Thatcher who murmurs in a throaty contralto: 'Of *course*, the government feels sympathy for the unemployed. *Of course* we do!'

The other is the Thatcher seen in the House of Commons and at rallies and Party conferences. She is a formidable parliamentary performer, and the moment when she rises from the government benches at question time causes a hush in the house. Strong men feel terror when she swings her cold gaze towards them.

At rallies and conferences she is a strong and forceful speaker, and might even, in different circumstances, have become a rabble rouser. She is immensely competent, and never falters or fluffs, though she usually makes sure she is not thrown off her stride by having admission to election rallies limited to ticketholders only.

She can, however, keep her nerve under difficult circumstances. I saw her at a Party conference watch unmoved as intruders violently burst through the door, and one, dodging the stewards, started running up the aisle towards her, shouting. He was not armed, but he could easily have been.

She stood unflinchingly at the lectern, and she also showed no sign of distress while the burly stewards dealt with the man and carried him bloody and half-conscious from the hall. 'These people probably only wanted to come in out of the rain,' she said with cold irony. 'They know it's always better where the Tories are.'

She sees herself as a radical reformer who will save Britain from degenerating into a third-class power. Her enemies say that she is nothing more than an old-fashioned political reactionary dressed in a few new, cliches. Only a longer-term assessment can provide the real verdict on Margaret Thatcher.

In 1984, a hint of rebellion arose in the Tory party for the first time since the pre-Falklands period. Labour, with its energetic new leadership, was creeping up on the Conservatives in the polls, at one stage even drawing ahead, and the Prime Minister herself was having serious family problems.

Her son Mark was retained as a consultant by the British firm Cementation International which was awarded a contract worth $500 million to build a university in the Sultanate of Oman.

Thatcher visited Oman in 1981 and Mark was also there at the same time though he did not travel with his mother. Thatcher did not deny that she mentioned Britain's interest in winning the contract in her talks with Omani officials, and she later had to spend a good deal of time inside and outside the Parliament fighting accusations of impropriety.

The 'Oman Affair' looked like casting a long shadow over her second term of office.

CHAPTER FOUR

HIGH AND LOW TORIES

After the election of June 1983, the Right in Britain entered a new historical period. It was the end of the *ancien regime* and the beginning of the reign of upward-thrusting, grammar school Tories.

'No more knights of the shires. Estate agents from the shires is more the style,' one political commentator said derisively.

The new epoch began in the usual way with a short burst of butchery. Thatcher sacked the Foreign Secretary, Francis Pym, and sent the Home Secretary, William White-law, to the Lords. She filled the key posts in her Cabinet with born-again Thatcherites, and when the blood-letting stopped, it became clear that something remarkable had happened.

The new Cabinet contained only one Old Etonian—the 75-year-old Lord Chancellor, Lord Hailsham, who could hardly be regarded as any sort of threat by the new breed of Low Tories.

In one sense, by trimming and slashing away at what she considered to be the dead wood in her Cabinet, Thatcher was only carrying out the usual reshuffle after a general election. This is a Prime Minister's privilege, and as this particular Prime Minister had been swept back to power on something close to a landslide, it is hardly surprising that Thatcher wanted to stack her Cabinet with her own men.

But the reshuffle was much more significant than that. It was signalling that High Toryism had become a casualty of the election of 1983. Thatcher, the grocer's daughter from Grantham, was not only leading the Party remorselessly rightwards; she was also taking it, electorally speaking, downmarket.

In a comment before the election, Thatcher had said somewhat patronizingly of her opponents that the Labour Party would not die of its present malaise. It would metamorphose.

The Tory Party in 1983 was in no danger of dying, but a metamorphosis was obviously occurring on the Right as well as on the left.

The purge of the Old Etonians aroused different re-actions in different quarters. Rupert Murdoch's *Sun* news-paper, which claims to fulfil an unchallenged *vox populi* role in today's Britain, ran a piece called 'Goodbye to the Old School Tie', in which it congratulated Thatcher on promoting 'hardworking ex-grammar school boys'. Echoing in a more popular form the verdict on Thatcher which had been given by the editor of the *Daily Telegraph*, William Deedes, it said: 'Privilege and rank count for nothing with the woman who was born above the grocer's shop.' (The *Sun* also rather maliciously pointed out that on the Left, Michael Foot, John Silkin and Tony Benn had all gone to expensive private schools, as had the Labour Party ex-ministers turned Social Democrats, David Owen and Shirley Williams.)

Not everybody, however, was happy about the new style Tory Party. The Labour leadership itself paid some sur-prising tributes to the old style paternalistic High Toryism, now sinking fast into the sea of history.

One of the most influential right-wing commentators in Britain, Peregrine Worsthorne of the *Sunday Telegraph*, gave voice to the doubts and fears of the Old Guard. In a column called 'Enter the New Men', written just before the 1983 election, Worsthorne pointed out that Thatcher was within reach of accomplishing what the Labour Party had been talking about for years: the elimination of Britain's old ruling class from the corridors of power.

Worsthorne is worth quoting at some length because he speaks with the authentic voice of High Toryism. It was not only the unskilled and unemployed in the depressed areas of the North who would lament the return to office of Mrs Thatcher, he said.

From the landed gentry of the shires will be heard just as bitter a volume of wailing and gnashing of teeth. For if the former (the unemployed) face material impoverishment at the hands of a triumphant Mrs Thatcher, the latter can expect a no less painful deprivation: loss of political influence, for which the continuation of fox hunting will be only scant compensation. In her eyes, neither group deserves much consideration, since she is ignorantly contemptuous of the values of the so-called idle rich as of the so-called idle poor. If Britain is to prosper, she says, both must be consigned to the scrapheap of history.

The new type of Conservative MP, whose like will flood into the House of Commons on Mrs Thatcher's coat tails is as different from, and inferior to, the traditional Tory as a Labour Trot is from the traditional socialist.

They are a narrow lot who have come up the hard way— thrusting, ambitious, tough-minded and short-sighted. How could it be otherwise? Clearly the view of the world and of the human condition, from the windows of suburbia, is bound to be different from the view from a stately home.

This is not mere snobbery. Broad acres do not guarantee broad minds, any more than a classical public school education guarantees a dislike for extremism.

But they help, and the best of the knights of the shires did indeed represent something very precious in this country's political culture, a certain tradition of public service and noblesse oblige which unquestionably sweetened and civilised the exercise of power.

Thatcherism is the Militant Tendency of the Tory Party and

henceforth it will rule unchallenged. Fasten your seat belts. We are in for a rough ride.

This rather astonishing summing up, in which the 'view from the windows of suburbia' is seen as automatically narrow and limited, and pragmatic management of the economy is regarded as less attractive than the tradition of noblesse oblige, shows that the class system is well and truly alive in the Britain of the Eighties.

The attitudes Worsthorne displays are typical of High Toryism, and their strength may help to explain Thatcher's own ruthlessness.

With her carefully chosen clothes (not too chic, not too dowdy), her pearls, her Tory Lady hairstyle, and her impeccable accent, she may look like the genuine article, but to a High Tory she will always be the daughter of a grocer and a dressmaker, with grandfathers who were, respectively, a cobbler and a railway guard. Worsthorne's 'knights of the shires' would undoubtedly echo an earlier verdict: 'Common as dirt'.

So Thatcher knew from the beginning that if she could not join the High Tories the only other thing to do was to beat them at their own game. What she is doing is reshaping the Tory party in her own image and making it basically lower middle class. It has become what one commentator called 'a party of the bourgeois radical centre', and it appeals to the upwardly mobile, and to small to largeish entrepreneurs. Thatcher's Britain could (no doubt ideally in her view) become again a nation of shopkeepers.

This has brought about some changes in tradition. 'In the days when we never had it so good, you knew that the Establishment had started its summer holidays when you saw newspaper pictures of the Prime Minister and his parliamentary colleagues relieving their political frustrations on the grouse moor,' the *Times* said in 1983 in an article on the Glorious Twelfth. 'Although today is the opening of the grouse season, it is not expected that

Mrs Thatcher or Mr Tebbit (then Employment Secretary) will take to the butts.'

In fact, it is significant that the only gun Thatcher has been photographed firing was a field weapon in the Falklands Islands, during her visit at the end of the South Atlantic war. No High Tory Prime Minister would have been seen dead doing anything so ostentatious.

The shape of things to come had been recognized by at least some of those who had encountered Thatcher in the early days of her political career. The Labour member Charles Pannell (later Lord Pannell) saw her in action when she stood unsuccessfully in Dartford in 1949, when she was only 23, and he said later that she obviously 'had a great appeal to the respectable working class'.

During her first term in office, Thatcher deliberately broadened out the appeal of the Tory party by introducing a scheme under which council house tenants were enabled to buy the properties in which they were living.

In the first four years of the scheme, half a million of the estimated six million council houses in Britain were sold in this way. If analysis of previous election results are accurate, these sales have proved helpful to the Tory party, as property owners have always shown themselves to be more likely to be Conservative voters than council house tenants.

Quite early in the first Thatcher government, it was seen that the Cabinet was dividing itself into two groups: paternalists and libertarians. The paternalists were the old Tories, who believed that noblesse indeed obliged, and that privilege carried with it the responsibility of looking after the less well-off members of society. William Whitelaw, Francis Pym and James Prior (the Northern Ireland Secretary) were all representative of this breed, who could also be roughly classified as 'Wets'.

The libertarians were led by the Prime Minister and included the new men in her Cabinet. Upwardly mobile themselves, they believed that most people could improve their situation in life if only they put their minds to it. They believed in money making, the free play of market forces, and, if necessary, the weak to the wall. After Thatcher, the two most prominent libertarians (or 'Dries') of recent years have been Norman Tebbitt and Cecil Parkinson. (A certain paradox emerges here. Thatcher has spoken more than once of Victorian Britain as a period when the prosperous played a useful role in helping the poor by building hospitals and workhouses. This does not altogether fit in with libertarianism, but it could indicate that in her later years, possibly when she goes to the Lords—someone suggested as Lady San Carlos—she may turn round and become a fully fledged paternalist.)

It is worth looking at a couple of specimens of High and Low Tories to see what motivates the two species.

Of the Low Tories closest to the Prime Minister, the present Trade and Industry Secretary, Norman Tebbit, is probably the most interesting, because he represents the tougher face of libertarianism. He is spoken of as a possible successor to Thatcher, though he will be hard to sell to the Party at large, because of the reputation he has gained as a hatchet man for his Leader.

He has been called Thatcher's pet piranha, a bovver boy, a skinhead, a street fighter and a standover man. In the flesh, close up, he is quite handsome; but in photographs, his baldness, his tight, skull-like face and pointed ears give him a death's head appearance.

Another of his innumerable nicknames is Count Dracula. The former Labour deputy leader, Denis Healey, meeting him late one night prowling along a House of Commons corridor, extended his arms wide in the form of a crucifix, and moaned piteously: 'The garlic! Bring me the garlic!'

'The most carefully crafted image since Boris Karloff,' said a profile in the *Guardian*. A civil servant in the Department of Employment was quoted as saying that, for relaxation, 'he bites heads off chickens'.

Tebbit is as much self made and upwardly mobile as

Thatcher. His father was not even a moderately successful grocer, but a tradesman who lost his job in the Depression and cycled round the dreary suburb of Chingford, in North-east London, offering to paint front doors.

At a Tory Party conference when unemployment was soaring to three million, Tebbit made an unfortunate speech urging the jobless to get out of the dole queues and onto their bikes like his father had done. He has been greeted by catcalls of 'on yer bike' ever since.

If the speech was less than tactful, yet it did, at the time, add to the Tebbit legend. Norman's father Lionel became something of a cult figure, and an enterprising *Guardian* reporter got on *his* bike and cycled round Chingford trying to find doors to paint. He wrote that he had sixty refusals before he gave up and decided that it was easier to go on the dole.

When Thatcher sent Tebbit to the Department of Employment, he succeeded James Prior, a red-faced, rotund gentleman farmer, who had clearly not enjoyed his job, and had showed obvious distress as the dole queues lengthened.

Tebbit proved himself much tougher. He had the advantage of not being any sort of gentleman, and certainly not pretending to be one, so his conscience was not over-troubled by woolly notions of noblesse oblige.

He was at first something of an outsider, for in a Cabinet in which, at that time, 80 per cent of the members were Oxford graduates, he was a grammar school boy, a former journalist, a former airline pilot, even a former union activist. Unlike Thatcher, who speaks what her enemies call 'phoney Belgravian', Tebbit retains the accent and manner of his lower middle-class suburban upbringing.

Possibly in self defence, he developed a savage line in repartee in the House of Commons. 'Why don't you go and have another heart attack?' he once shouted at an opposition member in the House. The MP did, and died.

When he set his sights on the trade unions, he described

them as being for 'lazy workers who prevent those who want to work from getting on with it'.

The then Labour Leader, Michael Foot, once described him as 'a semi house-trained polecat'. Bill Rodgers, one of the founders of the Social Democrats, said in the House: 'The Right Honourable gentleman has a nauseating manner. He made an ugly speech. This is because he is an ugly man.'

Tebbit does not seem to mind his street fighter reputation. He is aggressively right-wing in his attitudes, supporting capital punishment and arms for South Africa, and opposing the use of fluoride in the water supply.

He takes an ironic view of High Tories and their paternalism. 'Traditional grandees', he called them once, adding: 'They are not of a mind merely to hold on to what they have got, and to hell with the peasantry. They are extremely concerned about social issues. It is just that they view these issues from their experience, whereas people like me view it from mine.' Asked exactly what he meant, he said: 'Well, if one owns 20,000 acres, one has already got an inflation-proof pension.'

Tebbit's earlier task as a member of Thatcher's Cabinet was to try to bring the unions into line. The government made a start with the Employment Bills of 1981 and 1983, which were aimed at reform from within, with such measures as secret ballots, and compensation for workers who had lost their jobs for refusing to join a closed shop. Like Thatcher herself, however, Tebbit really started to flex his political muscle only in the government's second term of office. The real task still lay ahead.

He had another advantage over the usual Tory Cabinet Minister, in that he knew the unions from the inside as well as the outside. When he worked for BOAC, he was a union spokesman, serving on the 707 pilots' council. He was deeply involved in union affairs at a time in the Fifties when industrial relations in the airline industry were difficult, ending on several occasions in strike action. Tebbit has said that this experience has coloured his attitudes, but that it didn't persuade him that either management or unions were invariably right.

After the decline and fall of Cecil Parkinson (a startling episode in British Toryism, which we will look at in a moment) Thatcher took Tebbit away from Employment, thus abruptly halting what was looming up as a historic confrontation between the hardest man in the Cabinet and the equally tough union bosses.

She gave him instead Parkinson's greatly enlarged Department of Trade and Industry, thereby moving him up into a position of greater power and enhancing his 'favourite son' image.

* * * * * *

Though Tebbit is always ready to pay lip service to Thatcher's qualities as a leader, he is too idiosyncratic to be a real, 100 per cent gold plated Thatcherman.

Until late in 1983, that title would have gone to the former Chairman of the Conservative Party, the then Secretary of State for Trade and Industry, Cecil Parkinson.

The Parkinson story is fascinating. It is yet another chapter in the never-ending history of Sex in Politics.

Parkinson's sexual misdemeanour was neither unusual nor, by the standards of the Eighties, very grave: a straight, old-fashioned affair with his secretary, which ended in her becoming pregnant. Other politicians have carried off similar affairs without damage to themselves.

What brought Parkinson down was the reek of hypocrisy. Until his private life became public knowledge, he was seen as the archetypal New Tory. Apart from Thatcher herself, he was viewed as probably the finest living specimen of the breed, and certainly a vigilant guardian of Victorian values.

Like Thatcher, Parkinson looks the part. He is tall, clean cut, with regular features, and until his recent difficulties he had an aura of inner cleanliness and good health. At

Cambridge, he achieved only a lower second in English and a third in law, but he was a running Blue, and during his time in office he was often photographed on his daily jog.

He was believed to be an invaluable drawcard for Tory ladies. I remember a briefing at the Foreign Press Association when a Japanese correspondent asked him quite seriously if he expected his good looks to be a factor in winning the next general election. Parkinson gave a brief obligatory blush but did not look either really embarrassed or displeased. 'It is the Prime Minister's qualities and not my face which will win the election for the Conservative Party,' he said demurely.

Parkinson's resemblance to a handsome young officer of World War I vintage certainly did him no harm. But it was more his presentation of New Toryism in an agreeable and non-alarming way that made him so valuable to the Party.

Unlike Tebbit, he did not frighten anyone, for he did not look or sound like a tearaway. He had the idea, when he first went up to Cambridge, of taking Holy Orders; and though this ambition was only short-lived, his manner retained a faint unctuousness. One could imagine him as a popular vicar with his eye on a bishopric.

His blandness made some people rather underrate him. He was the subject of a winning entry in a *New Statesman* competition in 1983 which began:

Why should clean-shaven, pin-striped, Bryl-creamed Cecil Recall so perfectly an empty vessel?

In fact, the 'empty vessel' had shown himself even before he came into politics to be a good example of the upwardly mobile and get-rich-quick new men of the Thatcher era.

Born in Lancashire into a working-class family, he won a scholarship to grammar school and then went on to achieve the breakthrough of an Oxbridge education.

He started his business career as a chartered accountant. Then he went into the engineering business and made a good deal of money in a short time, having prudently married the daughter of a rich Hertfordshire businessman. They live in a 10-bedroom Queen Anne house near Potter's Bar.

In the days of the Old Toryism, Parkinson would probably never have progressed beyond some junior ministry. He did serve in that capacity at the Department of Trade, but his name was almost unknown to the public when Thatcher dramatically appointed him Chairman of the Party. He replaced an Old Tory, Lord Thorneycroft.

He also became in quick succession a member of the Privy Council, Paymaster-General, and Chancellor of the Duchy of Lancaster. Thatcher also brought him into the War Cabinet during the Falklands crisis. The move upset some of the Old Tories. They thought the Party Chairman had no right to be influencing decisions of life and death.

Thatcher's instinct for picking her own men proved to be justified, however, during the election campaign of 1983. It was run by Parkinson with enormous skill and with a ruthlessness that showed a very different personality lying behind the bland exterior.

While both the Labour Party and the Social Democrat—Liberal Alliance were muddling through somehow, the Tory campaign was carried out with the precision of a military operation. Buses and planes were laid on for the press, though transport was far from free, and the facilities provided had the added advantage of bringing in a handsome amount to swell the party funds.

Advertising was kept to simple, witty images—like the one which appeared on posters all over the country showing a foot-operated pump blowing up a balloon marked 'Inflation'. 'FOOT PUMP', the caption said tersely, a pun on the name of the unfortunate Michael Foot, then Leader of the Labour Party, who has suffered all his life from his surname.

After the election, Parkinson made another big jump. He went to the combined Departments of Trade and

Industry as Secretary of State. Just as Tebbit was appointed by Thatcher to do something about the unions, Parkinson was given what the Prime Minister regards as one of her government's most important tasks: the privatization of Britain's State-owned industries.

The Department of Industry in the past had been described as black hole which swallowed up billions of taxpayers' money, through such notorious loss-makers as British Leyland, British Shipbuilders and British Steel. It is the intention of the Thatcher Government to denationalize not only these nationalized industries, but to push even the most sacred public utilities into the public sector.

Parkinson, with his known administrative ability, his high reputation in the Party, and his well-concealed ruthlessness, was to have been the chosen instrument for carrying through this program.

What very few people knew, even those inside the Tory Party, was that Parkinson as he was settling into his new department was haunted daily by the fear that his affair with his former secretary, Sara Keays, was about to become a public scandal, and that his career would be blown sky-high as a consequence.

This is exactly what happened in the autumn of 1983.

It began, as many scandals have, with a small item in *Private Eye*'s 'Grovel' column which mentioned Cecil Parkinson's 'marital difficulties', and the fact that 'Parkinson's fun-loving secretary Ms Sarah [sic] Keays is expecting a baby in three months' time.' The *Eye*, however, suggested that Ms Keays had been having an affair ('an exploration of the jungles of Uganda') with an entirely different MP.

The *Daily Mirror* had already got hold of the story. But it didn't do anything much about it, as it was afraid of being accused of muckraking and of behaving like Rupert Murdoch's less scrupulous *Sun*. It seems certain that by this time Mrs Thatcher knew of the affair, though she may not have known that Keays was pregnant. And it was for this reason that Parkinson was taken out of the job of Party Chairman (which made him extra-vulnerable) and that he was given a tough ministry.

Probably, if both Ms Keays and her lover had kept their nerve, the scandal might have been a minor one. But Parkinson, fearing exposure, put out his famous statement admitting that he was the father of Sara Keays' child and that during their eight-year relationship he had given her assurances that he intended to marry her. In spite of all this, Parkinson said, he had decided to stay with his wife Ann.

Few statements by a serving politician can have been so rash and so ill-judged, especially as it then became clear that Cecil Parkinson felt that he had purged his offence and that he intended to keep his Cabinet post. The Tory Party, whatever its private feelings, rallied round him. And Parkinson set about, in a rather public way, playing the role of the repentent sinner over whom there will be much rejoicing.

All this was too much for Sara Keays, who did not care for the part of conniving mistress in which she was being cast, while Ann Parkinson, the wronged wife, had become a national heroine. Keays became possibly the first mistress in history to issue an official statement of her position, summoning journalists from the *Times* to her family's home in Bath, and presenting them with an elegantly prepared and set out exposition, outlining in numbered paragraphs the history of her affair with her boss.

It was a magnificent revenge, and the ghosts of deceived mistresses down the ages must have silently cheered. As an additional bitter stroke, Keays issued her statement during the 1983 Conservative Party conference, which had been intended to be an unalloyed celebration of the great victory of the Thatcherites in the general election.

As soon as Parkinson heard that the *Times* was publishing his lover's explanation of what had happened on the front page, he knew that he was doomed, and he resigned at once. Thatcher's loss was nearly as great as his own. The strong implication was that the Prime Minister had connived with her favourite in hushing up the affair and in trying to silence the by now bulgingly pregnant Keays. It did her reputation for Victorian rectitude no good.

The shock that the Parkinson affair sent through the Tory Party and through Britain was quite out of proportion to the affair itself. One reason for this that I have already advanced is that 'clean-shaven, pin-striped, Bryl-creamed Cecil' had a holier-than-thou image.

Moreover, not only was he breaching the conventional code of morality. He could not make up his mind to do it properly either. The present Chancellor of the Exchequer, Nigel Lawson, had also had an affair with a Commons researcher while he was still married, and the girl (now his second wife, Therese) became pregnant. But unlike Parkinson, Lawson left his wife, obtained a divorce, and married his lover as soon as he was able.

Cecil Parkinson wanted it both ways. He could not bring himself to leave his wife, though at the same time he was promising Sara Keays marriage. When Keays attempted to break off the affair—she left London and went to work in Brussels for a year—he persuaded her to come back. (Cynics suggest that his reluctance to terminate his marriage might be due in part to the fact that the business which gave him his present wealth comes from his wife's side of the family, and that she is trustee for his share of it.)

Whatever the reason, Parkinson's indecisiveness over marrying or not marrying Sara Keays alarmed the nation even more than his slipshod morals.

The main reason for the small earthquake the affair caused, however, was undoubtedly the shabby look it gave to Thatcher's shining new Victorian Era.

The Conservative Party has shown itself very vulnerable in the past to scandals involving sex. The most famous, of course, was the Profumo affair of 1963 when the Tory Defence Minister, John Profumo, was found to be sharing a callgirl with the Soviet assistant naval attaché. This helped to bring down the Tory government the following year, and had repercussions for years afterwards.

Edward Heath had similar problems when two Conservative ministers, Lord Lambton and Lord Jellicoe, were found in 1973 to be associating with prostitutes. (No one would really have known had not the police, who were investigating vice rings at the time, flushed out the ministers.)

Sex and politics often, in fact, seem to go together. Some Prime Ministers, even while in office, have been notorious philanderers. Lloyd George had a long-standing affair with his secretary, and no Prime Minister today would dare bring back prostitutes to Number 10 Downing Street as the righteous Gladstone did, on the grounds of saving their souls.

But Thatcher and the more pious of her supporters have made great public play of setting new standards. The new Chairman of the Conservative Party, John Selwyn Gummer, a Thatcherman *par excellence*, has written about the Profumo affair:

> The Victorians would have made no bones about it. They would have said quite clearly that public men should set an example in private morality. They would have seen such behaviour as harmful, *per se*.

Those who subscribe to Victorian standards must abide by them; and this was a lesson that both Thatcher and Parkinson, to their cost, learned in 1983. The affair clearly took its toll on Thatcher, and put a dint in her invulnerability and in her notorious good luck.

*   *   *   *   *   *

Among the High Tories, the greatest casualty of Thatcher's first five years of office was the former Defence Secretary and also former Foreign Secretary, Francis Pym.

If Tebbit and Parkinson are specimens of the new breed which has largely taken over the Tory Party, Pym could be usefully enshrined in a museum of political anthropology as Old Tory circa 1980.

Pym is not physically impressive. He lacks both Tebbit's street fighter energy and Parkinson's officer-class appearance. Short, round shouldered, grey suited, he looks more like a chartered accountant than Cecil Parkinson ever did. But anyone in Britain, where class consciousness is as part of physical make-up as a sense of smell, could tell you within two minutes that while Parkinson is *nouveau riche* (or a 'noove' in the current jargon), Pym is very much the genuine article.

This unassuming man comes from a long line of county landowners. One of his ancestors, John ('King') Pym, was a leader of the parliamentary revolt against Charles I. He was impeached for it, but he did not lose his head.

Pym's own career has followed along impeccable High Tory lines: Eton, Cambridge, 9th Lancers, MC at El Alamein, some dabblings in business (he was at one time a manufacturer of tents), and politics.

He is, though untitled, what Peregrine Worsthorne would undoubtedly call 'a knight of the shires'. His family have lived on their estate in Bedfordshire for more than 200 years, and five Pyms have been members of parliament. His whole tradition is the Old Tory one of noblesse oblige.

He first collided head on with Thatcher when he was at Defence. He was asked to cut £500 million from his department's budget. He refused, saying that he would resign first, and Thatcher was forced to settle for cuts of £175 million. When she could, she moved him from Defence. He became Leader of the House.

But when Lord Carrington resigned at the beginning of the Falklands crisis, Thatcher had no option but to push Pym hurriedly into the Foreign Office. It was an appointment which was to cause both of them a great deal of trouble, and ultimately it was to lead to Pym's sacking.

On the economy, he had already shown himself to be a 'Wet'. During the South Atlantic war, though a member of the War Cabinet, he clearly failed to match the Prime Minister in belligerence, or to echo her exuberance in moments of victory.

The Labour MP Tam Dalyell, who has called a number of times for an inquiry into the sinking of the Argentine warship *General Belgrano* claims that the *Belgrano* issue was only one of many on which the Prime Minister and her Foreign Secretary did not see eye to eye.

On more than one occasion, Dalyell says, 'a pale, horrified and livid' Pym went to consult the former Prime Minister, Edward Heath, about Thatcher's warlike behaviour.

If this is true, and if Thatcher knew about it, Pym's fate was already sealed. This was something she could never forgive.

After the Falklands campaign, the coldness between Downing Street and the Foreign Office continued. Thatcher appointed her own adviser on foreign affairs, a former ambassador to the UN, Sir Anthony Parsons. Parsons, who had played a major role in negotiations during the Falklands war, moved into Number 10 Downing Street as part of the special team which the Prime Minister was building up round her.

Even Pym himself, when he was still Foreign Secretary, agreed that the Prime Minister had felt 'let down' by the Foreign Office over the Falklands issue. Most political commentators in Britain said bluntly that after the end of the South Atlantic crisis the feelings at Number 10 were much deeper and bitter than that, and that actually Thatcher was suspicious and distrustful of the Foreign Office mandarins.

When I was in London, Foreign Office officials always denied that a rift existed, saying that Sir Anthony Parsons was, after all, 'one of our chaps', and that he had acted as a useful bridge between Downing Street and the FCO. Few people believed the disclaimer.

Whatever she thought about the Foreign Office as a whole, Thatcher showed no mercy towards Francis Pym, either before or after the election of 1983.

In the closing days of the campaign, she even reached the stage of humiliating him in public, correcting him when he gave what she considered to be an inadequate answer at a press conference.

'What the Foreign Secreary actually *means*...' she said derisively to assembled reporters, while Pym ducked his head and appeared to shrink even further into his chair. It has been said of him that as well as being an Old Tory, his problems with Thatcher have arisen from the fact that, as a gentleman, he was brought up never to take too hard a line with a woman.

An interviewer even asked him once if this were true, but he said that it was a question he found impossible to answer. It might very well be the answer to the Thatcher-Pym falling out. Like all natural bullies, the Prime Minister is impressed by people who are brave enough to shout back at her.

As soon as the election was over, Thatcher sacked Pym. She moved Sir Geoffrey Howe, the former Chancellor, in as Foreign Secretary. She is believed to have offered Pym his old job as Leader of the House, but he refused and went to the backbenches with the other casualties of the Thatcher era.

He did not go down without a struggle. He made a candid speech in the new Parliament which laid bare his pain and anger over being dismissed. Old parliamentary hands said that it was the best speech by an ousted minister in decades.

For the first time, Pym did not behave like an Old Tory. Not only was he emotional; he also fired a strong shot over the Prime Minister's bows, urging her to stop showing only the tough face of New Toryism to the world, and to exhibit some compassion towards the weak and helpless.

If Old Toryism makes a comeback, it is possible that the revivalist leader will be Francis Pym.

There is also, of course, Edward Heath—still dallying on the sidelines. Thatcher's old enemy was the leader of an abortive revolt against her economic policies at the Conservative Party conference of 1981.

But Ted Heath, ruddy cheeked and very portly, would be an unlikely standard bearer for a revolt these days. He also suffers from the disadvantage of being neither a New Tory nor a genuine Old Tory, his background making him as much of an *arriviste* as Thatcher herself. The man whom the party not so affectionately nicknamed 'The Grocer' is probably no longer a serious threat.

* * * * * *

Two other candidates for the succession, in the long term, are the Chancellor, Nigel Lawson, and the Home Secretary, Leon Brittan. But their day is still a long time off, and they have been, in any case, contemptuously described as no more than Thatcher clones. A better description would probably be Thatcher tools—instruments which she will use to bring about the changes she is determined to enforce. Their performance will be remorselessly monitored over the coming years, and if they fail to shape up, they will find that they are readily expendable.

But there is one other minister who constitutes a threat to Thatcher's supremacy. Like Heath, he does not fit easily into any category. Michael Heseltine, the Secretary of State for Defence, successor to Sir John Nott, is *sui generis*.

Unlike most Tories, Heseltine is not a grey man. He is flamboyant both in appearance and style, a passionate orator of the sort more usually heard at Labour Party conferences.

An athletic man, he has been nicknamed 'Tarzan' ever since the day in the House of Commons when he picked up the heavy mace and brandished it in the air to make a point in debate. He is also notorious for his hair, which is golden, and nearly as bouffant as Thatcher's own. At Party conferences, the two bright heads are electrifying among the bald pates and the grey marcel waves.

Heseltine, like Parkinson, is *petit bourgeois*, but is much grander in style. His background is Shrewsbury, Pembroke College, Oxford, and the Welsh Guards. As far as he can be classified at all, he is a paternalist, but he also has a strong touch of the populist.

While Tebbit remains obstinately suburban and while Parkinson, though rich, is still Home Counties middle class, Heseltine has elevated himself into the Tatler class, and lives in some splendour.

In a study of the possible future rivalry between Tebbit and Heseltine, the Conservative MP for Aldershot, Julian Critchley, wrote in the *Observer*:

> Heseltine and Tebbit are well matched. They are both vulgar and passionate, qualities essential to political success. Recently they have wrestled at Blackpool and Brighton for the laurel awarded annually by the party activists. The score is presently one all. Heseltine's rhetoric is the looser; he is the more glamorous, but he must rely as did his hero Iain Macleod upon a combination of piety (the poor and unemployed) and on invective. Tebbit is not quite as fluent, but he has the advantages of his prejudices, which increasingly coincide with those of his audience... I have watched them both perform. Heseltine can bring them to their feet: Tebbit to their knees.
>
> [Heseltine] is no intellectual. His flair is for presentation and administration. He is a gut liberal (in the Hampstead sense) whose beliefs were taken on board in the early Fifties when the ambitious Conservative modelled himself upon Macmillan, Macleod and R. A. Butler—party leaders upon whom Thatcherites now put the blame for many of our ills.

Heseltine, as Secretary of State for the Environment, had

his big chance when Thatcher gave him the job of bringing peace to the inner cities after the riots of 1981. He headed a task force on urban deprivation, and made himself very visible on tours of the worst hit areas. The end result was not particularly noticeable as far as the people of the inner cities were concerned. But there has been no repetition of the riots, so that his tactics have been considered to be at least negatively successful.

After the election of 1983, Thatcher moved him to Defence. His brief was to find a way of routing the peace movement, which at that time was mounting a big campaign to stop the siting of Cruise missiles in Britain, under the terms of the NATO two-track decision of 1979. Despite the marches and demonstrations, the missiles have been installed, and Heseltine has since turned his energies to providing Britain with a workable system of defence on a limited budget.

CHAPTER FIVE

ORWELL'S BRITAIN : 50 YEARS ON

The late Chairman Mao Tse-tung used to be fond of saying that the Chinese people were a blank sheet of paper on which he would paint beautiful pictures.

This is a fantasy in which many politicians indulge, ignoring the fact that nations are complex entities, composed of many layers, and that none of them offer any reformer a blank sheet.

Margaret Thatcher is not the only postwar political leader to see herself as changing the face of Britain. Harold Macmillan, Harold Wilson and Edward Heath all had messianic ideas.

And yet, their large claims aside, the face of Britain *has* changed over the past fifty years, not only because of the social revolutions of the Fifties and Sixties, but also because of a slow, hardly perceptible process which has started from within, working little by little on the national psyche.

Here is George Orwell writing in the early Forties, in *Inside the Whale*.

> ...as western peoples go, the English are very highly differentiated. There is a sort of backhand admission of this in the

dislike which nearly all foreigners feel for our national way of
life. Few Europeans can endure living in England, and even
Americans often feel more at home in Europe.

When you come back to England from any foreign country,
you have immediately the sensation of breathing a different
air. Even in the first few minutes dozens of small things con-
spire to give you this feeling. The beer is bitterer, the coins are
heavier, the grass is greener, the advertisements are more
blatant. The crowds in the big towns, with their mild knobbly
faces, their bad teeth and gentle manners, are different from a
European crowd...

Yes, there *is* something distinctive and recognisable in
English civilisation. It is a culture as individual as that of
Spain. It is somehow bound up with solid breakfasts and
gloomy Sundays, smoky towns and winding roads, green fields
and red pillar boxes. It has a flavour of its own. Moreover, it is
continuous, it stretches into the future and the past, there is
something in it that persists, as in a living creature.

The strong visual image that Orwell conjures up of the
British, with 'their mild knobbly faces, their bad teeth and
gentle manners', is brought to life in the old *Picture Post*,
the British news magazine which came to a much lamented
end in 1957, after nearly twenty years of reflecting the
world in its cameramen's lenses.

In a digest of *Picture Post* from 1938 to 1950 published in
1970 a pictorial feature on unemployment shows a line of
men standing outside Peckham Labour Exchange in the
winter of 1939. Caught in a time warp, they huddle
together waiting for the exchange to open. They are the
British of whom Orwell wrote: short, cloth-capped men
wearing mufflers at their throats (sometimes incongruously
tucked into waistcoats), their cigarettes turned inwards into
their palms in the traditional way of workers used to
snatching a surreptitious smoke on the job.

You know instinctively, though you cannot see it in the
photographs, that their teeth are bad or neglected. *Picture
Post* picked up one man, Alfred Smith, and followed him
through the day:

Alfred Smith lives at 52 Leo Street, Peckham. He is a little man, thin but wiry, with the pale face and bright eyes of a real Londoner. He wears a cloth cap and white muffler, old brown jacket and corduroy trousers. He talks animatedly, likes a joke, walks with his hands in his pockets, shoulders bent, head slightly forward. And he looks down as he walks—the typical walk of an unemployed man.

His face is lined, and his cheeks are sunken, because he has no teeth. He is only 35 years old. He has a wife and four children. He has not had a regular job for three years.

When Alfred Smith married 12 years ago, he was a skilled workman, a spray enamel maker, earning good wages. Things went well with him for nine years. But then the chemicals used in this work made his teeth rot, so that they had to be extracted. He fell ill, and was away from work for five weeks, and lost his job. He has not had a regular job since.

Before he lost his job, Smith had ordered artificial teeth and paid 15 shillings towards their cost. He has never been able to get them finished. That is why his cheeks are sunken.

When Alfred Smith was queueing outside the Peckham Labour Exchange, there were 1,830,000 registered unemployed in Britain, with many more not registered. Tom Driberg was to write some thirty years later:

> Mass unemployment was the greatest domestic disaster and disgrace of those shabby years... [It was] as shameful a blot on the record of a rich nation and its Conservative governments (one of them miscalled 'National') as the betrayal of Czechoslovakia and the appeasement of Hitler were on their record in international affairs.

The outbreak of World War II solved Britain's unemployment for the immediate and postwar period, and it was not until the Eighties that long dole queues again became a national disaster.

At the end of 1983, the unemployment figure remained obstinately at about three million, but there were profound differences between the Britain of Orwell and Alfred Smith and the jobless of the Eighties.

One important difference is that in the Eighties Alfred

Smith would not be toothless. He would have a full set of teeth by courtesy of the National Health, and he would not have lost his job because he had been on sick leave for five weeks. (If he had been sacked, he would have taken his case to an industrial tribunal.) If he was paid off for other reasons, he would also have redundancy money to cushion the first shock of unemployment.

A photograph taken outside any employment exchange (now called job centres) in the Eighties would astonish Orwell. The cloth caps have gone, along with the bad teeth, the mild knobbly faces and the 'gentle manners', by which I think Orwell meant the air of patient resignation with which the British working class used to accept whatever fate handed out to them.

What would Orwell make of punks with orange and green hair gelled into rigid spikes like the headdress of the Statue of Liberty? Or tatooed skinheads rattling with chains? Or young blacks on roller skates, with Sony Walkmans? Or dreadlocked Rastafarians? Or Sikhs in immaculately folded turbans?

How would he, or anyone else who was politically indoctrinated in the hard years of the Thirties, come to terms with a Britain in which working-class aspirations (of the young at least) are most credibly voiced by pop groups? It is hard to see Orwell as a *revenant* in the era of the Beatles or of the Rolling Stones, or of the androgynes like David Bowie or Boy George. (He would, however, have recognized as a recurring pheomenon the 'Oi' sound of the early Eighties, when skinhead groups with names like the 4-skins fought pitched battles with Asians in South London between gigs.)

There are, however, similarities between Britain then and now. A sub-stratum of poverty still exists, as it did in the Thirties, though the word itself is defined in a somewhat different way.

Orwell wrote of the unemployed existing on nothing but tea and bread and margarine (two slices three times a day);

of the poor living in the back-to-back houses of the industrial regions in which '. . . you not only had to walk a couple of hundred yards to the lavatory, but often had to wait in a queue when you got there, the lavatory being shared by 36 people'; and of the frightful 'caravan colonies' that he saw in Wigan. In *The Road to Wigan Pier*, he wrote:

> The majority are old single-decker buses. . . which have been taken off their wheels and propped up with struts of wood. Some are simply wagons with semi-circular slats on top, over which canvas is stretched, so that the people inside have nothing but canvas between them and the outer air. . . Each contains a tiny cottage kitchener and such furniture as can be crammed in—sometimes two beds, more usually one, into which the whole family have to huddle as best they can. It is almost impossible to sleep on the floor, because the damp soaks up from below. I was shown mattresses which were still wringing wet at eleven in the morning. Water is got from a hydrant common to the whole colony, some of the caravan dwellers having to walk 150 or 200 yards for every bucket of water. There are no sanitary arrangements at all. Most of the people construct a little hut to serve as a lavatory on a tiny patch of ground surrounding their caravan and once a week dig a deep hole in which to bury the refuse.

Poverty in Britain in the Eighties has a different face. In the summer of 1983, what was claimed to be the first detailed examination of poverty for more than a decade was carried out by *Market & Opinion Research* (MORI) for London Weekend Television, which was making a series called 'Breadline Britain'.

The survey did not look, as most poverty surveys do, at levels of income in relation to the national average. Instead, it defined poverty in terms of what the people who were interviewed considered essential to a reasonable life.

The researchers reported that according to these standards, about three-quarters of a million people in Britain, out of a total population of 55 million, are living in 'intense' poverty, while a total of 7.5 million people can be considered poor.

It was also clear, however, that items which in the Thirties, or even much later, would have been considered luxuries, are now classed by a majority of the population as essentials.

The MORI pollsters found, for example, that 51 per cent of those surveyed regarded a television set as a necessity. More than half the population listed as essentials two hot meals a day, meat or fish at least every other day, presents for family or friends, a week's holiday away from home once a year, and leisure equipment for children.

On a more basic level, two-thirds of the population regarded as essential the following items: a damp-free home, adequate heating, an indoor lavatory, a bathroom not shared with other families, a warm coat, two pairs of all-weather shoes, a fridge, a washing machine, and the traditional British Sunday joint.

The MORI survey showed that the 7.5 million people living in poverty in Britain in the Eighties are missing out on at least some of these things—with damp houses, poor heating, and the lack of a holiday away from home at the top of the list of complaints.

It is still a long way, though, from Orwell's caravan dwellers, or from the mining household in South Wales which Tom Driberg visited when he was a newspaper columnist in 1939:

Dai Davies was 39. He had once been a strong young boxer. Now he was nearly finished—out of work for seven years on end, coughing his lungs out with silicosis. ('Take it easy,' the doctor had said. 'Plenty of good food.') .... [When I called] it was two pm, after dinner time, but neither Dai Davies nor his wife Gwyneth had eaten any dinner that day. 'You've come on the hardest day,' she said. On the following day he would draw his weekly 45 shillings from the Public Assistance. (But she had managed a dish of faggots—5-1/2 ounces of diluted mincemeat; it had cost sixpence).

It is true that some comparable poverty exists in Britain today, but it now usually occurs among people who under any social system would find it impossible to manage their own affairs competently. At the same time that the MORI survey was published, the *Sunday Times* ran the story of a 23-year-old girl from Aberdeen who had spent most of her life in care, and who like many others before her, had come to London looking for a job.

She had an 11-months-old daughter, and was pregnant with her second child. She lived in a dirty bed-sit in London, with one bath and two toilets between eight tenants. The rent of £22.50 was paid by the State, and the girl's allowance for the week was £43.35, *of which she spent £10 on disposable nappies, and £2 on laundry*. But in her bed-sit she had also a colour television, a hi-fi, and a video recorder, all belonging to her Filipino boyfriend, presumably the father of her children. It was a sad and squalid little story, but one which failed to move a number of readers, who wrote in to point out that poverty of this sort was largely self-induced.

Others manage better. Another interesting sidelight on the Eighties is that welfare payments have made possible a new kind of single-parent family: girls and young women who actually choose to become unmarried mothers rather than work at unskilled and boring jobs. If they can find reasonable living accommodation, and if they are prudent housekeepers, they can manage well enough on what the State pays them, especially if they have more than one child. 'I like looking after my baby, and I am planning to start another soon. Why should I go out to work?' one of these girls said coolly when she was interviewed in the *London Standard* in 1983. This brought a flood of protests from irate taxpayers who said, with some reason, that that was all very well, but *they* had to go out to work to support *her*.

Orwell's tramps of the Thirties, who had their own sort of freemasonry and mutual help organizations, have been replaced in the major cities by squatter groups. Some of these are anarchic, and greatly feared by householders into whose neighbourhoods they move. (They have a tendency to burn down houses when they vacate.) Some are disciplined, and pool their dole money to set up their own variety of commune. In the early Eighties, the *Times* published a half-amused, half-angry account by a woman who lived next door to such a squatters' enclave. She complained that while she went out to work every day, her neighbours spent their time listening to Brahms and Beethoven, making pots and weaving, studying for Open University courses, and generally leading the good life.

Successive governments have launched their own schemes for the young unemployed, and in late 1983, the Thatcher government offered young people who did not take naturally to becoming punks or skinheads the radical alternative of spending a year in the armed forces.

The scheme provided for up to 5,200 teenagers in the 16 to 17 age-group to be taken off the unemployed register for 12 months to undergo training with the Army, the Royal Navy, and the Royal Air Force.

There were some cries of protest over this, as it was seen on the Left as either a total admission of defeat, or (more sinisterly) the prelude to the reintroduction of conscription —which, when Britain had its national service scheme, was mopping up 200,000 young people every year.

The government immediately denied that it had any idea of bringing back national service, but in spite of some stiff opposition from the armed services themselves who objected to being used as a dumping ground, it went ahead with the scheme.

In September 1983, the first batch of boys and girls were taken into a Hereford R.A.F. base. The thirteen girls and five boys had all been unable to find a job since leaving school four months before. They were the first irregulars to enter service life since national service had been abolished 25 years before. The RAF got its recruits cheap, as the Manpower Services Commission paid them an allowance of £25 a week each, deducting £10 for board and lodging.

This seemed to many people to be merely a variation of a previous idea of the Thatcher government, the one of using young people as cheap labour in factories so that Britain could compete with Taiwan or South Korea. But it proved more popular with the young themselves, and there were over 2,000 applications for the first year's intake.

* * * * * *

There are many other features of Britain in the Eighties which Orwell might not recognize. It is becoming more and more a nation of house owners, with (in 1983) 11 million out of 21 million households paying off mortgages, and with council houses eligible for sale to the 6.8 million families who live in them.

A remarkable 60 per cent of homes in Britain run one car, and 15 per cent have two. About 70 per cent of households have telephones, and in a country once notorious for its dank and chilly domestic interiors, 59 per cent now have central heating. A quarter of all households have video recorders.

Three-fifths of married women over 45 are now working, as are half those under 45, making a higher standard of living possible.

Possibly the biggest change has been in holiday practices. One-third of households still do not take holidays, but of those who do, one-third take them abroad. George Orwell wrote in *England Your England*:

> The English working class are outstanding in their abhorrence of foreign habits.
> During the war of 1914-18, the English working class were in contact with foreigners to an extent that is rarely possible. The sole result was that they brought back a hatred of all Europeans, except the Germans whose courage they admired. In four years on French soil they did not even acquire a liking for wine.

Times have changed. The British may still be insular and xenophobic, but since the introduction of cheap package holidays they have travelled abroad for vacations with an enthusiasm bordering on the manic.

Working-class people, who in the past have never gone further on holiday than Blackpool or Eastbourne, can now be heard arguing with passion over the relative merits of the Costa del Sol, the Costa Brava, or the Italian Riviera. More recently, they have ventured further afield, to resorts in Florida or the West Indies, to Sri Lanka, or even to the more salubrious parts of Africa. As some of the countries they holiday in tend to be politically unstable, they not infrequently become caught up in riots, in revolutions or in a change of government. But they are undeterred.

Television news regularly shows phlegmatic Britons sunning themselves by the side of hotel swimming pools while shots ring out outside the walls, or it features interviews with families from the Midlands who seem to have enjoyed their period under siege, even when the power was cut off or when armed guerillas burst into the dining room. That, after all, is what you expect of foreigners.

British insularity and suspicion of the outside world—the 'wogs begin at Calais' syndrome—finds, however, an enduring home in Butlin's holiday camps, founded in 1936, and still going strong.

Butlin's camps are a million light years away from that more contemporary phenomenon, the Club Med chain, with its blatant hedonism, its nudity, its easy amorality, its ever-flowing wine.

As much as anything, I suppose, Butlin's epitomizes the spirit of Britain Past. Billy Butlin, a Canadian immigrant with almost no capital, cashed in on the Bill of 1938 which gave a week's paid holiday to all industrial workers. In the postwar period, when millions wanted a break by the sea, the camps proliferated, and Butlin made a fortune.

Even in the Eighties, the Bultin camps offer the only sort of holiday that some families can afford. The recipe is the same as it has always been: togetherness in tight little chalets squeezed side by side, the sort of food that you can get at home, and non-stop entertainment of the traditional seaside variety. In Britain's unreliable climate, sunshine cannot be guaranteed, as the Butlin's song makes clear:

> All come down to Butlin's, all by the sea,
> Never mind the weather, we're happy as can be.
> Hi-de-hi! Ho-de-ho!

Butlin's is the old Britain of the seaside postcards, of enormous ladies with bulging, varicosed thighs, and of husbands with pot bellies and hairy legs, in baggy shorts and kiss-me-quick hats.

There are beauty contests with shivering girls in bathing suits and high heels, posing by the swimming pool, in which few people ever swim; there are bespectacled, blue-rinsed matrons competing for the title of Glamorous Grandmother, and Knobbly Knees contests for the men. There are non-stop quizzes and games, and bingo, and talent quests. For the middle-aged and elderly, there is ballroom dancing, now almost as archaic an art form as quadrilles or minuets. Bedhopping, it is said, is mainly confined to the staff, who regard the easy availability of sex as compensation for the relatively low wages paid at the camps.

One other great surviving relic of Britain Past is the country's most famous women's organisation, the Women's Institutes.

The WI well predates Butlin's. It was founded in World War I, imported from Canada where it was already well established. At that time, especially in the rural Britain, the standards of Thatcher's favourite Victorian era still largely prevailed. Women did not have the vote; contraception was unreliable, so that large families were the norm; childbirth was still a hazardous business; and in the countryside hygiene was primitive and social life was restricted.

The WI was an immediate success, and within a very

short time, villages and small towns all over Britain were sending delegates to the annual general meeting in London.

The catchphrase of the WI over the years has been 'jam and Jerusalem'. The jam is sold at the famous WI markets, which also specialize in cakes, all kinds of home produce, and handcrafts. During the recession of the early Eighties, the markets experienced a spectacular boom, with the annual turnover reaching £4 million. 'Jerusalem' is the WI theme song and cynics find comical the spectacle of middle-aged women in flowery hats singing:

> Bring me my Bow of burning gold
> Bring me my Arrows of desire
> Bring me my Spear, oh clouds unfold!
> Bring me my Chariot of fire.

But in fact, building the New Jerusalem has been a part of WI ambitions from the beginning. The Institute has lobbied for everything from better bus services in rural areas to the right of parents to visit their children in hospital. (It has never, though, tackled really controversial subjects like abortion or nuclear disarmament.)

But in the Britain of the Eighties, the WI is losing ground. Its top membership was 462,000 in 1956; today it is 360,000. The majority of its members are middle-aged and elderly, and it has little to say to the young or to ethnic minorities. It is stuck with the image of jam-making and tea cosies. The Queen Mother, herself in her Eighties, is president of the Sandringham chapter, but the young Princess of Wales is not a member.

In its struggle for survival, the WI launched a new campaign in 1983 called 'Women in the Community'. A WI song to be sung side by side with Jerusalem was commissioned. It begins with 'Prospects are sky high at the WI,' and ends with 'At work or leisure, we've got it together/ Knowing we're growing, and going on forever.'

The WI chairman, Anne Harris, appeared on television

kicking her legs up against a background of delegates massed on the steps of the Albert Memorial. A video put out by the WI included a sequence of black girls playing tennis. The WI, Mrs Harris said, was 'taking the biggest step forward in our history'. But others see the prospects of survival for a conservative, largely elderly, almost all white, women's organization which avoids awkward topics as being, in the long term, remote.

*   *   *   *   *   *

If Butlin's and the WI are Britain Past, the street movements of the Eighties seem much more to encapsulate Britain Present. Two of these groups, the punks and the skinheads, have proved surprisingly resilient, and have kept their identity while other cults have come and gone.

Skinheads are less interesting than punks, because they are really only another manifestation of that recurring phenomenon, the Street Tough. They are, in a less disciplined form, the same sort of thugs that attached themselves to Oswald Mosley in the Thirties, or who skirmish on the edges of the National Front today. Take them upmarket a bit and they become football hooligans or bikies.

Even if they are inoffensive and non-violent at heart, their intention is to frighten: hence their uniform of braces and halfmast trousers and heavy boots intended for kicking, though as often as not their only aggression is verbal. Foul-mouthed and shaven headed, they terrorize train carriages; or rather, attempt to. British phlegm comes into its own on these occasions, and other passengers simply pretend that they are both inaudible and invisible as the monotonous obscenities flow. They show no signs, however, of fading away. In 1983, when I left Britain, children of eight or nine with shaven heads and skinhead uniform were occasionally to be seen on the streets. (Presumably their parents had connived at their enrolment in the junior skinhead cult, for their scalps had to be shaved for them, and their clothes and boots specially bought.)

Punks are another thing again. Thugs we have always had with us, but punks are not thugs. While thugs are busy mugging pensioners and beating up Asian shopkeepers, punks are more harmlessly engaged in finding increasingly bizarre ways to embellish themselves.

In his television series, 'Civilisation', the late Lord Clark put forward the theory that at the peak of civilized eras, mankind became bored with the near-perfection it had created, and that it was then that barbarians came out of the swamps or the dark countries to overturn the established order.

Even in an age when this is less likely to happen, people still like to frighten themselves with the threat of the strange and the unknown, of the barbarians lurking beyond the fringes of the comforting firelight.

I have a theory that the punks are indulging in a kind of mock-barbarian fantasy. Like the skinheads, they wish to shock and alarm, but most of them, at least, do not seem to want to hurt.

Punk fashion has moved through many phases—from safety pins, through the septum, to dresses made entirely of rags and bandages wound round the arms and legs. Cockatoo hairstyles or semi-mohicans, combined with technicolour face painting, remain a constant. Hair gel has made possible the creation of hairstyles more *outré* than are usually seen (say) outside the central highlands of New Guinea.

There has also been something of a division between Low and High Punk. Low Punk is not cerebral; it is a way for young working-class boys and girls to put off, for a while, coming to terms with a life which will offer them not much more than low-paid, repetitive work, or the dole, an unglamorous marriage, and kids who will have little more chance than their parents of escaping the poverty cycle.

For Low Punks, decoration is all. It is a protest against

the drabness and monotony which soon will engulf them.

High Punks tend to be strongly into music and politics, and see themselves with something of a mission. 'We all believed Malcolm McLaren [of the Sex Pistols] when he said we could bring down the government, and the country would be run by people under 25,' a columnist on the alternative magazine *The Face*, Julie Burchill, said in 1983. Punks take part in marches for jobs and anti-nuclear protests.

But Burchill herself looks back on her punk years with some cynicism. 'What did it all mean? It meant putting off for two years the awful business of discovering the real world.'

In the early Eighties, the strength of punk, at least as a decorative style, showed itself in the emergence of Quasi-Punk. As we have already seen, even the glossies started featuring glamorized versions of punk hairstyles on their covers; and all over the country, young secretaries and office workers and clerks experimented cautiously with gel and shaving, and with the poison greens and lurid pinks and yellows of punk hair colouring. Punk face painting was echoed in the harsh bars of rouge and strong lip and eye colours of the Eighties as copied by former innovators like Mary Quant.

Chic street markets, which used to sell hippie gear, have switched over to punk, offering real rat skull earrings, fur bracelets, fishnet gloves, chest shields in goat's fur and leather, paint-splashed dresses, blouses which appear to be entirely in tatters. None of this comes cheaply. The well-dressed punk spends lavishly on clothes.

* * * * * *

If we go back to Orwell for a moment, the profound influence of street fashion and working-class music and culture on Britain over the past couple of decades appears to contradict his theory of the embourgeoisement of the proletariat. In *England Your England* he wrote:

One of the most important developments in England during the past 20 years has been the upward and downward extension of the middle class. It has happened on such a scale as to make the old classification of society into capitalists, proletarians and petit bourgeois (small property owners) almost obselete.

The tendency of advanced capitalism has been to enlarge the middle class and not to wipe it out, as it once seemed likely to do. But much more important than this is the spread of middle-class ideas and habits among the working class... In tastes, habits, manners and outlook the working class and the middle class are drawing together.

One of those who in the Eighties has quoted Orwell to support his theory that Britain is in deep decline is the writer Paul Johnson, the former socialist who suffered such a change of heart and is now so ardent a right-winger that he makes even Norman Tebbit look like a liberal.

Johnson pointed out in an essay in 1982 that in his masterpiece, *1984*, Orwell linked the decay in the physical fabric of life with the decay in morals. From this, Johnson goes on to deduce that just as (for example) small railway stations in Britain are no longer the clean, well-tended places that he remembers from his youth, but now have smashed windows and walls scrawled with graffiti, so society as a whole is more tolerant of vandalism, violence and sexual obscenities. 'I think (though one cannot be sure) that Orwell would have seen this as a confirmation of his belief that we were entering a new dark age,' Johnson said.

In his theory of the embourgeoisement of the proletariat, Orwell suggested that the working class would adopt middle-class values, and that the effect of all this would be a general softening of manners. But in fact, the exact opposite had happened. 'The middle classes were proletarianised,' Johnson said. 'Tolerance of violence, obscene language and theft, which had once been confined not so much to the proletariat but to a comparatively small section of it, now spread to the whole and then seeped upwards rapidly to engulf most of the middle class too.'

Johnson, one of the most entertaining and most exasperating of the British prophets of doom, goes on to outline what he sees as the two main reasons for this development.

One, he says, is economic, in that the gap between manual and professional workers has closed since Orwell's day. 'In 1914, university professors earned eight times the national average wage. Now it is scarcely 1.5.' Johnson quotes a survey carried out in 1975 by Professor G. D. Newbould which showed that a professor would have to reach the age of 47 before his aggregate earnings (plus interest) exceeded those of a manual workers of similar age.

(I can add a couple of relevant examples. In mid-1983, Fleet Street linotype operators were earning, with overtime, up to £650 a week, two or three times more than most journalists; and dockers at Immingham near Grimsby were paid £600 for three days work clearing a mountain of sugar from a record sugar beet crop in the Eastern counties. Salary for a qualified engineer at this time was £200 a week gross.)

'Human nature being what it is, poor economic performers are unlikely to be successful moral exemplars,' Johnson said. His other reason for what he sees as the malignant influence of the working class on middle-class manners and morals is cultural, and it goes back to the social revolution of the Fifties.

Up until then, the working class was more or less culturally invisible and inaudible. But in 1954, Kingsley Amis, with *Lucky Jim*, did for the novel what John Osborne was to do two years later for the theatre with the production of *Look Back in Anger*. The cultural domination of the middle class was over.

Johnson said that it was not that the new working-class writers rejected morality, but that they rejected absolute values, and that their heroes were anti-heroes. Didactic simplicity was replaced by doubt, and the only injunction was: 'Thou shalt not censor.'

'Once morality worked itself loose from its middle-class

moorings, it necessarily became relativistic, drifting on the tides of fashion,' Johnson said. Morals were not only relativized but secularized, and some moral values had now gone forever.

There is some truth in what Johnson says, particularly in regard to language. Walk down any British street and you will hear on the lips of the young a flow of obscenities which would make a docker blush. The middle class have adopted speech patterns once thought to be the prerogative of the proletariat.

But not all the middle class. The Eighties have also seen the re-emergence of other middle class sub-cultures, which have now been well documented.

These sub-cultures are of a timeless British kind, and they provide a constant in an era of restlessness and change. The most important of them is the cult of the Sloane Rangers, who, in the Thirties, when Orwell was writing, would have been known as Bright Young Things. Evelyn Waugh would recognize them instantly.

Sloane Rangers in one form or another have been about for decades—in fact, since the Twenties they have probably never gone away—and they were brought out into the limelight, and their habits and mores identified, when the ultimate Sloane, the then Lady Diana Spencer, became favourite in the Royal marriage stakes.

Now, as Princess of Wales (the 'PoWess' to fellow Sloanes) she adorns the cover of *The Official Sloane Ranger Handbook*, a runaway success when it appeared in 1982. (It has since run through nine impressions, and is still high on the best seller lists.)

The *Handbook* by Ann Barr and Peter York is sardonically sub-titled *The First Guide to What Really Matters In Life*. Despite its jokiness, it shows the Sloane Ranger cult as more significant than may at first appear, because it reveals the continuing existence of a large, influential, traditional, deeply conservative middle-class element in British life. Though non-political in itself, this class offers strong support to any conservative government in Britain.

Sloanes are Tories to a man and woman. They admire Mrs Thatcher, though she is clearly not One of Us, the ultimate Sloane accolade. Harold Macmillan or Alec Douglas-Home were more Sloane-type Prime Ministers, but Sloanes also revere Thatcher for her firmness in keeping at bay a Labour government, Reds generally, and other threats to the survival of Sloanedom.

Sloanes (according to the *Handbook*) live in town during the week, preferably in the SW area of London, of which Sloane Square is in the centre.

Further north—St. John's Wood, Hampstead or Highgate—is not favoured because intellectuals and left-wing politicians live there.

But the Sloane's heart is really in the country, where weekends are spent in the traditional Sloane dress, for both sexes, of a padded jacket or waistcoat known as a Husky and of trousers tucked into green wellies.

The sacred Sloane animal is the horse, which appears on Sloane table mats and ashtrays, and in hunting prints on Sloane walls. The Sloane dog is the Labrador, followed by Jack Russells, Sealyhams, boxers, Yorkshire terriers, King Charles spaniels, and dachshunds. But Sloanes never have 'yappy' dogs like poodles.

Sloanes have strong likes and dislikes. They are deeply enamoured of the Royal Family, but they detest intellectuals, politicians, trade unionists and academics with beards. All these people are described as 'chippy', 'bolshie' or 'stroppy'. They particularly dislike the left-wing Labour leader Tony Benn (formerly Anthony Wedgwood Benn, formerly Viscount Stansgate) whom they regard as a class traitor.

Sloane girls often train as cordon-bleu cooks, but Sloanes really like traditional British food, preferably of the nursery variety.

They also like coffee table books and 'sexy' books, but thereafter tastes divide. Sloane women prefer historical romances; Sloane men read thrillers, spy classics, and books about adventure. 'Anyone who has read Proust is not a Sloane Ranger,' the *Handbook* says firmly.

Sloanes talk a good deal about sex, and nowadays Sloane girls may be seduced before marriage, though the virginal style as epitomized by Lady Diana Spencer is also admired. After marriage, sex plays a less important role, and separate rooms come comparatively early.

Sloane wives rarely have affairs because they fear a marriage breakup, and their houses and their status are important to them. Sloane husbands may play around a little, usually with secretaries, nannies, or their wives' best friends. Keeping it in the family, so to speak.

Sloanes have had happy and protected childhoods themselves, and are anxious to have children, though, because they fear being thought sentimental, they usually refer to their offspring as 'ratlets' or 'sprogs'.

Sloane parents of the Eighties grew up in the perilous and restless, the uncertain Sixties and Seventies without being much affected by them. It would be very rare to find a Sloane who had taken part in a student protest, or had done anything more daring on the drug scene than smoke an experimental joint.

Sloanes are a bit of a joke (at least to everyone but themselves) but it would be unwise to take them too lightly. They represent a strong and continuing strand in British life; and short of war and revolution, they are likely to survive as a solid, property-owning class, even into the Space Age.

They do not think much about the possibility of Armageddon, and they confidently expect that their children will continue to walk along their own well-trodden path. Social anthropologists of the future will study their habits with intense interest.

It was the glossy magazine *Harpers and Queen* which backed the official *Sloane Ranger Handbook*, and it is planning to repeat this success with what it hopes will be another bestseller on the latest sub-cult—the Nooves.

Not that the Nooves are new, any more than were the Sloanes when the publishing world discovered them. They are the natural enemies of the Sloane Rangers, the *nouveau riche* businessmen and entrepreneurs who have managed to prosper even in the recession of the Seventies and Eighties. New Tory politicians are also Nooves.

They have been identified and classified by the deputy editor of *Harpers and Queen*, Ann Barr. She says that they are mainly accountants, builders who do up old houses, and burgeoning tycoons in the new electronic industries, producing video recorders and home computers.

There are specific differences between Nooves and Sloanes. Nooves believe that anything may be bought with money, while Sloanes value most what is inherited.

Nooves are much better behaved than Sloanes, who think it manly to get drunk at parties and to chunder and pee in the flower beds. But Nooves are far too socially pushy, and go in for kissing and first names on a very slight acquaintance.

Unlike Sloanes, who operate in very restricted geographical areas, Nooves tend to come from all over the country. They are a new and more fashionable manifestation of the 'Room At The Top' syndrome, or 'where there's muck, there's brass'. 'As soon as they've made money, they move out of town and get a second place, with ponies. They begin to ape the manners of the aristocracy,' Ann Barr says.

Given a few decades, Nooves may turn into Sloanes. Or, more ironically, they may become landed gentry in their own right; and Huskied, green-wellied Sloanes will go to stay with them at weekends.

CHAPTER SIX

THE SOFT CENTRE

...every boy and every gal
That's born alive
Is either a little Liberal
Or else a little Conservative

But not in the Britain of the Eighties. Infants who will be the voters of 2000 may also be little Social Democrats, if their parents joined in the rush to the centre ground of politics in early 1981.

On March 26 that year, I was one of 500 journalists, British and foreign, who witnessed the official birth of the Social Democratic Party. The launch was at the unfashionable hour of 9 a.m., and it took place in the huge mirrored halls of the Connaught Rooms, in Covent Garden. There were strenuous battles for places, the television lights competed with the glittering crystal chandeliers in brilliance, and even a correspondent from the *Peking People's Daily*, was there to witness the event.

On the conference room balcony, a Social Democrat claque had been carefully stationed to provide applause. The atmosphere outside was less friendly.

The anti-SDP demonstrators were numerous and noisy.

They waved placards which said, among other things: 'The Social Democrats are NATO's poodles', 'Williams the Euro-witch', and 'Jenkins the jerk—go back to Brussels!'

Inside, on the platform, under the newly designed SDP logo, were 'Williams the Euro-witch' and 'Jenkins the jerk' (Shirley Williams and Roy Jenkins) with the two other members of the founding Gang of Four, David Owen and William Rodgers.

All four were former Labour ministers. They had been among the Party's brightest and best. All four had left the Party because of what they considered (wrongly as it turned out) its unstoppable slide towards the extreme Left. All four were branded and vilified as traitors, and even two or three years later, when passions had somewhat cooled, the Labour Right and Centre still felt considerable bitterness towards the defectors. They should have stayed and worked to get the Party back in balance instead of deserting it, say their critics.

As they sat on the platform in March 1981, they looked an impressive joint leadership: Roy Jenkins, the rotund sybarite and claret fancier, fresh from four years in Brussels, where he had been a high-flying President of the European Commission; Dr David Owen, former Labour Foreign Secretary, a darkly handsome and charismatic man; Bill Rodgers, former Transport Secretary, the saturnine backroom strategist; and Shirley Williams, former Education Secretary, and one of the most personally popular politicians that the postwar period has produced.

They sat in a neat line, and only later was it discovered that Williams's chair—she is a short, dumpy woman—had to be raised on blocks so that the heads would all be on the same level. (Later, in standing group photographs, she climbed on a photographer's bag.)

Like royalty, the Four were flanked on both sides by their supporters, the members who had 'crossed over' to the SDP in the House of Commons and the House of Lords.

The numbers at that time were very encouraging: thirteen ex-Labour members and one ex-Tory in the Commons, nineteen supporters in the Lords. That meant that they already outranked the Liberals, who had in 1981 only eleven MPs in the Commons.

The line-up was even more remarkable when it is considered that at that time the SDP had no Leader (it was to be run by a steering committee of 15) and no clearly defined policies. It had only a few broad outlines to offer potential members. The collective leadership, for example, was committed to continuing membership of the EEC and NATO (hence the demonstrators outside the hall that day). It was against unilateral nuclear disarmament, and in favour of proportional representation. The EEC, NATO and disarmament issues were those on which the Gang of Four had parted company with their former colleagues in the Labour Party—or at least, with those on the dominant Left.

But if the new Party had no platform or detailed policies, it had a good deal of glamour; and, at the beginning at least, it had the capacity to attract media attention. It spent £170,000 on the 1981 launch, and as soon as the press conference at the Connaught Rooms was over, the Gang of Four fanned out by train and plane to launch the Party in the country at large. It has been estimated that the television coverage it received in its first week was worth £20 million in advertising time alone.

But the Social Democrats were offering a great deal more to the nation than a trendy new party with some attractive leaders. Their ambition was very large. It was, in the phrase which was to become the Party's rallying cry, to 'break the mould of British politics'.

At the beginning it was difficult for a journalist writing from Britain for a foreign audience to get readers to take the new Party too seriously. The example of Australia and of the great split in the Labor Party of the Fifties was often quoted as an example of the fate which awaits small breakaway parties. (The right-wing Democratic Labour Party, which split with official Labor in Australia in 1955 was extinct by 1978.)

Britain itself could offer an example of a third Party which had achieved very little for half a century or more. The Liberals, once a mighty power in the land, had been overtaken by the Labour Party after the demise of the Lloyd George coalition in 1922, and since then they had hardly provided more than an agreeable alternative for voters temporarily dissatisfied with the performance of the Conservatives or the Labour.

The Liberals, like the SDP in its early days, have always tended to be a rather glamorous and trendy party, beloved of media personalities. In 1956, they acquired an attractive new leader in Jo Grimond, and in the early Sixties, following the remarkable Orpington by-election, Liberal hopes of making a comeback rose. 'After that, some polls showed the Liberals getting over 50 per cent of the poll; and "Orpington Man" was hailed as the prototype of the new socially-mobile elector,' wrote Anthony Sampson in *The Changing Anatomy of Britain*.

But Orpington Man proved as unreliable a guide to politics as Piltdown Man was to anthropology. The actual number of Liberal MPs in the House of Commons remained low: only six in 1970, 14 in 1974, 11 in 1979. (The Liberals claim that their share of the national vote entitles them to a greater number of Members, and that they are being penalized by the inequities of the first-past-the-post-system. But that is another story.)

The Party suffered a serious setback when Jeremy Thorpe, who had succeeded Jo Grimond as Leader, was involved in a scandal as notorious as that of the Profumo affair in the Fifties. In 1976, he stood trial on a charge of taking part in a conspiracy to kill his former lover, Norman Scott; and the more sordid details of their affair, revealed in open court and published in every newspaper in Britain, put an end to Thorpe's political career once and for all. (He tried, in the early Eighties, to make a return to semi-public life as the chief executive of Amnesty International, but the outcry against him was such that he had to withdraw.)

David Steel, who took over from Thorpe as leader, has given Liberalism a very attractive new face, and in the election of June 1983 the Liberals won 17 seats, while their Social Democratic partners sank to a depressing total of six.

The Liberals were clearly holding their own, and even building up new support among disaffected Labour and Tory voters. But their experience has not offered much comfort to the Social Democrats since the first heady months when the SDP bandwagon seemed unstoppable. 'In a confrontation with the politics of power, the soft centre has always melted away,' the Tory Lord Chancellor, Lord Hailsham, said in October 1981; and there have been times in the SDP's short history when this verdict has seemed unassailable. But there are those who feel that the Social Democrats will continued to be a force to be taken seriously in the Eighties—they did very well in municipal elections in May 1984 at the expense of the Conservatives— and it is worthwhile taking a further look at their origins and policies.

*   *   *   *   *   *

The main reason for the formation of the SDP was the polarization of British politics as the Seventies turned into the Eighties. While Thatcher was leading the Tory Party hard right, the Left wing of the Labour Party was growing increasingly powerful. Tony Benn, the former Viscount Stansgate, became a popular bogey man, the Demon King of the Left; and it was said that the Bennites wanted to turn the United Kingdom into some sort of grey East European state, with parliamentary democracy reduced to a mere facade behind which authoritarianism lurked.

This left the centre ground vacant and ready for

occupation. At least this was how the former Labour Chancellor of the Exchequer, Roy Jenkins, saw it. Jenkins, sitting out a comfortable exile in Brussels as President of the European Commission ('The King across the water,' his followers came to call him) had already, in effect, parted company with the Labour Party; and long before the then Gang of Three (Williams, Owen and Rodgers) did likewise, he was talking about a new centre Party in terms of an aeroplane which might or might not get off the ground.

Shirley Williams took some time to come round to the idea. As late as May 1980, she was saying: 'I am not interested in a third Party. I do not believe it has any future.' Such a party, she said on another occasion, would have 'no roots, no principles, no philosophy and no values'. Rodgers and Owen seemed similarly uninterested.

There appears to have been two main events which drove them out of the Labour Party, and made them accept seats in the Jenkins' aeroplane. One was the vote at the Labour Party conference at Blackpool in October 1980 in favour of withdrawal from the EEC and of unilateral nuclear disarmament. The other was the election to the leadership in the same month of Michael Foot, the amiable Hampstead intellectual who was put in partly as a stopgap, partly in the hope that, as a left-winger more or less acceptable to the Right, he would be able to draw the Party together. The election of Foot was seen by the Labour dissidents as a disaster. They did not believe that he would be able to stop the headlong rush towards the abyss yawning on the Left. (In the event, they were wrong. By the time Foot left the leadership, the Party had lumbered back to a more centrist position, though it had also been dealt a frightful blow by the electoral disaster of June 1983.)

There was one other reason that a slightly left-leaning centre Party looked attractive. It would be a natural partner for the Liberals, themselves looking bright and fresh under the leadership of David Steel.

Steel had already made wooing approaches to the potential defectors and had publicly urged them to make up their minds to leave the Labour Party. To him, as to others, the prospect of an alliance was by no means unattractive. 'Dear Bill, Shirley and David,' he wrote in an open letter late in 1980. 'It is time surely for you to end your dialogue with the deaf and start talking to us with a view to offering a credible alternative government to the electorate in 1983 or 1984.'

But it was not until February 1981 that Shirley Williams led her colleagues out of the Labour party. In her letter of resignation from the National Executive, she said: 'The party I have loved and worked for over so many years no longer exists.'

The founders of the new centre Party were carried along on an almost hysterical wave of enthusiasm. Before the party was even officially launched, a Gallup Poll showed that the Social Democrats would take 31 per cent of the votes if an election was then being held, compared to 28 per cent for Labour, and only 25.5 per cent for the Conservatives.

Looking back, it becomes clear that the almost visible charisma of Shirley Williams was a vital ingredient at that time to the Party's success. This popularity held up for a long time, and as late as December 1981, I was writing in the *Sydney Morning Herald*: 'If you took a poll on who was the most popular woman in Britain today, the odds are that Shirley Williams would come in second only to the Princess of Wales. (No one can beat pregnant princesses.)'

She also had some powerful backers. When she left the National Executive of the Labour Party, the *Times* devoted a whole leader to her personality and prospects. It was written by the then editor, William Rees-Mogg, and because the rise and fall of Williams' personal fortunes are so bound up with the fate of the SDP, it is worth quoting at some length.

Mrs Shirley Williams would make a good Prime Minister. What is the case againt her? She has a good second class intellect rather than a good first class one....She is slow to make up her mind, and feels her way cautiously through problems, tacking this way and that. In a statesman, such caution is a virtue; undue decisiveness often causes disaster in a democracy.

It is also true that Mrs Williams holds a number of views which on the *Times* we do not share. She is an egalitarian, and we are not. She wants to abolish private education, and we do not. She believes in a wealth tax, which we believe would depress business investment still further...

Why, though, would we still say that this somewhat indecisive woman of middling intellectual attainments and mistaken views, would make a good Prime Minister? It is partly, of course, because she holds some very important opinions, very important principles which we share. There is no politician who is more completely a democrat, who understands better or is more fully committed to the idea of British representative democracy. She is a firm believer in the Atlantic alliance, and she is committed to Britain's membership of the European Community. She is a supporter of a mixed economy, with an important role for private as well as state ownership.

Yet a Prime Minister's opinions and principles are not all that matter. Mrs Williams has a personal character that very large numbers of British people can relate to, can give their confidence to...None of their other leaders talks to them in their own true language, a language of good nature, of friendliness, of fair dealing, of balance. Mrs Williams talks to the British people in their own accents, sometimes muddled, often courageous, always human and always kind.

Talking to foreign correspondents over lunch at about the same time, Rees-Mogg went even further. He said to us that he believed the proposed new British centre Party would win the next general election, probably with an absolute majority, and he repeated his views on Shirley Williams.

She was, he said, 'extremely charismatic, the most esteemed figure in British politics today. It is very unusual for most of the electorate to perceive a political figure as a good person. When you get a politician who comes across as better than the rest of us, you get a figure of immense power and force.'

In the future, Rees-Mogg said, the industrial workers would be in a minority, and the majority of the British people would be in service industries, and in jobs requiring a degree of skill.

The huge centre group of voters now emerging would be fairly prosperous. They would not be particularly compassionate, and would have their own interests at heart, not those of the rich or the very poor.

The number of wealthy entrepreneurs at one end of the scale would decline, as would the ideologically committed trade unionists—such as miners and dockers—at the other.

Rees-Mogg considered that left-wing conservatives, right-wing Labour and the Liberals could muster 70 per cent of the electoral vote between them, and would support a centre Party.

Rees-Mogg may have been wrong (at least in the short term; not necessarily in the long) but his views were shared by the 80,000 people who wrote to the newly formed Council for Social Democracy, inquiring about the new centre Party.

The comparison is often made between Shirley Williams and Margaret Thatcher, though they share little in common except their sex. In his *Changing Anatomy of Britain*, Anthony Sampson wrote:

> The contrast between the two women politicians, Thatcher and Williams, at the top of this male profession, was continually striking: Williams representing the compassionate, motherly side of womanhood; Thatcher standing for the more dominating headmistress side, and both talking more directly than most men. When Thatcher was first elected Tory leader, Williams thought that her chances of leading Labour were finished, since the House of Commons would not stand for two women protagonists. But Thatcher's obduracy soon emphasised Williams's attractions. 'Politics isn't all made up of

Mrs Thatchers and Richard Nixons,' she insisted. 'I don't believe in macho struttings and high noons.'

The concept of Williams as representing the compassionate, motherly side of womanhood is, of course, a very male point of view. Williams has never seemed to me to be particularly motherly, and it is doubtful that she would see herself as so. But she is famous for her ability to concentrate her attention on the people to whom she is speaking, so that, for a time, they and their individual problems are the most important thing in the world. She is also a natural campaigner (which is more than one can say for most politicians) and to see her working her warm, slow, absorbed way through a crowd on the campaign trail is an instructive experience.

Williams has one other great advantage: her appearance. One remark which is quoted in every profile written of her is that of Lady Astor, who, very early in her career, said to her: 'You will never get on in politics, my dear, with *that* hair!'

In the late Seventies, a London fashion expert designated her as Frump of the Year; and the Australian television commentator and wit, Clive James, said that her clothes looked as though they had been run up for her by a band of blind British designers.

Yet, with her perpetually untidy hair and her air of having hastily outfitted herself at the nearest Oxfam shop, Williams is a much more attractive figure than Thatcher. Margaret Thatcher, in her neat blue suits and pearls, with every hair disciplined rigidly into place, and her make-up a miracle of enamelling, is just too good to be true. She is too perfect. No one can compete with her or match her, whereas every harassed working woman in the country can identify with Shirley Williams.

She also has, unlike Thatcher, a very attractive speaking voice. It is husky and beguiling in personal conversations, but capable of dominating a noisy meeting. Thatcher is commanding, Williams is compelling.

Williams gets thoroughly bored with portrayals of herself as super-good and super-nice, but her friends insist that this is literally true. One of her former colleagues in the Labour Party said of her: 'Shirley is disproof of the old adage that there's something the matter with all of us. She is loyal, friendly, cheerful, sincere, intelligent, compassionate. Name a good quality and you can tack it on to Shirley. I'm afraid that I have to say that all the virtuous things that people say about Shirley are true.'

If this aura of sheer goodness seems a little off-putting, there is another side of Williams to balance it. She is capable of losing her temper and of attacking her enemies with a vehemence that makes Thatcher sound like an irritable school ma'am.

I once saw this happen at a fringe meeting at Blackpool, just before Williams left the Labour Party. She was being harassed by rent-a-thug interjectors who kept up a mechanical barrage of shouted slogans in an attempt to make her lose her nerve. Instead, she silenced them by the sheer force of her will. 'Let us never forget there is a fascism of the Left as well as a fascism of the Right,' she cried. The words cracked through the hall like a whip and the thugs became mute.

Like all politicians, she is something of an actor. When I was covering the historic Warrington by-election in 1981, I saw her come into the foyer of the hotel where I was staying. She was dragging a heavy suitcase, her clothes (as usual) were rumpled, and her hair (as usual) uncombed. She looked deeply fatigued, dispirited, ready to fall apart. But only a couple of hours later I watched her at a Party meeting, radiating charm, energy and optimism on the platform like a small powerhouse.

Unlike Thatcher, the lower middle-class girl who has perpetually to prove that she has made it to the top, Williams can afford to be untidy and *distrait*, for she comes from a class in which these things are counted as virtues.

Her father was Sir George Catlin, a professor of political science, while her famous mother was the writer and feminist Vera Brittain, author of *Testament of Youth* and *Testament of Experience*.

While Shirley Williams was making up her mind to leave the Labour Party, a television version of *Testament of Youth* was on view in British living rooms, adding to the dramatics of the time.

Vera Brittain and George Catlin were intensely political, and Shirley Williams spent her childhood sitting on the laps of the famous. As her parents were often away, she was dragged up rather than brought up by a succession of nannies and housekeepers, and went to all sorts of schools from the most posh to the very rough.

She cut a swathe through Oxford which is still remembered to this day, though even then her lack of dress sense was notorious. After Oxford she worked in a factory, on farms, in journalism, and lectured for a year in Ghana, before turning to politics—her true vocation.

In office, she is chiefly remembered for her term as a highly controversial Minister for Education, when she was vociferously in favour of the abolition of public schools. Some of her critics hold her personally responsible for the present relatively low standard of State education in Britain, and for the production of a generation of semi-literates.

She is still passionately opposed to private education, seeing it as the main tool by which the upper class maintains its supremacy; but she has had to moderate her public utterances on the subject since she joined the Social Democrats.

Untypically, for her politics and her class, she is a Roman Catholic. Her father was a non-practising Catholic, and his daughter was not baptized. Williams arranged that for herself when she was 18 and up at Oxford, and the story of how she entered the Church is typical of her own impulsive nature.

'I didn't have a great religious brainstorm, it just seemed inevitable,' she once told an interviewer. 'I found a priest, and went up to somebody on the street, a surprised passer-by, and asked her to be my godmother. She was quite an agreeable lady and obviously took her duties seriously, because the next day she came to see me and was so shocked to find me in trousers that she went away and never came back.'

Despite this somewhat perfunctory beginning, Williams has remained a Catholic, and is resolutely opposed to abortion on demand, a position which has caused her some difficulties.

Her religion also made the breakup of her marriage to the philosopher Bernard Williams extremely painful. They were divorced in 1974, despite Williams' own opposition to the liberalization of British divorce laws. The couple had one daughter, Rebecca, who has been kept resolutely out of the limelight.

Despite her personal popularity, Williams' political career has had some nasty checks. In 1976 she lost the election for Labour's deputy leadership to Michael Foot (a decision by the parliamentary Party which was to have consequences unimaginable); and in the election of 1979 she lost the safe seat of Hertford and Stevenage—one of the victims of the Winter of Discontent. She did not return to the House of Commons until she won Crosby for the SDP in 1982.

But it is her curiously patchy performance since she has left the Labour Party which has puzzled her admirers; and as I said earlier, it almost seems that the swings in SDP fortunes are linked with the falling off in Williams' public appeal.

Insofar as her enemies have been able to find fault with her, she has always been accused of being indecisive, slow at making up her mind, disorganized, and compulsively late.

It may be that after she joined the SDP, the trauma of

leaving the Labour Party (all four of the major defectors were haunted by the accusation of treachery) and the breaking of relationships which went back thirty years sapped her vitality and her political will.

The real turn in Williams' fortunes came when, after dithering for some time, she refused to stand in the decisive by-election of Warrington in 1981. In the event, Roy Jenkins stood; and though he was a totally unsuitable candidate (his inability to pronounce the letter 'r'—an engaging upper-class characteristic—made the very name of his chosen constituency a nightmare to him), he managed to turn a Labour majority of over 10,000 into a mere survival vote of 1,750. Williams, who would have been a far more popular figure, could easily have taken that seat for the SDP. Her decision not to run was gleefully described by her former colleagues as cowardice, and by her friends as the worst single political choice she has made in her life. She is believed to have had strong personal reasons for not wanting to run at that time; but in politics, it is notoriously understood that personal reasons come a poor second best to political expediency.

Williams had a famous victory in Crosby in the following year and returned in some triumph to the House of Commons. Then she again had one of her inexplicable fadings away during the Falklands war, a time when she might have been expected to put on a very good performance. But both she and Roy Jenkins sat uneasily silent, leaving it to David Owen to steer a clever course between militarism, patriotism and reasonable doubt. He was much in demand as a former Foreign Secretary, and the commentators said at the time: 'The doctor had a good war.' No one knew it then, but his speeches were laying the foundation of his future claim to the leadership of the SDP.

Whatever the reasons, the brilliance of Williams' star continued to fade. She occupies a safe and respectable place as president of the SDP, but she is again without a seat in the Commons, both she and Bill Rodgers having been knocked out by the election of June 1983.

She could still be a future British Prime Minister, but for the present the oracles are silent.

For the Party itself, its wildly euphoric launch and the strong early build-up to success was followed by a slow but steady decline. In the meantime, however, it has joined with the Liberals under David Steel in the SDP—Liberal Alliance. It was not a fully consummated marriage, both sides said—more a modern, living-together arrangement.

From the beginning, there was some awkwardness over who was going to lead the Alliance, but Roy Jenkins (by then back in the House of Commons as member for Glasgow (Hillhead)) was tacitly acknowledged to be the senior figure, because of his long experience in government.

In the lead-up to the general election of 1983, however, Jenkins showed himself to be a lacklustre figurehead. He looked too old-fashioned and conventional for a mould-breaking party, too much like one of yesterday's men.

While the SDP was only limping along, the Liberals were on the upward curve, with a stunning victory in Bermondsey in early 1983. Bermondsey, a tough dockland area, was a rock-solid and apparently untakeable seat which Labour had held for sixty years. Yet in February of that year, a Liberal candidate, 31-year-old barrister Simon Hughes, took it for the Alliance.

It looks in retrospect as if the Liberals built too much on this famous victory. It was not so much a swing against the Labour Party as a decisive repudiation of the candidate that Labour had chosen, against all advice from Party headquarters.

Peter Tatchell was not only young and inexperienced. He was also an Australian—and so, in Bermondsey eyes, a foreigner. He was an advocate of gay rights, and he had left Australia to avoid being called up for the Vietnam war. Bermondsey voters, polled on the streets, called him 'that bleedin' Aussie draft dodger', and posters appeared asking

'Which Queen will you vote for?'

The Liberal victory in Bermondsey therefore, while it was one of the most dramatic overturns in modern political history, was also a freakish event and not an omen.

Even so, right up to the general election, the Alliance cherished hopes of pushing Labour into second place. It was generally encouraged to do so by the polls. But it was a hope that came crashing down during the night of June 9. The Social Democrats suffered a massacre, with two of the founders, Williams and Rodgers, losing their seats. Only six SDP members survived to take their seats in the new House.

With hindsight, it must have been super-optimism for the SDP to think this would not happen. Apart from Williams and Jenkins, its membership in the House was made up of people who had been elected from solid Labour constituencies and who had 'crossed over' without any mandate to do so from their Constituency Parties.

The Liberals did much better. They increased their representation in the new Parliament from 11 to 17 seats, their best figure in a quarter of a century.

It was hardly surprising that as soon as the dust had settled, Roy Jenkins announced that he was stepping down as Leader, and that he was turning the job over to David Owen. He was, he said, in no way retiring from politics, and would continue to work actively for the Social Democrats. But it was clearly the end of his ambition—in a political life full of glittering prizes.

Thatcher would undoubtedly have been sorry to see Jenkins go. With his departure from the scene, she was confronted when the Parliament reassembled with a third Party which not only threatened to continue to be a strongly disruptive element in British politics, but with two Alliance leaders who were young in political terms (both in their mid-forties) and also very much New Men. Since Shirley Williams had suffered a falling away, David Steel had regularly topped the polls as the most popular politician in Britain; and David Owen was already known as a magnetic if uncomfortable performer, a radical visionary who had not yet had an opportunity to show his true calibre.

The Two Davids, as they came to be known, promised to give Thatcher a run for her money when serious business got under way. The main hope on both the Tory and Labour sides was that a rivalry would grow up between them which would cripple the Alliance and make it less of a threat. David Owen, at least, recognized this, and briskly denied the possibility in a television interview. The voters, he said, would find the conjunction of the Two Davids 'rather charming'.

There are superficial resemblances between the Davids. They are within a few months of each other in age; they are both of something of a physical size; and both are darkly good-looking. But there the similarities end.

David Owen is Welsh, the son of a Devon doctor. He followed his father into medicine before moving over to politics. His rise was rapid. At 28, he was a junior Minister, and at the almost unprecedented age of 38 he was Foreign Secretary. He is abrasive and combative, as the Foreign Office found to its alarm; and there is something slightly disconcerting about his good looks. He has been nick-named 'Dr Death', possibly because of a chilliness about his eyes.

Owen is appropriately trendy for the times. He has an American wife who is a literary agent, and he lives in a gentrified enclave in Limehouse, once said to be the haunt of sinister Orientals bent on slitting the throats of sailors. The famous document which led to a new start in British politics as the preface to the founding of the Social Democratic Party was called, rather pretentiously, the Limehouse Declaration.

The Alliance is self-described as 'tough but tender', and the toughness is supplied by David Owen. Since he succeeded to the leadership of the SDP, he has moved to the

105

Right, obviously with one eye on the Tory vote at the next general election. In his keynote speech at the 1983 SDP conference, he came out as an uncompromising supporter of a free market economy and attacked the 'monopolies' of the trade unions and of the nationalized industries. He departed completely from Labour policies by underlining the need to deploy cruise missiles in Britain in the continuing absence of an agreement with the Soviet Union at the talks on intermediate nuclear weapons.

However, he defended the National Health Service, and said that the Party was against State subsidies for private health schemes and private education. The SDP wanted, he said, to display a policy of 'love, charity and altruism' for the poor and underprivileged.

'Toughness and tenderness can go together, and it is this combination which is the key to the identity of being a Social Democrat,' he said. And in a sideswipe at Thatcher, he added: 'Victorian values? No, these are timeless values.'

David Owen remains something of an enigma, an ambitious man who is ready to tailor his policies to the climate of the times. But behind his slightly brooding exterior, there is a sense of real power, and he certainly must be accepted as a major political figure in Britain in the Eighties.

* * * * * *

David Steel also presents a slightly puzzling and ambiguous face to the world. At one moment he seems full of enthusiasm and hope, at another he appears uncertain of his own position.

In the latter part of 1983, he horrified the Liberals by announcing that he proposed to take a sabbatical from politics. He was said to be suffering from depression, a complaint not considered admissible in a politician.

This diagnosis was later amended, and it was said that he had been afflicted with some form of low-grade influenza.

Other rumours suggested that his married life had suffered so much from the demands of his political career that he was considering leaving Westminster for good and retreating to Scotland. Some commentators said that the ailment which was afflicting Steel was frustration over being the Nearly Man, presiding over a Nearly Party.

Certainly Steel had sounded confident enough, if not over-confident, in the preceding two or three years. At the Liberal conference at Blackpool in 1980, he was saying: 'I foresee a Liberal vote so massive and the number of Liberal MPs so great that we shall hold the initiative in the [coming] new Parliament. No government will be formed without us.'

At the first Liberal conference after the formation of the SDP—Liberal Alliance, he was telling his assembled faithful: 'Go back to your constituencies and prepare for government!'

That turned out to be a pipe dream, as the election debacle of 1983 showed, but the Liberals still believe in the possibility of a breakthrough if they can continue to occupy the centre ground.

Certainly David Steel would be a great loss to the Party if he did decide to pull out and go home to his country house at Ettrick Bridge. The 'wee Scot' is a very attractive figure; and the television cameras dwelt lovingly on him in the run-up to the 1983 election, as he perched on rough stone walls in Scotland, dressed in a thick white Arran knit sweater, jeans and sneakers. (This was bad luck for Roy Jenkins, who turned up for a photocall with him in a conservative grey suit. They looked like an ad for Today's Man and Yesterday's Man.)

In his middle forties, Steel appears even younger, with a boyish, smiling face only just starting to thicken around the jowls. A son of the manse, he is guaranteed to be one hundred per cent clean and pure, with a reputation for integrity that only a politician who has never held office can enjoy. He has brought the Liberal Party to the fringe of

107

power. How much further he can take it does not really depend on the Liberals or on their allies the Social Democrats. It depends on two things: the economic performance of the Thatcher government during its second term of office, and on whether the new Labour leadership can succeed in pulling the Labour Party together and making it look like a credible opposition at the next election.

Some political analysts believe that the Liberal Party has become too small and shrunken ever to make a comeback to the days of glory. According to this point of view, it has set its sights too low, and has become the Party of community politics, deeply involved in local government and in issues such as rates and drains. There are only 17 Liberal MPs in the House of Commons, but nearly 2,000 Liberal councillors throughout the country are slogging away to find solutions to grassroots problems. It has been called the 'upstairs-downstairs' party, lacking a middle level.

The Liberals and the SDP, joined in the Alliance, continue to look like a force waiting for a vacuum to fill. The electorate has until 1988 (if the Thatcher government runs its full term) to examine what it is offering, and to judge whether it should be taken seriously.

It might be useful at this stage to have a look at the Alliance policies as finally defined in the manifesto issued for the election of June 1983. The coalition pledged itself to:

- Continuing membership of the European Community and expansion of activity within the Community;
- Continuing membership of NATO, and multilateral rather than unilateral disarmament. Cancellation of the £10 billion Trident weapons program. The Polaris-armed nuclear submarine force to be included in disarmament talks.
- Introduction of proportional representation (a move which the Alliance regards as essential to its survival);
- Reform of the House of Lords, to include the election of

108

proportion of its members, balancing the hereditary and
life peers;
- Abolition of rates in favour of local income tax;
- Setting up of a Scottish parliament and an Anglo-Irish
consultative committee;
- A plan to reduce unemployment by a modest program of
public spending;
- Increased funding of the National Health Service and
social services;
- Trade union reforms, including compulsory secret ballots
and an end to confrontation politics.

These basic planks of the Alliance platform remain in
place, but there has been some disagreement between the
Liberals and the Social Democrats over disarmament
issues.

For the SDP, David Owen supports the deployment of
cruise missiles in Britain as a bargaining counter to induce
the Soviet Union to reduce the number of SS20s targetted
on the West.

But David Steel's position is much more ambiguous, and
he has tended to sit uneasily on the fence on defence issues.
He believes that Polaris should be included in the East–
West disarmament talks, and he has suggested that the
Alliance as a whole may harden up its position if this is not
done.

The Liberals are also well to the radical side of the Social
Democrats on Northern Ireland. At the 1983 Party conference the Party committed itself to the long-term objective
of a united Ireland, and called for the setting up of an all-
Ireland council.

The Liberal Assembly also urged the recruitment of a
multi-national force drawn from countries within the EEC
to take over peacekeeping duties in Ulster from the British
Army.

The Social Democrats were embarrassed and dismayed
at this plain speaking, as they had already agreed to set up

109

a joint commission with the Liberals to work out an Ulster policy. It was not wise to conduct difficult diplomacy at Party conferences, an SDP spokesman said angrily.

Obviously the two partners in the Alliance are going to continue to have their difficulties. It seems likely, though, that they will postpone any real power struggle until the late Eighties, as their only chance of being a credible opposition at the next election is to cling to each other with all their strength.

The Social Democrats may turn out to be the weaker partner in the Alliance. The bulk of SDP membership is white, middle aged and middle class. This makes it something of an anomaly in a society which is becoming increasingly multi-racial and multi-cultural.

Much the same could, of course, be said of the Liberals; but many of David Steel's followers are veteran workers at local government and constituency level. The overwhelming majority of Social Democrats have never before belonged to a political Party, and are often referred to, even inside the SDP, as 'virgins' or 'naives'.

CHAPTER SEVEN

BORN AGAIN LABOUR

On the night of Sunday, October 2 1983, in the main hall of the Brighton Conference Centre, another New Man stepped on to the stage of world politics.

Neil Kinnock, thin, ginger-headed, freckled, sky-high on euphoria, had just become—at 41—the youngest man to be elected to the leadership of a major Party in modern political history. He could not stop smiling, though the task that he had been given would have frightened most people into sobriety. He is committed to achieve nothing less than the rebirth of the Labour Party.

Kinnock, who knew in advance that his election was certain, had a prepared speech ready. But he glanced at it only occasionally, linking the carefully phrased sentences with bursts of the extravagant Welsh oratory for which he is famous. It was an astonishing performance and it did not please everybody. 'Sheer demagoguery!' some of the delegates murmured afterwards.

The speech did not offer any apologies for socialism, which the Tories have tried to turn into a dirty word, and which the Social Democrats have largely repudiated. (Even before the new Party had been launched, Roy Jenkins was saying that he hadn't really thought of himself as a socialist for years.)

111

But in this acceptance speech at Brighton, Kinnock used the word 'socialism' over and over again, brandishing it like a bright spear at his audience. He said:

> We have to commend the commonsense of socialism for that is how we get the maxim for socialism—the most rational, reasonable, emancipated creed ever put on to the agenda for the advancement of human kind. That is how we will win.
>
> If anyone wants to know the reason why we must conduct ourselves in this fashion, just remember how you felt on the dreadful morning of June 10, and think to yourself: June 9 1983—never, ever again will we experience that!

Kinnock is going to play a vital role in British politics in the Eighties, so it is worthwhile quoting a little more of his acceptance speech to get his flavour. After the customary tribute to his wife Glenys and his family, he said:

> I look at our children, I look at their future, and I look at the future of their generation, and it makes me determined that they must not know war. It makes me determined they shall not live in a world of want. I look at those children of mine and other people's children, and I say that no generation shall inherit idleness or ugliness or prejudices of racialism or sexism. I want these freedoms for my children and I know I cannot offer them unless we are about the business of seeing them for all people.
>
> Here in the crowded, dangerous, beautiful world there is only hope if it is together for all people. Our function, our mission as socialists, is to see we gain the power to achieve that, and there is no other way but by socialism—deliberate organization of all the resources of human kind and talents. That is the definition of socialism, productive, systematic, liberating socialism; socialism that doesn't count its greatness in nuclear warheads, socialism that will take real patriotism when the sick, old and young and poor have their just share of the wealth of this massively prosperous country.
>
> To get that, we have to win, and we must be of the people and for the people.

It was heady stuff, but it made Kinnock's audience thoughtful rather than ecstatic. With such a passionate, uncompromising Leader, there were obviously going to be some bumpy times ahead; and the right-centre delegates in the hall looked wistfully at the plump fair-haired man sitting (quite appropriately) on the new Leader's right-hand side.

Roy Hattersley, their chosen candidate, had just been elected deputy Leader, but short of Neil Kinnock being struck down by some malign fate, he was seeing that evening the end of his ambitions to lead the Party and become the next Labour Prime Minister. It was a dust-and-ashes evening for Hattersley, despite the cheers.

For the membership of the electoral college, which had been responsible for putting the two men together on the platform, the outcome was very satisfactory. Before the election a Kinnock-Hattersley partnership was called a Dream Ticket; and after it, it was called a Dream Machine.

The electoral college is made up of the trade unions, which have 40 per cent of the votes, and of the Constituency Parties and of the parliamentary Labour Party, which have 30 per cent each.

This system was forced through by the Left to replace the old practice of leaving the election of Leader and deputy Leader to the parliamentary Party. The Left said that the new system was more democratic. The right-centre was outraged by it, and this was one of the reasons why the Gang of Three—Williams, Owen and Rodgers—deserted the Labour Party.

This time round—after the disaster of 9 June—the electoral college was clearly interested in compromise. It wanted a balanced ticket, with Kinnock representing the soft Left and Hattersley the centre-right, though Hattersley's critics tend to see the amiable Roy as very much a man for all seasons.

Other sections of the Party, however, were appalled by the Dream Ticket, claiming it to be only a repetition of the earlier mistake which combined Michael Foot, the idiosyncratic old left-winger, with Denis Healey—who represents the Labour equivalent of the hard Right. This led to some embarrassing moments during the election of 1983, when Foot and Healey publicly parted company over some aspects of policy, especially defence. Kinnock-Hattersley would be a nightmare rather than a dream ticket, the objectors said. What the Party wanted was not balance but single-mindedness, either on the Left or the Right.

For all but a minority, however, there was one cause for satisfaction in the outcome of the leadership election. The hard Left suffered an ignominious defeat with its candidate for the deputy leadership, Michael Meacher, taking only 27 per cent of the votes, compared to 67 per cent for Roy Hattersley.

Nevertheless, there remained a slight doubt in some minds about this famous victory. The situation would undoubtedly have been rather different if the hard Left candidate had been Tony Benn, its acknowledged Leader and a man with a very strong following in the radical Constituency Parties.

But Benn was not able to stand at that time. He was one of the casualties of the 1983 election, having lost his seat of Bristol East in part as a result of redrawn boundaries. Had Benn been in the House of Commons, he would have been a candidate for either the leadership or the deputy leadership of the Party or both, and this would have made the contest for the top posts a bitter and divisive affair instead of the smooth procedure it turned out to be.

It is reasonable to assume, though, that the decisive rejection of Michael Meacher was a defeat for the hard Left, as he was largely seen as wanting to keep the chair warm for Benn. 'Benn's Vicar on earth' said the cynics.

In the run-up to the Party conference, a Kinnock-Meacher victory had been predicted, and it was strongly rumoured that if this happened there would be another exodus of right-centre MPs from the Party to swell the ranks of the Social Democrats.

Whether this rumour was true or false, it certainly had its

effects. The trade unions and the Constituency Parties deserted Meacher in the last few days before the conference opened. The trade unions gave Meacher only 4 per cent of their votes compared to 35 per cent for Hattersley; and the Constituency Parties gave him 14 per cent compared to 15 per cent for Hattersley.

The trade union vote was not so significant as that of the union barons, who are as powerful in their own way as Mafia dons, always tending to swing their weight from side to side. A number of the trade union delegates, though, did go against their own leadership's recommendations, and that was seen as a sign of a swing right at grassroots level.

The switch by the Constituency Parties was a much more important omen for the future. The Constituency Parties (CLPs) had been deeply radicalized in the late Seventies and early Eighties, mainly because they had been taken over at the top by ardent left-wingers (members of Militant Tendency among them) who drove out the comfortable old Party workers by their sheer energy and determination, and by their ability to continue branch meetings late into the night.

The old-style Party activists complained that, before the radicals took over, they had been able to get their business done quickly and go to the pub for a drink. Under the new regime, it was a case of black coffee from paper cups, and angry debates that raged until three o'clock in the morning. Many of them withdrew from committees, unable to come to terms with the changing face of Labour and leaving the field to the militants.

It was from the powerful bloc that the Constituency Parties made up at the Labour conference that the Bennite Left had drawn its strength. But 1983 was different. As expected, the CLPs gave Kinnock a high vote (27 per cent compared to 0.5 for Hattersley) but they were divided enough on the deputy leadership to deprive Michael Meacher of his chance.

Neil Kinnock himself made light of the difficulties which

the Dream Ticket was likely to present for the Party. The differences between him and his deputy were real enough, but they were neither deep nor enduring. 'We both want to win the next election,' he said.

On that night in October, the task before the two men looked formidable. In an essay in the Journal *Marxism Today*, the historian Eric Hobsbawm assessed the magnitude of the electoral defeat of 1983. Labour's vote, he said, while slowly eroding over the years, had not usually dropped by more than a couple of hundred thousand between elections. There had been no reason to suppose that it would suddenly collapse. Yet this is what had happened, and Labour had taken a terrible beating at the hands of the Conservatives.

It is not just that Labour lost one in five of its already low number of votes. It is the massive defection of supporters of all classes, ages and genders.

In 1983, Labour is larger than other parties only among unskilled/semi-skilled workers, the unemployed and trade unionists, but had majority support among none of these groups, not even the unskilled-semi-skilled workers and the unemployed. They had lost support since 1979 among all three. Only 35 per cent of skilled workers voted Labour: down by more than a quarter. Only 39 per cent of trade unionists supported the party they had founded: a similar drop. Women had shown a slight swing to Labour in 1979, but in 1983 they abandoned the party at a greater rate than men. Forty one per cent of the young (first-time voters aged 18 to 22) had chosen Labour in 1979, a modest enough result for a party which ought to be able to inspire young people. But in 1983, the situation is quite disastrous. Only 17 per cent of first-time voters chose Labour, 3 per cent less than chose the Alliance, 11 per cent less than the Tories, while almost half did not bother to vote at all ... Unless Labour can once again become the party of the majority of the working class, it has no future, except as a coalition of minority pressure groups and interests.

Hobsbawm, a respected and influential voice on the Left, is sceptical about the necessity for Labour leaders to have what he called 'image and charisma'. Labour's greatest triumph was scored under Clement Attlee, he said, who had 'the charisma of an average building society branch manager, against Churchill, who had star quality to give away'.

* * * * * *

How much, then, does 'image' count? A negative image certainly can affect electoral results. This was clearly shown during the 1983 general election, when the constant portrayal of Michael Foot in the media as a bumbling, ineffective old gaffer helped to drive voters away from Labour. In his famous editorial on the virtues of Shirley Williams, the *Times* Editor William Rees-Mogg called Foot 'a rum old ranter'; and even the most determined Labour voter had trouble, in 1983, in seeing Michael Foot as Prime Minister of the United Kingdom.

The New Men at the top of the Labour Party have very definite images, and they are complementary: the thin, quick-tempered but exuberant Neil Kinnock, the Welsh Wizard from the mining valleys; and the solid Roy Hattersley, fair and cuddly, the newspaper columnist and cricket buff.

If nothing else, they have restored wit and some humour to the British political scene, a quality which has been largely lacking in the Eighties. Wit is in short supply on the Tory side: those who exercise it tend to find themselves out of a Cabinet job, or else they are exiled to Ulster. (One of the main casualties was the former Leader of the House, Norman St John-Stevas, an elegant and acerbic raconteur. Thatcher did not mind him calling her 'The Blessed Margaret', but with 'The Immaculate Misconception' St John-Stevas went too far. His head fell.)

On the Labour side, lightness has also been lacking. Michael Foot's wit is too literary, and that of the deputy Leader, Denis Healey, is too cruel. If wit and humour exists on the far Left, it has only been exhibited behind closed doors. No flash of it appears in public.

The new Leader, however, has a temperament as volatile as his glaringly ginger hair suggests. The most astonishing thing about him—and one which his opponents continue to stress—is that he has no ministerial experience at all; and until after the election of 1983 he had hardly been mentioned as a possible Party Leader.

It was obvious that Michael Foot would have to step down, on the grounds of age if nothing else (he was then already 70), but it was assumed that the plum job would go to one of the Party veterans with solid Cabinet experience.

But the Eighties have been a time of upheaval, both on the Right and the Left; and there was a strongly-felt though only half-articulated feeling coming up from the grassroots of the Labour Party that it was time yesterday's men stepped aside and let a new generation take over. This was in part prompted by the fact that the Two Davids—in alliance a formidable threat to Labour—were still both in their forties, and that beside them the Labour Old Guard looked very stale.

Kinnock, then, was suddenly at the centre of the stage, without anyone quite knowing how he had got there. Unlike the older Party leaders, he has impeccable working-class credentials, and like his great hero Aneurin Bevan, he is a voice from the Welsh valleys. Kinnock was born in the mining town of Tredegar, where Nye Bevan worked on the coal face before becoming an MP. After Bevan's death, Michael Foot—whom Kinnock says he loves more than any other living man—followed him as Member for Tredegar and Ebbw Vale.

Kinnock was born in 1942, into a family which had migrated to South Wales from Scotland in the early part of the century. His father worked down the pit, but had to take a surface job after he had contracted dermatitis of the hands. His son remembers him having his hands bandaged, before he went to work on the blast furnaces at Ebbw Vale, so as to prevent further damage.

Kinnock's mother, Mary, was a district nurse, a woman of great energy who dominated the household. Neil was, by deliberate choice, the couple's only child, as they both knew by personal experience in their own childhood the hardship which large families can bring to working-class parents.

For a future Leader of the Labour Party, Kinnock's parentage could hardly be more suitable. Both his mother and father were socialists, and when his son was eight, Gordon Kinnock took him to hear Nye Bevan speak. It was his first political memory, and it was to lead him, thirty-three years later, to the platform of the Brighton Conference Centre, where as the new Leader of the Labour Party he called Bevan 'my inspiration'.

Mary Kinnock also took her young son with her on her rounds as a district nurse, and this gave him an intimate insight into the lives and difficulties of working-class people in the mining areas.

Both parents were ambitious for their only child, and Neil did well enough in the 11-plus examination to win a place at a good grammar school. He disliked its elitist atmosphere so much that he became what one of his friends was later to describe as 'a lazy sod', and from then on his academic record was consistently undistinguished. (The 11-plus examination and most grammar schools have been abolished in Britain, and with Neil Kinnock as Prime Minister no future Labour government would be likely to give way to calls for their restoration.)

He was reluctant to stay at school, but under continuing pressure from his parents he finally managed to win a place at University College, Cardiff. Here he spent so much time on politics and social activities that he failed to graduate first time round, and finally he achieved only a very mediocre Arts degree.

Kinnock, however, already knew what his life's work was to be. He had joined the Labour Party at 15, lying about his age to get in. In his second year at university he became secretary of the Socialist Society, and it was then he met a railwayman's daughter called Glenys Parry, whom he was later to marry.

His friends have been quoted as saying that Kinnock fell totally and absolutely in love with Glenys when they met, and has remained so ever since. Her father was the secretary of the Anglesey Labour Party, and like Neil, she had been steeped in socialism since early childhood.

Glenys Kinnock is a pretty and vivacious woman, a teacher. She has the reputation of being more politically acute and sophisticated than her husband, thus providing a cooler balance to his wild Welsh enthusiasms.

Neil Kinnock himself says that when he asked his wife if he should lead the Labour Party, she replied: 'Someone *like* you should.' It was a wistful way of saying that while she approved ideologically, she also regretted the havoc that the new job was going to bring to their personal life.

(Kinnock's children—he has two, Stephen and Rachel— seem less reluctant to move into the limelight. Rachel has already been quoted as asking how she will get to school from Number 10 Downing Street, and has written a song about her father which she sings to guitar accompaniment.)

Kinnock honed his debating skills after university by taking a job as a lecturer with the Workers' Educational Association, teaching adult pupils who were always ready to argue and challenge any easy assumptions.

About this time he met Michael Foot and his wife Jill Craigie; and the Foots, who were childless, adopted him almost as a son, encouraging his political ambitions. In 1970, aged twenty-eight, he finally arrived in the House of Commons, as member for the mining constituency of Bedwellty (now Islwyn).

If, after more than thirteen years in parliament, Kinnock has not had any experience of office, it is not for want of opportunity. Within his first few years in the Commons, the abilities of the fierce young orator from Wales were already being noticed, and two ministers offered him a job as Parliamentary Private Secretary. To avoid difficult refusals he did become Michael Foot's PPS for a short time, but neither of them took this too seriously. He was also offered junior ministerial posts in the departments of Industry and Prices and of Consumer Protection during the Callaghan government, but he turned them down. He claims that this was because he was generally out of sympathy with the government; but those who believe Kinnock to be a good deal more calculating and devious than he appears to be suggest that it might have been part of a long-term plan to keep his hands clean, and to increase his reputation.

In 1978, he was elected to the National Executive Committee of the Party; and a year later, with the Party out of office, he agreed to become the shadow Education spokesman. He was, by now, an outstanding and popular speaker at the Party conference, capable of bringing an audience to its feet, cheering.

There were, of course, those who remained impervious to his charm. ('I don't like Welsh windbags,' one Party stalwart said to me.) And if his reputation was high in the Party, few members of the general public before mid-1983 would have named him as a possible Leader of the Labour Party. Kinnock himself, asked in 1980 if he had any such thought for the future, said that anyone who even considered the idea of succeeding to the leadership at his age would be 'some sort of obsessive nut'.

But three years later, a bunch of dark red roses clutched in his hand, he was acknowledging the cheers for him as the new Leader at the Party conference. 'No leader of the Opposition since the war has started out looking less like the next Prime Minister,' the political commentator Peter Jenkins said in the *Guardian*. Jenkins went on:

> That is due not merely to his own inexperience, but also to the fact that the party he leads has never looked less like an alternative party of government.

He is starting virtually from scratch in his attempt at the moral conversion of Thatcherite Britain to the values of democratic socialism he learned at Aneurin Bevan's knee, and he will need every ounce of that zealous energy and Welsh charm to do it.

It is true the task confronting Kinnock is formidable. He himself has spoken of the 'unmitigated adversity of the last three years', and he has taken over a Party which not only has lost majority support in the country at large but which is also in grave financial trouble, operating on an overdraft (in 1983) of half a million pounds.

In his more messianic moods, Kinnock takes his role very seriously, declaring that he sees the purpose of socialism as gaining liberty for mankind. 'I want to be Prime Minister,' he said after the 1983 Labour Party conference, 'for that will mean the Labour Party has won, and then we can rescue our country.'

If he lacks ministerial experience, he still has considerable assets to help him carry out this crushing task—not least of which is the charm of his own personality, sunny and stormy by turns.

Even by the high standards of Labour Party conferences, his oratory is impressive.

He does, however, sometimes become carried away, as in the 'guts on the ground at Goose Green' episode. In another famous outburst he described Margaret Thatcher as 'corrupted by arrogance' and 'flattered and fawned upon by spineless sycophants, the boot-licking tabloid knights of Fleet Street, and placemen in the quangos'.

He has the advantage of not being over-modest. On one occasion when his lack of experience was being brought up against him, he mentioned that President Kennedy had suffered from the same disadvantage, but that his youth had given him an appealing dynamism. His aides have also cited Castro and Lenin as fresh new faces who made good.

His ideological commitment has been described as soft Left, or by others as 'marshmallow Left' or 'moderate extremism.' It is, in any case, undefined enough to allow for changes in position—or as he himself has put it, 'changes in nuance rather than dramatic changes of policy'.

He told socialist members of the European Parliament even before he was confirmed as Party Leader that the Labour Party was unlikely to carry out its present commitment to leave the EEC. A socialist party, he said, did not suffer from 'policy paralysis'.

Kinnock received a final gift, bestowed by whatever Welsh spirits attended his birth. This is his talent for falling into clownish situations and turning them to his advantage.

Practically every newspaper in Britain ran photographs of him slipping on the pebbles at Brighton during the 1983 Party conference, falling into the sea, and being picked up by his wife. 'It would never have happened to Maggie!' he said ruefully as the cameramen went berserk with delight.

A famous story is told of how, having suffering a *coup de foudre* at the first sight of his future wife, he set out seriously to woo her at a dance—only to fall at her feet, felled by two pints of beer on top of the effects of a couple of violent blows received on the rugby field that day. Instead of stepping over him, Glenys picked him up on that occasion as well, and took him home to his lodgings.

His critics say that his main personal defect is that he is too straight-down-the-middle, to much a man's man, full of ingrained working-class prejudices. Peter Tatchell, of Bermondsey fame, stung by a reference to 'fairies' ('woofters' is another Kinnock phrase), diagnosed him as suffering from 'macho-heterosexualism'. In spite of his own wife's radicalism, Kinnock appears to have little real sympathy for feminists, even though he publicly attacks the evils of sexism. And though Glenys works full-time he is not renowned for helping her round the house.

What he has so far offered the Party, however, is a fresh and flexible approach laced with old-style Labour romanticism, and the mixture is a very attractive one.

His election as Leader makes the forces ranged against

Thatcher even more threatening. A cartoon in the *Guardian* in the autumn of 1983 showed the Prime Minister lining up political brands of cosmetics and iron pills to fortify her while she gazes anxiously at photographs of Steel, Owen and Kinnock, all displaying themselves in macho poses.

* * * * * *

Roy Hattersley, now serving as deputy Leader under Kinnock, is not nearly as flamboyant as his Leader. But he is an interesting and complicated man, from an equally romantic background.

His mother, Enid, was for a long time more famous than he, for she was Lord Mayor of Sheffield—an achievement which, for a woman of her generation, is almost comparable to climbing Mount Everest.

Hattersley is a Yorkshire man, with the obsessive interest in cricket that this usually implies. The story is told of him that when he was out of office, he was seen at Lords cricket ground, perched in a lonely place, speaking quietly into his cupped hand. He was, he told an anxious inquirer, not deranged but simply seeing if he could improve his skill as a cricket commentator.

Hattersley, despite his present large size and apparent blooming health, was a sickly child, and also an only child. He was made much of in a household which included his grandmother and two uncles as well as his parents.

There was a special reason for this extended family setup; and Hattersley did not know it until he was forty years old, when it came as a considerable shock.

His father had been a Roman Catholic priest who had fallen in love with one of his parishioners (Roy's mother, Enid) and for her sake he had left the church. His two brothers, both of them seminarians, followed him. All of them set up house together, but as ex-priests with no qualifications they were not much in demand on the employment market. And thus, in the early years, Enid Hattersley was the main force in pulling the household through to some form of prosperity.

Like Kinnock, Hattersley became involved in politics at a very early age, and he started campaigning when he was sixteen. 'From the moment I knocked on my first door and announced I was calling on behalf of the Labour candidate, I was infatuated with politics,' he said.

After reading economics at Hull University, Hattersley went into local politics, and then into the House of Commons as the member for Birmingham Sparkbrook. It is a mixed-race, inner-city constituency; and Hattersley has had no difficulty in holding it for the Labour Party. He increased his majority even in the dreadful year of 1983.

His wife, Molly, is an educationalist with a distinguished career of her own, and she takes some trouble to keep out of the limelight. They have no children, and Hattersley is able to devote his energies obsessively to politics. He has said publicly that he enjoys nothing so much as campaigning, a statement which even other MPs greeted with groans and incredulity.

Unlike Kinnock, Hattersley has solid ministerial experience, serving in a junior capacity at Defence, at the Foreign Office, and at the Department of Labour, before entering the Cabinet as Prices Minister. Out of office, he has been shadow Education spokesman, and shadow Home Secretary.

Unlike Kinnock, he is a literary man, a writer rather than a passionate orator. The author of five books, he also has written for *Punch*, the *Listener*, and the *Guardian*, and in 1981 he was named Columnist of the Year. He is as compulsive a communicator through the written word as Kinnock is through haranguing an audience.

He has something of a reputation as a compromiser (David Owen once called him 'the acceptable face of opportunism') but, like his Leader, he is passionate about socialism. He quotes the late Anthony Crosland, then

Labour Foreign Secretary, as defining socialism in a way which, Hattersley says, has guided his own political thinking ever since. Socialism, Crosland said, 'is about the pursuit of equality, the protection of liberty and the understanding that until we are all equal we shall not be free'.

Hattersley undoubtedly passionately wanted to be Leader of the Labour Party, and, next time around, to become Prime Minister. He is, however, nine years older than Neil Kinnock; and, unless Kinnock steps seriously out of line, the Labour Party is likely to allow him two chances to win back electoral power. In another ten years, Kinnock will be only fifty-one and still in his political prime, but Hattersley will be sixty, and a little past his.

CHAPTER EIGHT

WHAT HAPPENED TO LABOUR?

'I am deeply ashamed that we should have allowed the fortunes of our country and of the people who look to us for protection to rest with such a government as we now have in Britain,' Michael Foot, the retiring Leader, told delegates to the Labour conference at Brighton in October 1983. It was the farewell speech of the man who had led the Party to ignominious defeat in the general election earlier in the year. But Foot, while accepting personal responsibility for the debacle, rejected any idea that Labour's socialist policies were to blame.

There were, he said, three main reasons for Labour's rout: the defection of the Social Democrats, which had caused a split vote on the Left; the 'debased' capitalist press which had presented a consistently false picture of Labour policies; and the dishonesty of the Conservative Party campaign ('the biggest Dr Goebbels exhibition we have had in this country this century').

This is part of the truth, but not the whole truth. In the years when I was in Britain, I witnessed the depressing spectacle of a Labour Party apparently intent on committing suicide. Some quite respectable commentators even floated the idea that the Left wing of the party was deliber-

127

ately out to destroy Labour's electoral chances in 1983 so that the Left-Right compromise would come to an end, and so that the membership would have to make up its mind whether it wanted pure socialism or not. (As it turned out, nothing of the sort happened. The membership gazed into the abyss, and retreated hastily from the edge, voting for a soft Left and centre-right leadership ticket.)

Many people in the Party itself did not agree with Foot's assertion that the blame lay elsewhere. In late 1983, the Labour MP Austin Mitchell brought out a book called *Four Years In The Death of the Labour Party*, in which he analyzed the disasters which had occurred between 1979 and 1983. He said moodily after its publication that he was still not optimistic about the Party's chances, as 'the same crazy ideas are being forced on us'.

The shadow Chancellor, Peter Shore, who stood for the Leadership and was defeated, blamed the National Executive Council (the Labour Party's governing body) which swings intermittently from Left to Right and back again.

Shore, in a burst of plain-speaking made possible only by the bitterness of the 1983 defeat, called the NEC 'factious, introspective, quarrelsome and irresponsible'. It had presided for a decade over the decay of the organization, the emptying of the Party's coffers, and an assault on the Party constitution, he said. It had damaged the performance of both the former Prime Minister, James Callaghan, and that of Michael Foot.

Shore said that the new Leader, Neil Kinnock, would also be damaged and affected if the Party was once again cursed by an NEC which was dominated by those who neither represent nor respect the interests and wishes of the plain and good men and women who form the electorate.

Earlier, one of the Party's most eminent women MPs, the shadow Health Secretary Gwyneth Dunwoody, said that the Labour Party was dying on its feet:

The body of the party is dying at every level, in every limb.

We have become a Party of talkers, instead of a Party of action.

The first rule is that without power, we are nothing more than a bunch of tired academics endlessly discussing what should be—and never bothering to make it happen.

A confidential analysis prepared by a senior Labour researcher after the 1983 election said that if Labour did not beat off the Alliance's challenge it would go into the 1988 election as a third Party. There had been a massive shift away from Labour to the Alliance in 1983 ('an electoral earthquake'); and if the same thing happened in the local government and European Assembly elections in 1984, it would be a major disaster for Labour!

The next general election may be five years away but the decision about which is to be the third party in that election will almost certainly be decided within one year... Unless we have broken the back of the Alliance within 12 months— unless we have firmly reestablished ourselves in second place in public opinion—we have the real prospect of a steady erosion of our already massively depleted vote.

The strongest attack of all came from Denis Healey, the Party's deputy Leader until late 1983. He declared:

The election was lost not in the three weeks of the campaign, but in the three years that preceded it. In that period Labour managed to lose about 20 percentage points in the opinion polls. In that period, the party itself acquired a highly unfavourable public image, based on disunity, extremism, crankiness and general unfitness to govern.

The party also managed to express many of its policies in terms remote from the lives and hopes of millions of voters, and rendered itself politically vulnerable to attack on many issues.

* * * * * *

What happened, then, to the British Labour Party, model

of middle-of-the-road socialism, architect of the welfare state, a Party which for decades enshrined the hopes of millions of ordinary men and women?

Whatever happened in those disastrous three years happened after 1980, when James Callaghan resigned as Opposition Leader and handed over a Party already torn with internecine warfare to the far from decisive hand of Michael Foot.

In the autumn of 1980, I went to the first Labour Party conference of the new decade, and saw how the splits and divisions were already physically tangible.

Party conferences are always extraordinary affairs. The Conservative Party conference is ritually stage-managed, with the traditional outburst by the hanging-and-birching brigade, a speech by a token 'radical' (usually a working-class Young Tory), and a rapturous ovation for the Leader (in this case Thatcher) at the end. In between these highlights there are enormous *longueurs*, and it is not surprising that Denis Thatcher tends to nod off on the platform.

The Labour Party conference is much more enjoyable, especially when it is held at Blackpool, in the decaying glory of the Empress Ballroom, ablaze with chandeliers which are reflected in great cloudy mirrors. The sanitized modernity of the Brighton Conference Centre is much more suited to the Tories.

The Labour conference is very dramatic. To enter the hall, delegates and journalists have to run the gauntlet of lines of agitators on behalf of any one of a hundred causes, shouting and thrusting leaflets into reluctant hands. In the lobby are gruesome blowups in full colour of Tories at play—disembowelling stags, or encouraging eager hounds to pull small furry creatures to bits. The display is that of the League Against Cruel Sports and of other anti-blood sports bodies.

Unlike the Tories, who tend to be cosily domestic, the Labour Party conference attracts observers from all over the world. The Soviet Union sent an official Party delegation for the first time in 1981, and in the Eighties there have been observers from Bulgaria, Romania, Czechoslovakia, Hungary, Yugoslavia, Chile, Cuba, Egypt and El Salvador, Guyana and Nigeria.

Liberation movements have also been well represented: the People's Liberation Front of Eritrea, SWAPO, the African National Congress, the Black Consciousness Movement of Azania (South Africa) the Polisario Front, the Movement of Popular Unity from Tunisia, and so on.

Inside the conference hall, at the conference of 1980, there were the usual divisions into three blocs: trade unions, Constituency Parties, and the Parliamentary Party, all sitting in their own sections.

That year, the trade union delegates further enlivened the already passionate proceedings when they came to blows during some disagreement over voting procedures.

But to me, having been away from British politics for some years, the most amazing features of that conference were the radicalism of the Constituency Parties, and the low state to which the Parliamentary Party had been reduced.

Sitting forlornly huddled together, far outnumbered by the other blocs, constantly under attack, and often ignored by the chair when they tried to speak, the MPs looked not unlike the wild creatures at bay in the blood sports posters outside. It was as though the Constituency Parties were in full cry, and the Parliamentary Party was the hunted.

What was the guilt of the MPs? They were being seen as fat cats, as Westminster mandarins bloated with affluence and out of touch with grassroots sentiment.

This was by no means mere rhetoric from the now predominantly hard Left Constituency Parties. They meant to do something about it, and they did.

At that conference, the two reforms most heatedly debated were the removal of the power of the Parliamentary Party to elect the Leader and deputy Leader, and the introduction of mandatory reselection. This awkward

131

phrase meant that a sitting Member must present himself for reselection between elections, so that his Constituency Party could sit in judgment on his performance.

Mandatory reselection was like a lightning bolt to those MPs in safe seats who had gone into the House of Commons expecting to stay there until they either died or retired. It was the overthrow of centuries of tradition.

On the face of it, it was very hard to argue against either of these reforms. The election of the Leader and deputy Leader by an electoral college was undoubtedly more democratic than leaving it to a couple of hundred or so MPs. As for mandatory reselection, honest, hard-working MPs should have nothing to fear from it. It was only intended to weed out those who were not doing their jobs, its sponsors said.

Both reforms were in fact pushed through at a special conference a few months later, and mandatory reselection was practised before the 1983 election—to deadly effect in a handful of cases.

To date, the machinery is working smoothly, but the centre-right of the Party has never been really reconciled to the changes. It sees them not as a democratizing process, but as a serious attempt to emasculate the power of the Parliamentary Party and ultimately the parliamentary process itself.

These two issues represent, perhaps more than any other, the struggle between the centre-right of the Party, and the Bennite Left.

The hard Left, the centre says, wants to change Britain from a parliamentary democracy to a country of 'democratic centralism', where the Party is dominant, and where the parliament is simply a harmless debating shop.

In a ferocious attack on Tony Benn, held to be the main exponent of this view though he would undoubtedly deny it, Michael Foot said that he seemed to want to turn the House of Commons into a 'castrated House of Lords'.

MPs, Foot said, must be 'not Honourable midgets or

Right Honourable marionettes, but real men and women exercising their own independent power of judgement on the great complex issues of the age'. He challenged Benn to stand against him as Leader, and put their respective concepts of democracy to the test; but Benn never took up the challenge, though he stood for the deputy leadership and was defeated by Denis Healey.

Benn, however, takes a different view of what is happening in Britain. In his book *Arguments for Democracy*, he set out what he called 'the case of a constitutional premiership', in which he argued that the range of powers at present exercised by a British Prime Minister, both in that capacity and as Party Leader, 'is now so great as to encroach upon the legitimate rights of the electorate, undermine the essential role of parliament, and usurp some of the functions of collective Cabinet decision-making.' He went on:

> In addition, a Labour prime minister can neutralise much of the influence deriving from the party's internal democracy— which is necessary to serve the interests of its membership. In short, the present centralisation of power in the hands of one person has gone too far, and amounts to a system of personal rule in the very heart of our parliamentary democracy. The prime minister and party leader must be made more accountable to those over whom he or she exercises power, so we can develop a constitutional premiership in Britain ...
>
> Democracy means that the electorate can remove their government. It does not mean that political leaders can take over power from the electors because they are disappointed with the electors' performance in exercising responsibility for their own affairs. Power and responsibility must necessarily go together, and it is my argument that if the people are supposed to lack responsibility, it is because they have too little power. Perhaps the remedy lies in decentralising power by moving it down from the top, instead of shifting more of it to the top.

One of the main grievances of the Left at that time was that the Parliamentary Party worked out its own politics as it went along, tailoring them to suit day-to-day needs instead of following the guidelines set down at the Party conference each year.

Denis Healey, whose liking for a *bon mot* often gets him into trouble, has been quoted as saying that drawing up a Party manifesto is like masturbating: it really does you no harm. In late 1983, he was obviously still adhering to this cynical view as he said then that the reaffirmation at the 1983 Party conference of a policy of unilateral nuclear disarmament was likely to be changed later.

But what the Left claimed was largely true. Time after time, the Party conference voted for abolition of the House of Lords, withdrawal from the Common Market and scrapping of the nuclear deterrent, but without any real certainty that a Labour government would carry these policies through.

(After the 1983 election, though, the centre-right was able to point out that these promises had indeed been included in the manifesto, and had undoubtedly helped to lose the election for Labour.)

* * * * * *

During what Austin Mitchell called 'the years in the death of the Labour Party', the struggle was wide and deep and ran through all levels; but there were only two main protagonists, the Party Leader, Michael Foot, and the darling of the Left, Tony Benn. Their personalities were to have a decisive effect on the outcome of the 1983 election, even though by the end, the Foot Factor was dominant over the Benn Factor.

If Neil Kinnock has been called an unlikely Leader for a major Party, Michael Foot was an even more unlikely one. When he was elected, he was already 67; and he looked a great deal older than that carefully preserved elder statesman across the Atlantic, Ronald Reagan.

Michael Foot's wild white hair, his habit of trying to put on two pairs of spectacles at once, his uncoordinated movements, and his daily practice of clumping about on Hampstead Heath accompanied by a woolly dog named Dizzy while brandishing a heavy stick, made him the delight of photographers and cartoonists. He looked like the Mad Hermit of the Moors.

Almost his first act after being elected Leader was to stumble and break his right ankle, thus allowing political columnists unlimited opportunities for punning. Not long after that, he fell down an organ well while walking across a stage, and this led to a good deal more jokiness.

Yet, in the long hard years of the leadership, he was to prove astonishingly enduring. I went out with him on the campaign trail on a day which had started at half past six in the morning, and which was crammed with travel, television appearances, and speaking engagements; but at eleven o'clock at night, speaking to a crowded hall in a London outer suburb, he was still fresh and full of fire, while the journalists who had followed him round were wilting and anxious for bed.

As a Leader, he was conspicuously eccentric, and made few concessions to what is regarded as conventional political behaviour. Travelling by plane once, he seized the intercom and harangued the amazed passengers on Labour policy. He caused a scandal by turning up at the Cenotaph on Remembrance Day in a donkey jacket, while everyone else was in solemn black.

Addressing a meeting at the Royal Institute of International Affairs, he spent a great deal of time reading to the audience (of which I was one) extracts from a poem by Byron, which—he said—forecast the terrible consequences of a nuclear explosion. Only British good manners kept people in their seats while the interminable recital went on.

He has a considerable reputation as a parliamentary orator, and he can undoubtedly call the thunder down from heaven when he is in good voice. But his rambling, old-fashioned style contrasted badly with Thatcher's brisk aggression in the House, and the columnists made gibes about her cruelty in beating up an old-aged pensioner with her handbag. He prefers to speak without notes. This often leads to his becoming entangled in circumlocutions and sub-clauses, a thicket of words from which he sometimes finds it hard to escape. (He has said himself that his wife, Jill Craigie, warns him to remember Beethoven when he steps onto a platform—Beethoven being supposed to specialize in unfinished works.)

No one could, however, ever doubt his sincerity. The *Economist* once described him as 'hunched over a lectern, his jaw rigid, his eyes ablaze, his lips flecked with spittle. Words and sentences spill out as though driven by some superhuman force. Had he lived in ancient Greece, he would have been one of those, such as Cassandra or Teiresias, through whom the immortal gods speak to man.'

His physical courage is also considerable. A sickly child with poor eyesight (hence the thick pebble glasses which he still wears), he also suffered in his adult life from asthma and from a disfiguring eczema. Sometimes the outbreaks on his face and arms were so bad that he could not go out in public. Those close to him say that he spent much of his life feeling ugly, uncomfortable, and shy, and deeply vulnerable to physical distress.

The fact that he was able to overcome these handicaps and go on to make a career in public life is probably due to the robust qualities of his family background, plus sibling competition.

His father Isaac was Lord Mayor of Plymouth and a Liberal MP, a puritan who held morning prayers for his household and would not allow alcohol under his roof, an accomplished lay preacher, and a passionate home reader and reciter.

Michael Foot says that his father was a 'bibliophilial drunkard,' and the house was so crowded with the 60,000 books he collected that there was hardly room for the family. His library included 450 Greek testaments and 2,000 books on the French Revolution alone. When his second wife put her foot down and forbade him to buy any more books, he smuggled them secretly into the house.

Of Isaac Foot's seven children, four were to become eminent. The oldest boy, Dingle Foot, was a minister in the Wilson government, and was knighted. Hugh Foot, now Lord Caradon, was Chief Secretary of Nigeria and Governor of Cyprus. John, now Lord Foot, became a Liberal peer. (The only younger Foot of any note is Paul, son of Hugh, a radical and crusading journalist.)

Michael broke the family tradition of law and diplomacy and became a journalist, working for Lord Beaverbrook on the *Evening Standard* and the *Daily Express*. Foot's devotion to Beaverbrook, who is regarded as a monster in left-wing circles, has continued to puzzle and dismay his friends. But Foot refuses to recant even to this day. 'I love him, not merely as a friend, but as a second father,' he has said.

When Foot was thirty-six, he married the film maker Jill Craigie, who largely gave up her own career to support him physically and emotionally. Sessions under a sun lamp cleared up his eczema; and rather mysteriously, a car crash in the sixties cured his asthma, though it left him with his characteristic Charlie Chaplin walk.

As a politician, Foot's reputation until late in his career was always that of an outsider, a non-conformist, the Party's gadfly, the Left's conscience. One of his principal interests was the cause of nuclear disarmament, for which he campaigned indefatigably. 'I am an inveterate and unrepentent peacemonger,' he told a Labour Party conference in the Eighties.

He was also fastidious about staying out of office, preferring the independence of the backbenches, and though he entered Parliament in 1945, it was not until 1974—nearly thirty years later—that he accepted his first portfolio, as Employment Secretary.

After that, he became Leader of the House of Commons, but when he was thrust into the leadership of the

Party, his actual experience of government was hardly more than than that of Mrs Thatcher, and a great deal less than of those who served under him.

There are some who believe that in allowing himself to be talked into accepting the leadership, Foot did a serious disservice to the Party which he had served all his life, and that he would have done far better to stick to the role of the blind prophet Teiresias. It has been said that he was pushed towards acceptance by his wife, though he himself has denied this. Saying that his wife would never forgive him if he didn't take the job was a mere throwaway remark, he claims.

But if Foot, the eternal rebel, was betrayed in old age by vanity, the ultimate responsibility for making him Leader lies with the Party itself, and for this it paid a heavy price. Writing in the *Guardian* (a mildly left-wing paper, though lately more committed to the Social Democrats), the columnist Peter Jenkins said that Foot's election was an act of treason, and that he had served his Party 'as a kind of walking obituary'.

Anger should be directed not at Foot but at those who made him king, Jenkins continued. 'A majority closed round Mr Foot, united only in fear of losing their seats at reselection conferences. "Much loved" he was by some, but scarcely loved at all by others, who voted for him nevertheless.' Jenkins wrote:

> Some of them had hitherto regarded him as a spoilt child of his class who had indulged his conscience in literature and oratory while not troubling, until the age of sixty, to acquaint himself with the gritty stuff of bread-and-butter politics, or sully his knees in the compromises of office. They chose him knowingly, as a Quixotic leader.

The real reason Foot was elected was that, unlike other candidates, he was acceptable to the warring factions within the Party. As an idiosyncratic and idealistic left-winger, he did not frighten either the hard Left or the centre right. It is also quite probable that in November 1980, when MPs chose him under the pre-electoral college system, he was seen as a caretaker leader, more or less in the way that the college of cardinals saw Pope John XXIII. But like the Pope, Foot stayed.

During the (nearly) three years in which he led the Party, Michael Foot did indeed partly succeed in his mission of healing; and he proved himself a better strategist than most people anticipated. In October 1983, when he handed over to Neil Kinnock, the Party was shattered by the electoral disaster which it had suffered four months before—but the fearful divisions between Left and Right were less obvious. If the Bennites had not been routed, they had at least prudently drawn off a little way to regroup their forces, and the leaders of the Trotskyite Militant Tendency had been expelled from the Party.

A new National Executive had been elected, with a reasonable balance of Left and Right, with the centre-right plus the soft Left strong enough to give the new Leader a small but workable majority on most policy matters.

It was true that the Party had just received a near-fatal electoral rebuff, that its finances were in an alarming condition, and that its membership was less than one-third of what it had been thirty years before. Yet it is only just to point out that Foot left it in better shape than when avuncular Jim Callaghan made his farewell as Leader in the autumn of 1980.

Why, then, is Michael Foot held to be at least in part responsible for Labour's massacre at the polls in 1983? Probably because he was never able to overcome, in the public's mind, the image of himself as what *NOW* magazine (*NOW* is defunct) once called 'a slightly deranged toff'.

His supporters also saw with terror that, though as Leader he had automatically become a world figure, yet he was not about to emulate Mrs Thatcher and undergo a rapid course of self-education on world problems.

He remained obstinately stuck in the role of the Hampstead intellectual—preferring to discuss, even with his political associates, great books and long dead heroes rather than the sordid and day-to-day Party affairs.

He took holidays in Italy, but showed little other interest in travel. As Leader, he did not embark on any world tours; and it was pointed out that, though he spent a good deal of time attacking the United States for its nuclear policies, he has not visited America since 1954.

Another omission was even more glaring. Although he has been a confirmed socialist all his life, he did not set foot in Moscow until he was sixty-eight, and then only for a very brief visit. Geographically, his world has been a very narrow one.

Just before the 1983 election, the *Economist*, in a profile of Foot, charged him with invincible ignorance. It said:

> Mr Foot does not know anything about anything. He knows no economics, no sociology, nothing at all about international relations except that peace is better than war. He scarcely knows M3 from MX.
>
> Mr Foot will probably go down in history as a great backbencher who did himself a disservice by his ambition. He is literate, amiable, loyal and a very old-fashioned political eccentric. There are precious few such creatures left at Westminster. But he has been unsuited to be Labour's leader and he is even more unsuited to be prime minister.

The electorate felt the same way on polling day.

* * * * * *

If Michael Foot came over as a warm and lovable nut, his opponent in the struggle for the soul of the Party, Tony Benn, tends to chill the blood. He has an inexplicably mesmeric effect on his followers, but non-Bennites find his cold eyes and his ostentatious asceticism strongly off-putting.

In 1981 Benn's challenge to the leadership of the Party was interrupted by an illness that lasted several months. He was diagnosed as suffering from Guillain-Barre Syndrome, a form of polyneuritis, and though he eventually recovered, it was a serious setback for the Left of the Party.

It came at a vital time, when the centre-right had been reduced to putting together the so-called Wedgiegate Tape, in which Benn was heard denouncing the leadership for not incorporating in the Party manifesto declarations on such issues as a wealth tax, the need for more public spending, and a cut in the arms program.

It would be difficult, I think, to find another example in British political history of a tape being produced by Party officials to discredit a member of its own National Executive.

So when Benn fell ill, the leadership sent him a 'Get Well' card, and heaved a sigh of relief. The joke round London was that Benn's complaint was not really poly-neuritis, but that he was suffering from the Shrinking-Name Syndrome.

'Wedgie' Benn is the son of a former Labour minister who accepted a hereditary peerage. On his father's death he became Viscount Stansgate, but he managed to shed his title and revert to being Mr Anthony Wedgwood Benn.

Even that sounded far too upper class, so he made it known that he was becoming plain Tony Benn—though his contemporaries still call him Wedgie, and some of the quality papers continue to give him the full family version.

As well as shrinking his name, he reduced his entry in Who's Who bit by bit, taking out all reference to his parentage and his education. Then, eventually, he disappeared from Who's Who altogether, though he has since been reinstated (without, he says, his knowledge or consent).

He is sometimes referred to by his enemies as a wealthy aristocrat, and it is thrown up against him that he holds a sizeable block of shares in the family publishing firm and that he is married to a rich American wife. To offset these disadvantages, he drinks proletarian tea incessantly from a cheap mug, and has been photographed eating fish and chips in a proletarian Blackpool caff.

He is a teetotaller and an ascetic, though he continues to live in Holland Park, one of London's more elegant areas. When his wife's wealth was brought up against him some years ago, he replied that it had been put into a family trust and that his parliamentary career was not being supported by it.

Benn held six ministerial posts in five Labour governments, a fact which Michael Foot was once able to turn neatly against him. As Benn railed on about the lack of accountability at the top, Foot said satirically: 'You should know, Tony, you have been in a great many more Labour Cabinets than I have!'

As Minister of Technology, he became famous for forcing through the ill-fated merger between Leyland and the British Motor Corporation. In *The Changing Anatomy of Britain*, Anthony Sampson quotes one of his former civil servants as saying: 'I've been trying to work out which has cost Britain more, the Second World War or Tony Benn.'

Out of office, Benn consolidated his position as spokesman for the Left. As anyone who has heard him at a fringe meeting knows, he has a hypnotic effect on the young, working them up with his cold passion to a high peak of emotion.

He and the media have had for years a great love-hate relationship. Benn seizes every ounce of prime time to attack the press, radio and television; the cameras dwell on him compulsively while he does it because he is guaranteed always to be provocative. (Oddly enough, the only job he has ever held is that of a BBC producer, at the beginning of his career.)

Benn and his followers delight in his reputation as a bogey man. In his introduction to Benn's book *Arguments for Democracy*, his editor and close associate Chris Mullin said in May 1981:

No one in British public life is more roundly vilified by the establishment than Tony Benn. Mention of his name is liable to send a wave of hysteria not merely through the boardrooms of the City of London or the drawing room of the Athenaeum, but even through the smoke-filled rooms where the establishment of the Labour movement prefers to do business. There have been times during the last few months when the entire resources of Her Majesty's Opposition seem to have been devoted, not to opposing the Tories, but to stopping Tony Benn becoming deputy leader of the Labour Party.

Yet outside the golden triangle bounded by Fleet Street, the Palace of Westminster, and Hampstead, quite a different appreciation of Mr Benn prevails. His public meetings drew larger and more enthusiastic crowds than those of any other contemporary politician. His last book, *Arguments for Socialism*, became a best-seller. Year after year he tops the poll in the elections for the constituency section of the Labour Party exeutive.

Certainly Benn has a talent for grabbing the headlines, for he is another of the messianic breed of politicians. Pressing at a Party conference for unilateral nuclear disarmament, he said that he was looking forward to being the British minister who would go to Washington and tell President Reagan to get all US nuclear bases out of Britain.

His 'kamikaze peers' proposal was another long-running attention stealer. He announced it at the Party conference in 1980, and I can still remember the tangible shockwave which ran round the hall.

The Labour Party is committed to the abolition of the House of Lords, but no one, up until then, seemed to have thought of an effective way of doing it. Benn's proposal was that as soon as a Labour government achieved office, it would immediately create 1,000 new Labour peers, who would then vote for their own abolition. A sort of mass suicide, in fact, in the manner of whales.

This idea, to which Benn obstinately clung, caused the Party a great deal of anxiety. It was seen as involving the Queen, who would have to give her Royal Assent. Constitutional experts pointed out that in any case the Lords themselves could defer the day of reckoning almost indefinitely by refusing to admit more than one or two new peers a week.

The Left fell in behind's Benn's idea of a sudden and dramatic end to the Lords, but the centre-right of the Party remained wedded to the concept that Their Lordships should be allowed to wither away. The main proposal from the Right was that the legislative powers of the Lords should be gradually removed, thus allowing the majority of bills passed by the Commons to reach the statute books. 'Once that has been achieved,' said the plan put forward at the time by the shadow Leader of the Commons, John Silkin, 'the House of Lords will be increasingly seen as an irrelevance, and the logic of its eventual abolition will become unanswerable.'

The 'kamikaze peers' proposal was, in fact, eventually thrown out by the Party. The Labour manifesto issued for the election of 1983 merely repeated previous pledges. It said that Labour would 'take action to abolish the undemocratic House of Lords as quickly as possible and, as an interim measure, introduce a Bill in the first session of parliament to remove its legislative powers, except those which are relative to the life of a parliament.'

In 1981, six Labour left-wingers belonging to the Bennite school put forward another radical proposal—this time to impose a ceiling of £28,000 a year on salaries paid in Britain, no more than four times the average wage.

To anybody wedded to the concept of social justice, this idea was by no means unreasonable. At the time, the average man in Britain was earning £7,000 a year, the average woman considerably less.

But the chairman of British Leyland, Sir Michael Edwardes, who was running a company making gigantic losses, was being paid £100,000 a year, and (as I mentioned in a previous chapter) he was taking a 38 per cent increase himself while insisting that the workers should be limited to a 3.8 per cent pay rise. The chairman of British National Oil Corporation was then earning £58,000 a year and the head of British Shipbuilders £48,000; and earnings of over £50,000 for stockbrokers and solicitors were not uncommon.

The sponsors of the upper limit plan pointed out that wealth distribution in Britain is totally inequitable, with 60 per cent of all land in England and Wales being owned by less than half of one per cent of the population, and with one per cent of the top people owning 80 per cent of privately held stocks and shares.

The authors of what they called 'a radical strategy for Britain's future' claimed that Benn himself did not actually have a share in drawing up their manifesto; but inevitably, he was blamed for it.

It was seen as additional evidence that the Left was preparing plans for conversion of Britain into a grey, egalitarian Eastern European-style state. An editorial in the *London Standard* warned that Benn, 'a dangerous man', was clearly behind the proposal, and that his followers were 'a new breed of extreme socialists within the Labour Party who, when given an inch of political power, take a mile.'

The chairman of National Oil, Philip Shelbourne (himself named as one of the highest salary earners in Britain), commented that such a proposal if put into effect could 'only lead to a mass exodus of Britain's most talented people'.

However, the group of left-wing economists and academics who put forward the idea had already seen this difficulty for themselves. A Labour government which brought it in would be accused of driving the best and brightest from the country, they said. There would certainly be a good number of highly publicized and well-known exiles, but presumably they thought this was a price which would have to be paid.

The idea of a top ceiling for salaries progressed no

further, but its memory lingered on as an element of Benn demonology.

Benn's opponents in the Labour Party saw him as a humourless and simplistic ideologue, and therefore a nuisance to the Party if nothing worse. The charge was often made against him (and it must have annoyed him considerably) that he greatly resembled Mrs Thatcher. Both, Benn's critics said, were political primitives rather than sophisticates. Both saw life in terms of black-and-white, with no grey areas. Both believed in simple solutions to complex problems.

Benn was also seen, rather more seriously, as allowing himself to be set up as a charismatic front man for groups of sinister left-wing activists, who were working to destroy the Party from within and bring about a Marxist Britain.

He was accused of condoning the activities of the bully boys who turned up at political meetings to shout down the moderates. They were the sort of political thugs whom I saw in action against Shirley Williams and who provoked her famous attack on the 'fascists of the left'.

The interjectors were particularly active when Tony Benn was standing for the deputy leadership against Denis Healey, and there were ugly scenes whenever Healey was speaking.

Benn was repeatedly asked to disown the rent-a-thug groups but though he made a few mild noises of reproof, he never brought himself to the actual point of repudiation. What sometimes happened at political meetings might be regrettable, he said, but he was in favour of free speech.

On the Right, Benn mania reached, in the early Eighties, hysterical proportions. One of its oddest manifestations came when it was announced that the owner of Land's End, Charles Neave-Hill, planned to auction off the 300 acres at the western tip of England, though it had been in his family since the days of William the Conqueror.

Why? A close friend explained: 'Charles is worried stiff about Mr Benn taking over in Britain. He said to me this week: "I would rather sell Land's End than have it taken away from me by that man!" '

Tony Benn is also, in retrospect, blamed for making possible the early success of the Social Democratic Party. A cartoon in late 1981 showed Benn shaking the Labour Party tree, and apples falling off in great numbers into the laps of the Social Democrats waiting below.

Even today, Tony Benn remains a difficult man to assess fairly. Time, circumstances, and the illness which took him out of action for months at a critical moment of his upward thrust, seemed for a while to reduce him to a shadow of a bogey man.

The Constituency Parties, which gave him his greatest strength, have edged to the Right. This was shown at the Party conference in 1983, when they voted for the centre-right candidate for the deputy leadership, Roy Hattersley, rather than for Benn's 'vicar on earth', Michael Meacher.

Now that Labour has a boyish new Leader and what one commentator has called 'a young and happy face', the grim ideologues of the hard Left, still preaching class war, tend to look old-fashioned; and Tony Benn is in danger of becoming a Yesterday Man. He will find it hard to make a comeback in the Kinnock-Hattersley era.

Peter Jenkins, writing in the *Guardian* as the 1983 conference ended, commented on Benn's position:

> Mr Benn is no longer champion of the broad left, no longer a rival for power, but reduced to leading the hard left sectarian minority. He himself seemed determined to play this role, as at one fringe meeting after another, he adopted the losing causes of the last general election, and identified himself, like a valiant officer in a hopeless situation, with the routed factions of the party.
>
> Strange and wild remarks have been flowing from his lips—he describes Britain as 'occupied by a foreign army which can do what it likes in our territory'—and this man of abundant political talents who might well have led his party, begins to look as if he has exiled himself to the barren fringes of British politics, another Enoch Powell.

However, Tony Benn cannot be written off at this stage in the Labour Party's history. In March, 1984, he reentered the Parliament, easily winning the Labour seat of Chesterfield.

During the campaign, reporters who followed him about on the obligatory door-knocking exercises remarked with surprise that he appeared to have considerably mellowed. He and his old enemy Denis Healey appeared on platforms together, and sang My Old Man in unison in a pub.

Healey has made it plain he now regards himself as an unambitious elder statesman, and the Right hopes, though without much conviction, that Benn will also come to accept this role.

The situation in the Labour Party in the early Eighties has been the subject of a satirical essay by Richard Heller, the then political assistant to the deputy Leader, Denis Healey. (Well, the pen is the pen of Heller; but the voice undoubtedly is that of the old master himself, Healey, whose bitterness breathes through every line.)

Heller explains the Left-Right struggle in terms of a contest between two rival tribes, the Dirty Hands and the Virtuous Ones. The Dirty Hands, he says, are the politicians who believe that the duty of the Labour Party is to win office, because they think that a Labour government is better than any other form of government. They may also, less nobly, want to do something for themselves; but whatever their motives, they throw themselves into elections, kissing babies and dancing with pensioners, and trying to keep in step with their electors' feelings on major issues. For the Dirty Hands, statements and policies are aimed at winning elections.

Virtuous Ones, Heller says, are lineal descendants of an earlier tribe, the High Minds. Like the High Minds, the Virtuous Ones believe that statements and policies are ends in themselves, and should be spooned down the electors' throats like castor oil, whether they like it or not.

High Minds tended to be homogeneous, but the Virtuous

Ones are split into minority groups, each of which insists that the minority is always right. They believe that all ministers, all MPs, all people in office are potential traitors (though this causes some difficulties when they are in office themselves). This distrust tends to extend into the whole world; so they see everything as a conspiracy against them.

In an obvious gibe at Tony Benn, Heller says:

> Those who have had the disadvantage to be born and brought up outside the working class will endeavour to conceal the fact in their speech, with vowels not so much flattened as steam-rollered. They may make other attempts to adopt the trappings of workerism, whether in clothes, or in recreations, or even in drink. They change their names.

The Virtuous Ones, Heller says, are energetic, obsessive and uncompromising. In 1983, they made no compromise with the electors—and in the end, nearly three out of four electors did not compromise with them.

The whole essay is a cry from the heart. The consensus politicians of the centre-right fear that the puritans of the hard Left may keep them in the electoral wilderness for decades to come.

CHAPTER NINE

THE NEW JERUSALEMS

I shall not cease from Mental Fight,
Nor shall my Sword sleep in my hand
Till we have built Jerusalem
In England's green and pleasant Land.

Yes, but what sort of New Jerusalem? Tory-style, with
minimal State interference, the nationalized industries
restored to the private sector, private education and private
medicine in the high-growth sector, immigration only a
memory, and law and order imposed with Victorian
severity? Or Labour-style, with Britain out of the Common
Market and unilaterally renouncing nuclear weapons, with
private medicine squeezed and economic penalties against
private schools, and the House of Lords sent to historical
oblivion?

*　　*　　*　　*　　*　　*

At a Conservative Party conference in the early Eighties, a
resolution was put forward asking the government to
recreate a Britain in which 'a virgin leading a child and
carrying a bag of gold could pass safely on foot from one

end of the kingdom to the other'. Just when this golden era existed was not made clear, but the motion showed that the concept of a New Jerusalem is embedded in the collective minds of a section of the Tory Party.

Some of Thatcher's close aides have specifically denied that she shares this vision, saying that she is a short-term pragmatist who excels in dealing with the here-and-now. But as time goes on, it seems more and more likely that Thatcher has a conception of an ideal Britain. And it seems to be very different to the one which she inherited after the election of 1979.

We have already seen how she attempted to reshape the Tory Party in her own image, turning it from the Party of privilege into the Party of competition; and how, on the most basic level, she would like to rid Britain of what she calls 'State socialism,' and rebuild it as a nation of property owners and small business men.

Her dislike of consensus predates her coming to office. At an election meeting in 1979, she declared:

> The Old Testament prophets did not say 'Brothers, I want a consensus.' They said, 'This is my faith. This is what I passionately believe. If you believe it too, then come with me.'

For this reason she has no time for Butskillism, which derives from the names of the Tory and Labour Party strategists 'Rab' Butler and Hugh Gaitskill. It stands for the unwritten agreement between Right and Left that the reforms which brought about the welfare state are so worthwhile and so electorally popular that no Tory government would try to undo them.

Institutions like the National Health Service and State education have been considered by all postwar governments as sacred cows. The New Tories do not necessarily share this view, though the Conservative Party as a whole has clearly been unnerved by the preliminary Thatcherite assaults on them. The Prime Minister, in her reshaping of

Britain, will have to move cautiously in these areas, concentrating on issues like law and order, trade union reform, and privatization of industry—issues on which she knows that she commands popular support.

Of these, law and order is a great favourite with the Tory Party. Every year, at the annual conference, the hanging-and-flogging debate is the most emotional, as the scenes of delegates calling for the return of the gallows and of the cat are ritually reenacted.

Viscount Whitelaw, now safe in the Lords, must still recall with anger and shame his time as Home Secretary— when he had to stand on the conference platform at Brighton or Blackpool, and defend the government against the furious accusations from the floor that it had failed to fulfill its 1979 election promise to restore the era of the virgin and the bag of gold. More than once the delegates bayed for poor William Whitelaw's blood.

It comes as something of a shock that well-conducted Britain has the highest prison population of any country in Western Europe, and that its prisons are disgustingly overcrowded and archaic. In the early Eighties, the governor of Wormword Scrubs resigned in sheer despair, saying that the prison had become nothing but a penal dustbin.

British experiments with penal reform have been tentative and relatively unsuccessful. I once was allowed to visit one of the 'short sharp shock' centres set up by the Thatcher government to deal with young offenders. It was very like the old concept of 'give 'em a spell in the army and it will make men out of 'em'. In this case suitable teenagers were sentenced to short spells in centres resembling army training camps, where they followed a regime of early-to-bed, early-to-rise, and were drilled and exercised remorselessly. Their hair was cut short, and they were required to keep their bodies and their belongings immaculately clean and tidy.

Both the staff and the kids themselves seemed to take a cynical view of all this. I asked one prison officer what he thought of it, and he raised his eyes to heaven and said: 'We've seen it all before. As long as they don't ask us to actually torture the boys, we go along with anything.'

The kids I talked to (some of them, in their mid-teens, were already professional burglars) were weedy, hollow chested, white-faced and sharp-witted: Britain's big industrial areas still produce this traditional type. Most could hardly wait to return to the inner cities, to the amusement arcades and the discos, and to a life of petty crime. 'They won't even let you 'ave a fag in 'ere,' one boy said furiously.

The government has also talked of introducing curfews to keep young offenders at home at night and on weekends, and of making parents responsible for paying compensation to victims of their children's crimes.

All this has failed to impress Party conferences which tend to see capital and corporal punishment as, if not part of the New Jerusalem, at least a necessary pre-requisite for its eventual coming.

The Right wing of the Tory Party has not, however, realized its ambition of bringing back the gallows in the Eighties. The great hanging debate in the Parliament in 1983 was a striking example of how, in a democracy, the elected body can go directly against the expressed opinion of the electorate.

Public opinion polls taken before the debate showed that the majority of British people were in favour of a return of the death penalty in specific cases—notably for terrorist crimes.

But when Thatcher, as she had promised, allowed a vote on the reintroduction of capital punishment soon after the House of Commons reassembled, she had already guessed the abolitionists would win the day.

It was a highly charged and emotional debate, preceded by an amount of media type which showed (not for the first time) that the idea of execution retains its old fascination for the British. Perhaps it is because the practice of public executions persisted late in British history, and because the British seem to have been unusually adept at devising slow and frightful methods of death—hanging, drawing and quartering, for example.

One of the most popular tourist sights in Britain is the Tower of London, where arrogant Tower ravens (whose upkeep is paid by the State) strut around the bloodsoaked site of the execution block. Instruments of torture and execution axes are on display. I remember peering closely at one which appeared to have a pattern of exquisite engraving, only to find that the finely drawn motifs were actually quite disgusting scenes of naked victims being tortured to death.

When the Commons debate on hanging was coming up, the press dealt in loving detail on famous executions of the past, and shook out old hangmen from their peaceful retirement to give their views on the efficacy of the noose. A Tory MP was found anxious to say that if the gallows was brought back, he would be quite willing to do the job of topping criminals with his own hands.

Quite apart from public bloodlust, the hanging debate of 1983 had special significance because of the complication of Ulster. The introduction of the death penalty, especially for terrorist crimes, would mean that the scaffold would be in regular use in prisons in Northern Ireland—possibly as often as once or twice a week.

If that happened, it seemed certain that the province would be engulfed in an outbreak of violence, one far worse than any which had gone before in the whole unhappy history of the Troubles.

Abolitionists forecast that, far from acting as a deterrent, the reintroduction of capital punishment would spur on insane acts of martyrdom on both sides of the religious war, as Ulster caught fire.

Judges who put on the black cap in Ulster would also be signing their own death warrants, for the sole responsibility for sentencing would depend on them. In Northern Ireland, the difficulty of inducing juries to convict has resulted in the setting up of the so-called Diplock courts, in which a judge alone hears and decides a case.

The death penalty would certainly cause an outbreak of hostage taking, and dawn deaths in the Maze or any other Ulster prison would be accompanied by the matching 'execution' of innocent men and women.

It was strongly hinted before the hanging debate that a vote in the Commons for restoration would be swiftly followed by the resignation of the Secretary of State for Northern Ireland, Jim Prior, and one or more of his junior ministers as well.

But the debate in July 1983 was thought to be more significant than previous ones principally because of the landslide Tory victory only a month before, and of the dominance of the Right wing in the Party itself. If this parliament did not restore the death penalty, it was said, the issue could be laid to rest for ever.

In the event, though Thatcher herself led the way into the 'yes' lobby followed by eight members of her Cabinet, the 'no' vote prevailed six times.

MPs were asked to decide whether the death penalty should be restored for the following: murder by terrorists; murder of a police officer; murder of a prison officer; murder by shooting and explosion; murder in the course of theft; and, finally, if they approved of the death penalty in principle. Majorities against ranged from 81 for the category of murder of a prison officer to 175 for murder in the course of theft. Even the category of murder by terrorists was rejected by a majority of 116.

The vote was a free one, and though eight Cabinet ministers voted 'yes', another eight voted 'no', while four abstained. The split was predictable, with Thatcher-men like Tebbit, Parkinson, Leon Brittan and Nigel Lawson voting with the Prime Minister, and the wetter end of the Cabinet voting 'no'.

The Commons debate revealed one little known aspect

of British justice, which is that the death penalty is still (theoretically at least) in existence for treason, violent piracy, and arson in the Royal dockyards.

The gallows and other trappings of execution are still kept ready at Wandsworth prison, and could be used if anyone was convicted of those crimes. During the hanging debate in 1983, a group of Labour MPs tried to push through an amendment calling for the abolition of this last vestige of capital punishment, but did not succeed in getting it debated.

Though restoration of the death penalty looks like a lost cause, the Conservative Right wing may very well have its wish for a harsher enforcement of law and order come true in the middle or late Eighties. Some judges appear to think the law too lax, including the Lord Chief Justice himself, Lord Lane.

In a speech to the National Association of Prison Visitors in London in May 1983, Lord Lane echoed Thatcher by urging a return to Victorian morality, with its social sanctions against crime and violence. If Britain did not return 'a little way' to Victorian standards, things were going to keep on getting worse, he said. He added rather ominously that while he would not wish a return to pre-welfare state days, there was no doubt any potential criminal would then think a long time before consigning his wife and children to the workhouse.

At the Conservative Party conference in October 1983, the Home Secretary, Leon Brittan, gave notice of what the *Daily Express* gratefully called 'a tough new blitz on crime'. One of the government's proposals was to introduce mandatory or fixed-term sentencing, so that murderers of policemen for example would serve a minimum of twenty years, without any possibility of remission.

This idea has been bitterly opposed by those (including the Lord Chancellor, Lord Hailsham) who believe that the independence of judges is a priceless asset of the British legal system. But it is likely to prove popular both with the electorate and with a large section of the Conservative Party.

One aspect of the law and order debate in Britain in the Eighties which has not much been touched upon is the emergence of a new breed of senior police officer: tough, ambitious, probably incorruptible, and often, in a broad sense, political.

One of the most striking specimens of this new breed is the man whom Thatcher appointed as Commissioner of the Metropolitan Police, Sir Kenneth Newman. Newman is a small, neat, cold-eyed man who probably would not have met the physical requirements of a selection board if he had come into the force in the orthodox way; but he entered via the Palestine Police. He became famous as a 'hard man' when he was Chief Constable in Ulster at the time of the Troubles, and his appointment to head the Met caused a renewal of efforts by the Left-dominated Greater London Council to itself take control of the police. (This was a lost cause, for in any case the government announced at the election of 1983 that it intended to abolish the GLC and some other large metropolitan councils.)

Some of Newman's methods in Ulster were not tender, and they could only be introduced in mainland Britain with difficulty. But there are those who believe that even his velvet glove tactics will, in the Eighties, give civil libertarians even more to worry about.

In 1983, Newman set up in London what the Met called Neighbourhood Watch schemes. These were intended to prevent petty crime, burglaries and break ins.

In theory, what this meant was that neighbours would keep an eye on each others' premises and report any suspicious activities to the police. But after the Neighbourhood Watch schemes were launched, *Time Out*, one of Britain's best-sourced 'alternative' magazines claimed it had been leaked confidential documents which showed that Newman's pet project had a hidden face.

The scheme's true nature, *Time Out* said, is 'an intelligence operation in which teachers, local authorities, social services and youth workers will be required to spy on their charges, as they did in Newman's last area of active service, Northern Ireland'.

The magazine said that while media attention was directed towards the more benign aspects of Neighbourhood Watch, teachers and youth workers were being given instructions to supply 'useful' information to police about their pupils and charges. Any knowledge or suspicion of crime should be immediately passed on, along with any details which might point to an offender.

This is seen as a repetition of Newman's methods in Ulster—where he introduced 'blue lamp' discos for both Protestants and Catholics, where policemen took slum children on holiday, and where police were instructed to establish friendly relations with community workers.

All very innocent and worthwhile. But from these contacts (according to *Time Out*) 'everything went into a Big Brother filing system at HQ'. The magazine quoted Newman himself as saying, when he took over at the Met: 'Intelligence and targeting methods developed in the fight against terrorism will be employed in the fight against crime'.

Time Out ran a satirical little cartoon showing a friendly, old-fashioned bobby riding on a bike through a slum area. A sign on the bike carrier says 'Stop me and shop one'.

Well, in Britain, 1984 is a great year of paranoia. But anyone who has seen in China how the famed street committees acted as a policing arm of central government (reporting not only on crime but on morals, marital difficulties, and over-enthusiasm for parenthood) must look at Neighbourhood Watch schemes with suspicion, however benevolent their intentions.

Not, one would think, that there is much danger of this sort of thing catching on in Britain, a nation with an unusual devotion to the sanctity of the individual household, and a dislike of neighbourhood interference. The most detested term in England, George Orwell once said, is Nosy Parker.

Whether or not Newman and other police chiefs intend to use methods evolved in Ulster on the mainland, there is no doubt that the early Eighties largely saw the end of the traditional British bobby. Instead of the tall figure in a helmet majestically pacing the beat, police in Britain have started to resemble their Continental counterparts, and since the riots of 1981 there have been constant demands for sophisticated methods of crowd control. Water canon, plastic bullets, and CS gas are now available to metropolitan and provincial forces, and in the summer of 1981 police in Liverpool fired riot gas cartridges directly into the crowd, despite manufacturers' warnings that the particular kind of CS gas bullets supplied were for use only in sieges and had been designed to be fired through doors.

* * * * * *

'If the Conservative revolution has an infantry, it is the self-employed. It is in the growth of self-employment, spreading out to small family businesses, that the job opportunities of the future are going to come.' The Conservative MP for Guildford, David Howell, Secretary of State for Transport until he was sacked by Thatcher, said this in September 1983. (Despite his summary treatment, he nevertheless paid tribute to Thatcher, appearing to give her the credit for changing the Conservative Party from 'a grandees' party', and pushing it onto 'common bourgeois ground'.)

Howell was voicing one of the articles of faith of Toryism in the Eighties, namely that small businessmen will be a major factor in bringing about the British economic recovery.

The Tory Party introduced new methods of encouraging small businesses, projects with names like the 'Business Expansion Scheme' and the 'Business Start-up Scheme', while in the first four years of the Thatcher government the 'Loan Guarantee Scheme' backed lending of over £300 million to about 10,000 small firms.

Thatcher herself is enthusiastic about small businesses, urging (as we have already seen) the unemployed to take their redundancy money and start up for themselves.

It is not hard to trace back the origins of Thatcher's obsession with the small man. Her own father, the remarkable Alfred Roberts, saved furiously from his wage as a shop assistant, and delayed his marriage to Thatcher's mother, Beatrice Stephenson, until between them they had enough money to buy a business of their own—a small sub-post office and grocery store in Grantham, later to become famous as the Thatcher birthplace. Alf and Beatrice even delayed having their first child for four years (a long time in the pre-Pill period) so that the business could get on its feet.

Is Britain then (New Jerusalem or not) to become a nation of small businessmen, as the might of the Industrial Revolution becomes a memory?

Certainly the collapse of the traditional heavy industries like shipbuilding and steel make diversification seem desirable. The spectacle of the giants in their death throes was not comforting.

According to a survey carried out by the *Economist*, there were 4,100 manufacturers in Britain with more than 200 employees twenty years ago. By 1979, the year in which the Tories came to power, that figure had fallen to 2,900; and it has continued to decline.

Correspondingly, in the Seventies, the number of firms with less than 200 workers rose from 27 per cent of the total manufacturing sector to 30 per cent. But in America, the figure is 40 per cent, and in Japan, it is nearing a rather staggering 70 per cent.

The *Economist* quotes a British venture capitalist as saying that 'there has been a dramatic change in the culture'.

Certainly there was a net gain of nearly 18,000 new small firms in 1981–1982, but doubts are frequently expressed about their staying power. It still remains to be established how many of the firms were set up out of a genuine entrepreneurial spirit, and how many were set up out of desperation, since this was the only way of staying out of the dole queue.

Local authorities are setting up enterprise agencies to encourage small businesses, but advisers say that a number of people who come to them for help are simply making the best of a bad situation.

'Reports of the birth of British small business are much exaggerated,' the *Economist* said in its summing up. 'The best hope lies in industries like electronics and biotechnology that have germinated a fresh but so far scant crop of entrepreneurial firms, encouraged by venture capitalists and academics debagged by cuts in industry grants.'

The shining example in the first half of the Eighties is the handful of businessmen who are making a fortune for themselves and for Britain in the field of electronics—notably Sir Clive Sinclair, whose Sinclair Industries has beaten the Japanese at their own game.

Sinclair, knighted by Thatcher in 1983, has sold more small computers than any other manufacturer in the world. He completely undercut Japan when he produced the first cheap pocket-size television set with a two-inch screen. After an extremely modest beginning, he is now on the way to becoming a billionaire tycoon, and in lordly fashion he has already endowed a literary prize for a novel of sociological significance. Last year he unveiled a plan to set up his own think tank, offering salaries to scientists going beyond the dreams of avarice.

In other areas, though, many symptoms of the British malaise still remain. Cunard, in 1983, sent its flagship Queen Elizabeth II to a German shipyard for a refit, claiming that British Shipbuilders' subsidiary, Vosper Ship Repairers, couldn't guarantee to complete the refit on time.

Even Thatcher, whose rallying cry is 'Buy British,' said glumly that British firms had to compete in a tough world.

British manufacturers continue to complain that they must go abroad for many of their needs, because small British firms either cannot or will not supply them. In September 1983, the Confederation of British Industry actually helped set up a trade exhibition called 'Can You Make it?'

Nothing was for sale. On the contrary, the exhibitors, in this topsy-turvy trade fair, were anxious to become buyers. They showed on their stands an enormous variety of equipment, ranging from industrial gloves to small electrical connections, which had to be bought from foreign firms because no British companies were bothering to produce them.

During its first term, the Thatcher government played for a time with the idea of remedying this sort of situation and of encouraging the 'Buy British' drive by using unemployed teenagers as cheap labour. The idea was the brainchild of Norman Tebbit, who is never averse to trying out a controversial scheme.

Young people in Britain, he said, were unemployed because they were pricing themselves out of the labour market. He thought they should be willing to gain experience and enter the labour market by accepting very low wages for a beginning.

The Tebbit plan for promoting smallish industries involved setting up special factories, subsidized by the State, to produce goods cheap enough to compete with imports from countries such as Taiwan and South Korea.

Tebbit at first suggested that trainees should be content with £15 a week, but he later agreed that £25 a week might be a more realistic figure.

The Tebbit plan also originally proposed to make working in the subsidized factories more or less compulsory. This would have been done by withholding dole money from those who refused to participate.

To a chorus of cries of 'slave labour', this scheme died a quiet death like many others before it. Britain was not ready for drafted labour in peace time. It is worth recalling here, though, as an example of the thinking of the hard men of the Thatcherite New Right.

* * * * * *

On the issue of the denationalization of major industries, the Thatcher government finds itself on firm ground, for even the Labour Party is divided on the wisdom of continuing to pour billions of taxpayers' money into unprofitable undertakings.

Denationalization or, in the jargon word, privatization is therefore an important part of Thatcher's plans for building the New Jerusalem. She appears to see the nationalized industries as debris or rubble which must be cleared away —or, more precisely, as undergrowth which needs chopping out to allow the growth of taller and healthier plants.

One of her close advisers has been quoted as saying: 'The second Thatcher term will be the Privatization Period.' Tentative moves towards this goal had already been made in the first term, against union resistance, but without much popular outcry.

In its first term, the Thatcher government sold majority shareholdings in British Aerospace, Cable and Wireless and Amersham International. The postal monopoly was broken, with the profitable Telecom being separated from the postal services and with the private sector being allowed to compete in areas like equipment sales and special deliveries.

Work forces were savagely cut back in the nationalized industries: 82,300 jobs were lost in British Steel; 20,266 in British Shipbuilders; 20,241 in British Airways; 32,198 in British Rail; and 36,500 in the National Coal Board.

The scene was thus set for much more drastic privatization; and loud cries of encouragement came from the

Right of the Tory party and from press commentators and columnists like George Gale, who has acted as one of Thatcher's principal Fleet Street cheerleaders. Writing in the *Daily Express* in July 1983, Gale said:

> A bill is now going through Parliament to enable the government to sell a majority of British Telecom shares to the public for £400 million.
>
> This...is the biggest step yet in the Thatcher revolution, which should make a return to socialism impossible. Most successful revolutions lock themselves in by breaking up the wealth and estates of the few, and giving property to the many.
>
> Giving land to the peasants makes revolutions irreversible.
>
> In a different guise, but on precisely the same principle the Thatcher revolution can make itself irreversible here. It has already been very considerably secured by extending home ownership breaking up the vast council estates, and encouraging tenants to become owner-occupiers.
>
> If it handles its privatisation plans bravely, resolutely, intelligently and swiftly, it can break up and massively distribute the ownership of State monopolies, so that these modern versions of the great fiefdoms of the past can never be restored again.
>
> With ownership scattered among millions of workers and consumers, no government would contemplate renationalising, unless it was bent upon establishing a totalitarian dictatorship of the Left or Right.
>
> The British electorate would never vote for such a dictatorship.

This concept of privatization as a guarantee of the irreversibility of the Thatcher revolution is obviously shared by the Prime Minister herself—if, indeed, the Gale article was not inspired by her. But selling off state-owned industries is easier said than done. First they have to make a profit, or at least show that they are capable of doing so under the right management.

So far, the main success story in turning round a state-owned lossmaker is that of British Leyland which, in late

1983, began trading in the black for the first time in four years.

In September 1983 the company announced that it had made a trading profit of £1.3 million in the first half of 1983, compared with a loss of £61.3 in the same period in 1982. (It is true that after allowing for taxation, interest payments, and other items, BL still made a loss of £48.4 million; but this was comparatively modest compared to the loss of £143.4 million in the first half of 1982.)

After the results had been announced, Cecil Parkinson, then Trade and Industry Secretary, said that the privatization of viable parts of BL was now a matter of top priority for the government.

Thatcher cannot but have been delighted with the result, but it is ironic that her government cannot claim full credit for it. The man largely responsible for pulling BL round and bringing it somewhere near break-even point, Sir Michael Edwardes, was, in fact, appointed head of British Leyland by the Callaghan government in 1977. But Edwardes is the sort of man of whom Thatcher approves, a strong pragmatist with a ruthless streak.

Edwardes spent five years with BL before he handed it over to other hands in 1982. When he took it over, BL workers were making an average of six cars each a year, while BL's competitors in Japan were turning out 60 a year for each man on the shop floor. Industrial relations were calamitous, with ideological war raging at the Longbridge and Cowley plants, and disputes numbering up to 13 a day.

The very name of British Leyland became synonymous with 'the British disease'. As late as 1980, Thatcher's chief economic adviser, Professor Alan Walters, told Edwardes that it might be better for the government to let the company collapse.

But that would also mean that the government would have to find another £1 billion in closure costs; and, more seriously, a quarter of a million motor industry workers would join the dole queues, at a moment when unemployment was becoming something of an electoral nightmare.

Thatcher decided to put her faith in Edwardes, but it took the loss of 90,000 jobs and a transfusion of £2 billion of taxpayers' money to keep the company going. Edwardes bypassed union officials and ballotted the workforce direct on reduced wage offers and further job cuts. Aided by the hidden threat of unemployment, he won his point on each occasion.

By 1982, the company was still making losses, but productivity had gone up to 25 cars per man—still less than half the Japanese average, but a remarkable improvement on the years of non-stop industrial strife.

Edwardes, a short, combative South African, has written the story of his turbulent years at BL in a semi-autobiography called *Back From the Brink*. He tells in it the story of how, as a teenager in South Africa, he lost an outboard motor on a fishing trip.

His father left him alone at a bush camp with food and supplies, and with instructions not to come home until he had found the motor where it lay on the seabed and fished it up again. It took the boy eight days, but he did it.

'You make your own mistakes and you correct them yourself. No one looks after you from the cradle to the grave,' Edwardes says in *Back From the Brink*. It is a sentiment of which Thatcher herself would unreservedly approve.

After British Leyland, the next best improvement in the nationalized industries has been shown by British Steel, and once again, the turnaround was forcibly brought about by a ruthless outsider.

The man Thatcher appointed as chairman and chief executive of British Steel, Ian MacGregor, was Scottish-born and educated, but he has spent his adult life in the United States. Sometimes he is called 'the Scottish Hammer', but more often, 'that Yank'.

He had had a long career in international business behind him when Thatcher made him head of British Steel in 1980. She caused something of a scandal by 'buying' him from the New York investment bankers, Lazard Freres, for £1.8 million.

Thatcher wanted a hatchet man and this is exactly what she got. In 1979–80, the workforce in the steel industry was 166,400. By 1983, it had been reduced to 77,000. And before he left British Steel, MacGregor said that he would like to see another 10,000 jobs made redundant.

The effect, in human terms, was staggering, but the tactics paid off. In January 1983, losses were still running at £8.6 million a week, but six months later they were down to £2 million a week; and in 1984, British Steel is expected to break even. Wasting the labour force has brought productivity to a level where British workers have even overtaken the industrious West Germans.

As he left British Steel, MacGregor said: 'Despite all the terrible things which have happened to the workforce, we have emerged with a group of people who want to work. This is an indication of the change in the somewhat demoralised crew I inherited.'

Another piece of pure Thatcherism. It is hardly surprising that the Prime Minister promptly moved MacGregor over to the National Coal Board with (so the National Union of Mineworkers believe) a mandate to close pits and sack miners.

A Coal Board document which was leaked to the press in 1983 appeared to show that the government was planning to shut down unprofitable pits, mainly in the traditional mining areas of Scotland, Durham, Northumberland and South Wales. This would mean the loss of 70,000 jobs from in between 70 and 80 pits (about one third of the British total).

MacGregor seemed an unlikely choice as Coal Board chairman. At seventy he was already five years over retiring age, and in addition, he was very expensive. Thatcher had to pay another £1.5 million to Lazard Freres for the privilege of keeping him in Britain. But the Prime

Minister obviously had confidence in his ability to do at the Coal Board what he had already achieved at British Steel.

In shaping up to the National Union of Mineworkers, MacGregor was in any case meeting an adversary whose militancy and industrial muscle have been much reduced by the years of recession. As we have already seem, its president-for-life, the fiery red-headed demagogue Arthur Scargill, had been unable during Thatcher's first term of office to fulfill his boast that the miners would bring her down as they had done Heath in 1974.

However, in 1984, the situation in the mining areas grew much tenser. In February, McGregor, now 71, was knocked to the ground by furious miners during a visit to Ellington colliery in Northumberland.

The announcement in March, 1984, that 20,000 jobs would be lost by the end of the year brought a call for a national strike. But Scargill was again unable to rally the nation's miners solidly behind him.

The union was split wide open, with some fields striking and others remaining open. Police reinforcements had to be brought in as miner fought miner on the picket lines.

The mineworkers' union knows that if Thatcher can push through her plans for denationalisation, then the coal industry, like the steel industry, will return to the private sector.

Thatcher's plans for the short term are much brisker. The nation's telephones will feel the effect late in 1984, when the government sells off British Telecom. The State airline, British Airways, will come on the market in 1985, though the chairman of BA, Sir John King, has said that it should be profitable enough to be sold by the autumn of 1984, a year ahead of schedule.

The government in 1983 sold off another chunk of its holding in British Petroleum, and it also appeared to be planning to speed up its program to sell the North Sea oil assets of British Gas.

Apart from the workers directly involved, few people in

Britain will mourn the government's decision to stop injecting billions of pounds into the bloodstream of the ailing giants.

Where Thatcherism is really going to affect the person-in-the-street is in the apparent intention of the Prime Minister to sell off public transport—a move so radical that few countries would contemplate it.

In 1983, the Secretary of State for Transport, Tom King, said bluntly that he expected large-scale private investment in British Rail within the next few years. A White Paper put out by King's department has also been interpreted as meaning that London's bus and underground services could be offered for sale to private investors within two years, and commuter services in the populous south-west of the country within five years.

The government is expected to sell off parts of London's historic railway stations, including Victoria, Waterloo and King's Cross. It has already made a start with that masterpiece of neo-Gothic glory, St Pancras. Sections of the station, which is famous as possibly the most extravagant example of railway architecture in existence, have been sold to an insurance company.

Thatcher and her ministers have repeatedly insisted that the Tories have no intention of dismantling the National Health Service, the proudest achievement of socialism in the postwar years. 'The NHS is safe in our hands', was the slogan before the election of 1983.

But hardly was the election over that the government started hacking away at the health service manning levels, and pushing ahead with its plans to privatize some of the ancillary services.

Even before the June election, an estimated 2,000 doctors were on the dole; and it soon became clear that other doctors and many nurses were to join them in the ranks of the unemployed.

Lopping away at the NHS, even in a tentative manner, was a very dangerous course for Thatcher to follow; and that she risked it at all is a measure of her nerve. On the Left, it has been seen as a warning of further butchery to come if the government finds that it can get away with it.

The NHS has many defects. The service that it provides is uneven, ranging from the magnificent to the dreadful; and for non-urgent operations, the waiting lists are appalling. An old person with an arthritic hip may very well die in some regions of the country before he or she can be accepted into hospital for a replacement operation.

Surgeons have been known to put their patients' names in a hat and draw out one where there are a number of cases of equal need, even for operations as serious as hysterectomies.

But it is also fair to say that any man, woman or child in Britain, who is in desperate need of medical help, will be given it—no matter how involved and expensive the procedure and without any cost to the family. Anyone who has seen the domestic tragedies caused by medical bills in the United States can hardly fail to stand back and applaud Britain's National Health Service, whatever its flaws.

The Thatcher government's aim, however, has been to encourage a two-tier health service. This is diametrically opposed to the Labour Party's ambition of wiping out private practice altogether. Labour insists that the very existence of a medical private sector downgrades the National Health Service.

Labour's contention is that if there were no private doctors, the rich and powerful who now go to private clinics would demand (and would be in a position to do so) that the NHS be brought to a much higher peak of efficiency.

The Left says that if Thatcher has her way and an official two-tier health service comes back in Britain, then the bottom tier, the emasculated version of the NHS, will be only for the poor and the chronically ill who are unable to get cover from the private medical insurance schemes.

Already, these are the people who suffer most. A recent

program made by Yorkshire Television in 1983 showed that
between 2,000 and 3,000 kidney patients who are suitable
for treatment die every year in Britain because of a short-
age of kidney machines.

The program-makers claimed that those being (in the
euphemism) 'deselected for treatment' tended to be of
below average intelligence, or over sixty, or immigrants
with poor English, or patients who lived in the Midlands
and North—the poorer of the two nations into which
Britain is increasingly divided.

In Britain in the Eighties more and more people have
been turning to private health insurance, and the funds
have reported a sharp increase in business. In the five years
up to 1983, the number of private insurers doubled to more
than two million. There were red faces among trade union
officials when it was revealed that some unions were taking
out private insurance for their staffs.

Under the present system, however, the worker or
householder who insures privately is charged twice for
health care, for he or she is already paying a large national
insurance levy in addition to tax, and part of this goes to
fund the NHS.

In 1982, the Central Policy Review Unit, the government's official think tank, came up with a proposal which
got no further at the time but which showed in which direction the government may move in its second term.

The think tank suggested that the NHS could be virtually
abolished, leaving it only as a safcty net for the poorest in
the community. In the short term, the policy makers said, a
start could be made by charging for visits to doctors (now
free) and for drugs on prescription (now heavily subsidized). In the longer term, a comprehensive scheme of
private health insurance (possibly compulsory, though
Thatcher might not approve of that) could be introduced,
cutting down government spending to less than half the
present figure. At that stage private insurance would cost
the average family of four an estimated £600 a year.

When these proposals were leaked to the *Economist* magazine, the outcry was such that they were hastily disclaimed. But that was before the government was returned with a large majority at the election of 1983.

Thatcher has repeatedly shown that she will not abandon a goal which she has set herself; and since the election, what would have been unthinkable even two years before has happened. The first assaults on the NHS began within three months of the government's victory at the polls. In September, the Social Services Secretary Norman Fowler sent out orders to regional health authorities to cut 5,000 jobs.

Not only were the jobs of doctors and nurses among those lost, but the cuts were the first reductions in National Health service manpower for thirty years.

The government made it plain that this was only the start, as in the short term, up to 8,000 jobs would have to go. Norman Fowler pointed out that the NHS had become Europe's biggest single employer, with over a million full- or part-time staff. He said that the government had the right and the duty to seek a more efficient use of this enormous manpower.

The British medical Association has already estimated that 3,500 doctors will be unable to find jobs in 1984, quite apart from those being weeded out under the Fowler redundancy plan. 'We are horrified and appalled at the wastage of trained doctors,' the BMA's under secretary Dr Frank Wells said in 1983. 'The career prospects of school leavers going into medical school have never been bleaker.'

If the medical profession is no longer a sacred preserve under the new Tory radicalism, what else is safe! Certainly not education—another dangerous area, full of pitfalls, but again one which the Thatcher government is quite likely to tackle seriously in its second term of office.

This is also a subject on which Right and Left find themselves totally opposed. The Labour Party wants to eradicate private education in Britain, which it sees (not without reason) as the last formidable bastion of the class system. Its manifesto at the 1983 election contained specific proposals for financially penalizing parents who wished their children to be educated at 'public' (i.e. private) schools.

The Conservatives want to do just the opposite. The document drawn up by the Central Policy Review Unit suggested, among other things, ending free tertiary education. Any family wanting to put a child through university would have to find £4,000 a year for fees, books and other expenses. The proposal envisaged a small number of scholarships which would be awarded to the most gifted and for which there would be fierce competition.

This would have the side-effect of reducing the present overcrowding in universities and the current unemployment among graduates. In the Tory Party's ideal Britain, a university education would once again become the province of the rich or of the unusually talented.

This idea would obviously appeal to Thatcher. She herself was once a scholastically precocious child, fiercely competitive, and she gained her own secondary and tertiary education through scholarships.

At that time, only two per cent of the population managed to do what she did and find a place at university. Even in the Eighties, the proportion of young people going on to higher education in Britain is lower than in most developed countries—13 per cent of the eligible age-group compared to 19 per cent in West Germany, 39 per cent in Japan, and 42 per cent in the United States.

In 1982, the government think tank also looked at the possibility of abolishing State education at primary and secondary levels. But with an election on the horizon, such a concept was too radical for the Cabinet to swallow.

However, the Prime Minister's advisers did come up with the idea of a scheme of educational vouchers. It was suggested that these might be as high as £950 per child per year. They would be awarded to suitable parents so that they could, if they wished, take their children out of the State system and send them to private schools.

Any gap between the amount of the voucher and the fees charged by the private school (these can run as high as £5,000 a year) would be made up by the parents. Obviously such a scheme would be of benefit to the relatively well off; more so, probably, than to working or lower middle-class parents.

The voucher scheme had a very mixed reception, even among the Tory faithful; and it was rather ostentatiously disowned before the election of 1983. But it would surprise no one if it resurfaced during the remaining years of Thatcher's second term.

The New Jerusalem, or the Tory vision of it, is still a long way off. There are signs, however, that Thatcher would like to be around to watch its development.

In 1982, she was talking sardonically about 'not being able to take more than another ten years'. The next year, she went even further in a television interview. 'It's a great comfort to many of us,' she said, 'that Walpole stayed [as Prime Minister] for 21 years.'

* * * * * *

If Thatcher's New Jerusalem means a return to the Victorian virtues of self-help, Labour's plan for Britain in the Eighties envisages the State playing an even greater role in the life of its citizens.

When the Labour Party manifesto was published before the election of 1983, the Tories purported to be outraged by it, calling it a Marxist blueprint for Britain. In fact, it contained few surprises, and, for once, it took serious heed of decisions made at Party conferences.

Scattered through the great many worthy and worthwhile proposals the manifesto contained, however, were a number of highly explosive issues, all due to go off at some future date like little time bombs.

In theory at least, the Labour Party is committed to the phasing out of both private medicine and private education in Britain. As we have already seen, many people in the Labour Party, on the centre-right as well as on the Left, believe that the National Health Service will never reach maximum efficiency until private practice is abolished. I remember hearing a delegate at a Party conference, a doctor himself, shouting angrily from the rostrum that private practice was 'a cancer eating away at the health service'.

No one doubts that Labour will receive maximum popular support in its attempts to stop Thatcher dismantling the NHS. Whether a move to wipe out private practice altogether would succeed is open to doubt. In the Thatcher era, private medical insurance has become a growth industry; and if, or when, the Tories introduce some active financial encouragement for those willing to take care of their own health problems, the floodgates will open.

The Labour Party is, however, pledged to oppose the return of a two-tier health service, where the rich will be able to jump the queue. If it comes to office at the general election of 1988, it will stop NHS doctors treating patients privately on request, as some of them now do. (The health service does not, for instance, give patients complete medical checkups unless some serious problem needs to be tracked down. Dentists under the NHS provide an excellent basic service, but people wanting elaborate work done for purely cosmetic reasons must pay hefty fees.) Labour said rather vaguely in its last manifesto that it would also take into the NHS 'those parts of the profit-making private sector which can be put to good use'.

The boom in private health insurance and the influx of wealthy Arabs from the oil kingdoms during the Seventies and early Eighties means that Britain now has a growing number of luxurious private hospitals and clinics. They have drawn away from the National Health Service many doctors and nurses, among them NHS-trained consultants who have left to set up their own private clinics.

Short of a complete overthrow of the Establishment, it is hard to see any future government taking over these lucrative hospitals (some of them American owned) and opening them up, with their expensive and modern equipment, to NHS patients. That aspect of the socialist New Jerusalem is still a long way off.

Labour is also dedicated, in the long term, to the phasing out of public schools. This objective will prove even more difficult to achieve than socializing all forms of medical practice.

'Private schools,' the Labour manifesto says, 'are a major obstacle to a free and fair education system, able to serve the needs of the whole community.'

The next Labour government has promised to abolish the assisted places scheme, and to withdraw all public subsidies, tax privileges, and even charitable status from public schools. Fees paid to such schools will attract VAT (Value Added Tax), and local authorities will be authorized to take over private schools where they see fit.

Sections of the Party would like to see an even more radical surgery on Britain's education system. Before she switched allegiances, Shirley Williams (then a controversial Education Secretary) voiced the feelings of the reformers when she wrote: 'It is with reluctance that I, for one, conclude that the freedom to send one's children to an independent school is bought at too high a price for the rest of society.'

Tony Benn has recommended that children at school should be formally taught about the history, principles, organization and work of trade unions, with active trade unionists themselves taking some of the classes. This would prepare school children for their life's work, Benn said.

The argument of the Labour Party Left is that it is

impossible to break down the class system in Britain and to stop the concentration of power in a few hands unless a more egalitarian educational system is introduced.

Anthony Sampson, whose series of books on the 'anatomy' of Britain has been largely concerned with analyzing the sources of power in the community, believed at the beginning of the Seventies that far-reaching changes were taking place and that a new breed of men, the Meritocrats, were consolidating their position.

But in *The Changing Anatomy of Britain*, published in 1982, he wrote:

> The upper reaches of many British institutions, from banking and industry to politics and government, are still largely populated by the products of a handful of old schools...and more than ever by two of the oldest mediaeval foundations— both over five centuries old. Far from weakening their hold, they have extended their influence into new areas over the last twenty years.

The two schools which Sampson is talking about and which still maintain their traditional hold are Winchester College and Eton. Sampson continued:

> It is said of Wykehamists that, once given a ladder, they will climb to the top of it without questioning its purpose. Certainly their record of worldly success is second only to Eton's though it has only half its school population.

The headmaster of Winchester, John Thorn, has furiously attacked Labour's plans for reform, claiming that in the State system 'the education of 94 per cent of the nation's children is being allowed to languish and decay'.

'Abolish the independent schools and you abolish some of the riches of European civilisation,' he said.

The role of Eton in providing Britain's politicians with a training ground is well known, though Etonians are spread as well throughout the nation's whole power structure.

177

Lord Poole, of Lazards (the merchant bankers), when once he was asked how his firm had kept out of trouble in the financial crash of 1974, said: 'Quite simply, I only lent money to people who had been at Eton.'

The two dominant schools are matched by the two powerhouse universities, Oxford and Cambridge. James Bellini wrote in *Rule Britannia*, another survey of the British power structure:

> If there is an Establishment in Britain, Oxbridge is at the heart of it, turning out the leaders, the captains of industry, the opinion formers of today as confidently as it has ever done.
>
> Oxbridge's values and traditions have been preserved as carefully as its architecture. It has proved remarkably resistant to change, even in a Britain which, since 1945, has had 17 years of Labour governments supposedly committed to smoothing out inequalities in education. One reason is probably that the majority of members of those governments were actually educated at Oxford. In fact, despite the expansion of higher education, the two 'blue brick' universities have actually tightened their hold on the top jobs.

It is ironic that though it is Labour which is committed to the eradication of class privilege through the abolition of public schools, it was Margaret Thatcher who actually ushered in the age of the grammar-school Cabinet Minister. In 1979, she started off with seven Old Etonians in her Cabinet. Now they are down to one—the Lord Chancellor, Lord Hailsham. But Oxbridge seems to be maintaining its grip. In 1966, there were ten Oxford graduates in Harold Wilson's Cabinet. Oxbridge supplied Ted Heath with fourteen ministers; and the first Thatcher Cabinet had sixteen, including the Prime Minister herself.

* * * * * *

A Britain still sheltering under the NATO nuclear umbrella, but itself unilaterally disarmed—or a Britain offering a base for US-supplied cruise missiles, and with an updated nuclear deterrent of its own? This is the alternative being given to the nation in the Eighties by the two major parties. And in the likely event of the worsening of East-West relations it will be an enormously important issue.

The Conservatives, all hawks under Thatcher, have the advantage of being in office, and of being able to push through at least the preliminary stages of their defence policy before the next election. The fact that their policy is well-defined and capable of being clearly set out is also heavily in their favour. Probably no single issue did the Labour Party more harm in the election of 1983 than the confusion over defence issues, and disagreements in the leadership over what the policy meant.

Labour's situation is also made uneasy by the fact that the Party wants Britain to remain in NATO, even though it is firmly committed to unilateral nuclear disarmament. The only really logical position is that taken by the Left of the Party, which says that Britain should secede from NATO. The Left has succeeded in drumming up considerable support for this position at Party conferences, though it has not gained the two-thirds majority which would make it Labour policy.

The Conservative position, by contrast, is perfectly clear. Under the NATO two-track decision of 1979, Britain is committed to the deployment of 160 Tomahawk missiles with nuclear warheads at British bases, and the first of these were installed in the silos at Greenham Common Airbase at the end of 1983.

Public opinion polls taken before the June 1983 election showed that a majority of British people were opposed to the installation of the missiles, but Thatcher took the general election victory as a mandate and went ahead.

The main objection to the nuclear missiles in the public mind appears to be that the decision to fire the missiles remains in the hands of the US administration. If cruise missiles are fired from British soil against the Soviet Union, the finger on the trigger will be American not British, though there will be consultation between governments.

In 1982, efforts were made to urge the government to revive the dual-key system which existed for Thor missiles in the late Fifties and early Sixties. At that time, the British held a 'key' which launched the missiles, and the Americans had a 'key' which armed the warheads.

The Thatcher government turned this idea down on the grounds of extravagance, as a dual-key system would mean that Britain would have to contribute to the actual cost of the missiles instead of having them supplied by the United States.

The other reason for allowing the US to retain full control is strategic. Cruise and Pershing II missiles are being deployed in West Germany, Italy, Belgium and Holland as well as Britain, and the prospect of a single finger on the trigger is seen as a more credible deterrent to the Soviet Union than the possibility of five separate nations hesitating over whether or not to fire their missiles.

The Thatcher government's major defence expenditure over the rest of the decade will be its preparations for the replacement of the Polaris nuclear submarine fleet with the new Trident system.

The cost of Trident is steadily rising—the estimate rose from £6 billion to £10 billion in the first three years of the Eighties—and shocks even some Tories. Labour has been able to make effective propaganda out of the huge expense of the program at a time, when savage cuts are being imposed in the areas of public health, education and social services.

The government points out, however, that the expenditure will be spread over fifteen years, and that in the Nineties Britain will have a fleet of four new submarines each equipped with sixteen missiles. At that time, Polaris can be phased out.

The Thatcher government is also planning to spend hundreds of millions of pounds on a submarine complex at Coulport on Loch Long, to prepare it to receive Trident.

The base will be enlarged to eight times its present size, with nine miles of new roads and new facilities for missile storage and testing.

One of the main reasons for Labour being anxious to regain power in the last general election was that it saw the election as its only chance to stop Britain racing headlong into an era of nuclear build-up.

It went into the election on a platform of unilateral disarmament. But its defence policies sold badly on the doorstep—with the Leader, Michael Foot, and his deputy, Denis Healey, publicly at odds over their meaning. It was difficult for the voters to put their faith in a Party whose deputy Leader had once been quoted as saying that he would not serve in a Cabinet which tried to put unilateralism into operation.

The public was also confused by the Labour Party's apparent intention to go unilateral while remaining inside NATO, an organization whose whole defence posture is based on its ability to fight a nuclear war. Explanations that Britain could remain as a non-nuclear state within NATO, like Canada or Norway, failed to get across to bewildered voters.

In the post-mortem after the 1983 election, the Right of the Labour Party insisted that Labour lost on two main issues: unilateralism, and withdrawal from the Common Market. The EEC issue is now in some sort of limbo, and is likely to stay there; but the commitment to unilateral nuclear disarmament remains. It was strongly reaffirmed at the Labour Party conference in the autumn of 1983, despite pleas for a rethinking of the whole question by such right-wingers as the former Prime Minister, James Callaghan and the new deputy Leader, Roy Hattersley.

The proposals put forward by the National Executive commit the Party to a freeze on the testing, production and deployment of nuclear weapons. This means no acceptance of cruise missiles in Britain and cancellation of the Trident program. The conference declared:

We commit ourselves here to putting our existing Polaris system into the arms talks so that Britain can have a voice in negotiations which are of vital importance to humanity, but which are now the exclusive preserve of Washington and Moscow.

We commit ourselves to moving NATO strategy away from dependence on nuclear weapons to defence through conventional forces, and to cutting the Conservative plans for an annual increase of three per cent in defence spending.

There was also a vaguer commitment to 'working for a nuclear-free Europe and the dismantling of foreign bases in Britain'. It was rather a long way from Tony Benn's brave words about being the Minister who would go to Washington and tell President Reagan to get his bases out of the country.

The vagueness did not satisfy the new deputy Leader, who said that the removal of foreign bases would again be a vote-loser at the next election. Such a move would effectively mean withdrawal from NATO, Roy Hattersley argued—but without success.

Despite the rejection of Labour policies at the 1983 election, however, the Tories have not had a trouble-free ride on defence. One of the most fascinating phenomena of the Eighties has been the revival of the Campaign for Nuclear Disarmament which, after the great days of the Fifties and Sixties, had dwindled away to almost nothing.

It started to recruit new members at the turn of the decade, and its numbers increased with astonishing speed as the decision to deploy cruise missiles was firmed up by the Thatcher government. By the end of 1983, it was enrolling 400 new members a week, and it had already passed the 70,000 mark.

This was in part due to the personality of its secretary general, Monsignor Bruce Kent, a Roman Catholic priest of unassailable personal virtue and of unshakeable obstinacy in pursuit of his goals. Bruce Kent is an attractive and forceful speaker, with an easy, throwaway wit. He is not, as he himself puts it sardonically, 'a woolly mind in a woolly hat', nor is he the familiar, burning-eyed prophet of Armageddon. It is strikingly unlikely that he would ever read long extracts from a Byronic epic at a public meeting, as Michael Foot did.

He has also a remarkable knack of keeping himself in the public eye. In this he is unwillingly aided by his own Church. The Cardinal-Archbishop of Westminster, Cardinal Basil Hume, agonized in public in 1983 as to whether it was proper for a priest to be involved with a political lobby. Monsignor Kent immediately became, in the public's mind, a crusading priest about to be crushed by the full might of the Church, and Cardinal Hume had no option but to retreat.

Then the Papal Nuncio to Britain, Archbishop Bruno Heim, made the mistake of suggesting that Monsignor Kent was 'a useful idiot', a 'blinkered idealist', or 'a Soviet dupe'. The British do not care for one of their own being attacked by foreigners, and Kent rose another notch or two in the popularity polls.

However, the way of the publicist is strewn with deep pits, and Bruce Kent fell into one of them when he was quoted in *Woman* magazine as criticizing the Church leader with the heaviest line of all in personal charisma, Pope John Paul II. He did not think, Kent said, that a man with the Pope's background and high level of Polish nationalism was able to meet the needs of the whole Church. 'I don't think the amazing focus on one man is healthy,' he said. 'Within the church, his whole attitude towards women and his view of the life of the clergy is unbelievable.'

Later, in the autumn of 1983, there was another hiccough when Bruce Kent appeared on the platform at the annual congress of the Communist Party of Great Britain, and praised the Party (along with the Quakers) for keeping the flag of disarmament flying 'during the lean years, when others had gone away'.

These incidents apart, Kent's image has remained fresh

and likeable, despite the efforts of the powerful forces marshalled against him. The worst that has been said of him is that he is an unwitting front man for more sinister forces, and even then it has been impossible to make that charge stick.

During the early Eighties, the rebirth of CND was parallelled by the growth of a much more anarchic peace movement, the women-only peace protest at Greenham Common.

At its peak, the Greenham women's peace camp attracted world-wide publicity; and seeing this, CND and other peace groups tried to take it over. But the women would have nothing of that, fighting their own lonely—and uncomfortable and squalid and much criticized—battle on a muddy stretch of land outside the gates of the RAF-USAF Airbase near Newbury in Berkshire.

The Greenham Common peace camp began in 1981 with a march by a handful of men, women and children from Wales to Newbury. Some of the women stayed, and set up the peace camp, living in appalling conditions through one of the worst winters of the century. No one expected the camp to survive; but it is still there, and though its numbers rise and fall, the nucleus always remains.

The women have been evicted from the camp site a number of times, most recently in May 1984, when bailiffs hired by Newbury district council and backed by hundreds of police cleared the site of all its encampments. But by next morning, the women were back again, this time in a field just across the road from the old peace camp.

Protest, arrest, and jail sentences have become a way of life for some of the women, as they were once for the suffragettes. At one stage, it was estimated that ten Greenham protesters a week were passing through the courts.

By the end of 1982, the peace camp was able to attract 30,000 women from Britain, Europe and the United States, who joined hands and 'embraced the base', decorating the perimeter fence with baby clothes, family portraits and crocheted and knitted peace slogans.

No men were allowed in the demonstration, but thousands of them turned up to set up creches and take over the traditional female role of making the tea.

To the embarrassment of the British government—and no doubt to the fury of far-away Washington—the women appeared earlier to have no difficulty in breaching the base's security, and more than once they broke in to dance on top of the missile silos and to plant flowers and bulbs.

The spectacle of women, young and old, joining hands and dancing at dawn on the sites where nuclear missiles were to be stored made for some quite remarkable television footage.

In mid-1983, the women broke in again and daubed paint on two US planes at the base. One of them was the sophisticated SR71 Blackbird surveillance aircraft.

Authorities at the base estimated that the cost of re-painting the Blackbird with a special type of paint used to prevent detection by ground radar would be £250,000, and the arrested women expected heavy jail sentences. But in fact the case against them was dropped, the authorities no doubt thinking this alternative to be the less embarrassing.

The Greenham Common women have come under ferocious attack, often being described in the right-wing press as 'burly Lesbians' or harridans who have abandoned their husbands and children to live in communal filth and squalor.

Their living conditions are certainly atrocious, but miraculously the women stay on. They have extended their activities to protests outside the House of Commons against the arrival of cruise missiles, and they have sent delegations to peace meetings in Europe and America.

The Greenham women have failed, as CND has also, to block the installation of the missiles in the silos at the RAF-USAF base. But they have forced the government to turn the base into a fortress guarded by soldiers and by police with dogs. The peace camp is a constant nagging reminder that the bunkers at Greenham now hold nuclear warheads, each with a killing power many times greater than that of the bomb which wiped out Hiroshima.

The presence of the woman has even elicited a reluctant admission from the Defence Secretary, Michael Heseltine, that demonstrators might be shot if they break into the base again. The possibility that this will happen sooner or later is a continuing nightmare for the government.

CHAPTER TEN

HARD MEN AND LOONIES

Extremism, whether of the Left or Right, does not flourish under an English heaven. The individuality of the British character, the national dislike for show and ostentation, the distrust of naked emotion, have kept it in check. George Orwell pointed out in *England Your England* that the goosestep could never be used in Britain even on army ceremonial occasions, 'because the people in the street would laugh'. Writing in the early years of World War II, he said:

> Like all other modern peoples, the English are in process of being numbered, labelled, conscripted, 'co-ordinated'. But the pull of their impulses is in the other direction, and the kind of regimentation that can be imposed on them will be modified in consequence. No party rallies, no Youth Movements, no coloured shirts, no Jew-baiting, or 'spontaneous' demonstrations. No Gestapo either, in all probability.

That largely remains true forty years on, though ugly outbreaks of racial prejudice have intermittently occurred during the periods of the build-up of the immigrant population and are likely to continue as a social and political problem in the remaining part of the century. The ghosts of

Sir Oswald Mosley and his Blackshirts still haunts the British psyche.

In the early Eighties, though, the emphasis has been mainly on infiltration of what are considered sinister elements into the main political parties. 'Entryism' was and still remains the buzz word, whether it applies to Trotskyites or to 'Britain First' fanatics. The Parties take all this seriously enough; but for the public and the media, there has also been enormous diversion in the activities of the Left and Right, both hard and loony.

As it turned out, 1983 was a vintage year for connoisseurs of fringe political activity. The Labour Party, at its autumn conference, at last brought itself to expel the top five of the Trotskyist organization Militant Tendency; and the Young Conservatives, on the very eve of the Tory Party conference, spoiled what their elders intended to be a victory celebration by announcing that the Party had a serious problem with entryism from the far Right.

Labour's expulsion of the Militants was a Court of Star Chamber affair, conducted behind closed doors, though the television cameras and the microphones were waiting outside to record the expellees' fury.

'Five flee as the Tsarists rampage', the *Guardian*'s political columnist said gleefully. 'This is not the end,' cried the expelled Trots. 'We will be back. We will be reinstated in one, two or three years.'

Militant Tendency is a small but highly interesting organization to any student of politics. If, as the Right frequently warns, the ambition of the Left is to turn Britain into a grim copy of an Eastern European state, with Parliament reduced to a sham and the Party dominating every aspect of daily life, then such a process could begin with infiltration by Militant.

Militant itself makes no secret of its aspirations. If it were in a position to do so, it says, it would at once abolish the monarchy and the House of Lords.

It wants the next Labour government to nationalize all

newspapers, radio and television and bring them under State control immediately, though it adds that political parties should be given access to the media in proportion to their share of votes at general elections.

Militant calls for 'nationalization of the top 200 monopolies, including the banks and insurance companies which control the commanding heights of the economy, through an Enabling Bill in Parliament, with minimum compensation on the basis of proven need. This would allow a socialist plan of production to be democratically drawn up and implemented by committees involving the trade unions, shop stewards, housewives and small business men.'

Committees of shop stewards, housewives (again) and small shopkeepers should have the right to inspect the accounts of monopolies, the Militants say. One of their other proposals, which would prove less than popular with MPs, is that all Labour Members of Parliament should receive only the wage of a skilled worker, plus expenses—the surplus to be given to the Labour movement.

In the manifesto which sets out these aspirations, Militant Tendency says plaintively that in the past, this program 'was dismissed as the ravings of archaic Marxism'. It still is by large sections of the Labour Party, which see the Militants as living in an outdated world of class war.

The centre-right of the party and even the soft Left visibly winced when Militant organized a huge rally at the Wembley convention centre in 1982 and pledged the radical Left to 'end the nightmare of capitalism in Britain and to rescue the country from the grip of a decrepit, rotten, corrupt, infamous ruling class'.

A new-style Labour Party was emerging, speakers said, which would prepare the way for a socialist Britain, a socialist United States of Europe and a socialist world.

Militant Tendency has always insisted that it is not a political organization as such. It has no 'members' but only 'readers'—who subscribe to its magazine, *Militant*.

But the conference at Wembley in 1982 seemed to indicate a certain degree of organization. Delegates filled the 2,600 seat convention hall, which is more than the official Labour Party had managed to do in the past. A member of the Party's National Executive, Leslie Huckfield, looked triumphantly round the hall and said: 'This *is* the Labour party!'

How much of a threat are splinter groups like Militant to the future of Britain? Well, the Labour Party itself takes them seriously enough. Michael Foot called the Militants 'a pestilential nuisance'. Denis Healey has said they are 'space invaders'. They have been called 'political Moonies', and Labour's Red Guards.

The Labour Party has held two official inquiries into Militant Tendency, to try to establish whether it is just a 'pestilential nuisance' or a secret conspiracy working methodically towards the goal of overthrowing parliamentary democracy in Britain.

The original report in 1979 by the then National Agent of the Party, Reg (later Lord) Underhill, saw Militant as a serious threat. But it was shelved—a decision which was to be later bitterly regretted.

The second report, by the general secretary of the Labour Party, Ron Hayward, and by the National Agent, David Hughes, concluded that Militant was clearly in breach of Labour's constitution, and that it was 'a party within a party'.

'It is clear to us,' the report said, 'that Militant Tendency is a well organised caucus, centrally controlled, operating within the Labour Party; and it is equally clear that supporters of this Tendency are in control of Labour Party Young Socialists at national and regional levels.' The report went on:

We believe that the Militant Tendency is not a group formed solely to support a newspaper. It has a hard core of supporters (including its own full time employees) who form an organi-

190

sation with its own program and policy for distinctive and separate propaganda which is determined outside the structure of the Labour Party and its annual conference.

Critics on the Right go further, claiming that Militant Tendency receives its funds from 'foreign sources', though it is hard to make this charge stick, as the Militants are ardent Trotskyites and so presumably are not being financed from Moscow.

A special report in the *Daily Express* (admittedly not the most unbiassed of sources) claimed that at the end of 1981 Militant Tendency was actually just a front for the Revolutionary Socialist League, which intends to turn Britain into a Trotskyist state.

Far from receiving funds from abroad, the *Express* said, Militant (or the Revolutionary Socialist League) is so rich that it sends financial help to Trotskyist groups in other countries. Its money comes not only from sales of *Militant* and from open fund-raising among readers, but also from weekly tithes on the salaries of the membership, averaging between 10 and 15 per cent of the gross amount.

Members were often reasonably well off, for universities, notably Sussex University, had proved important recruiting grounds in the turbulent Sixties for Militant. These were the new elite, the grammar-school educated radicals, who have since remained supporters of Militant Tendency.

Just how sinister and secret an organization Militant is remains a matter of argument, but the Labour Party's own official report said that there were indeed two kinds of supporters. There is an 'indeterminate number who are aware of the nature and objectives of the organisation; and another larger group, who are not fully aware, and believe themselves to be working for socialist objectives, and for the party. We are concerned to distinguish between these two groups.'

The build-up to the 1983 election showed that the Labour Party was right to be concerned about Militant, for

Militant itself was in deadly earnest. No less that eight Constituency Parties selected Militant candidates to stand, and this fact was a rich propaganda gift to the Tories.

It was in the Constituency Parties that Militant found its strength. As we have already seen, a number of CLPs were taken over by young energetic activists, who captured them by sheer drive—and, it has been claimed, by intimidation and bullying. Old Labour Party supporters, worn out by late-night sittings, alarmed by the ferocity of the verbal attacks launched against them, in many cases quit the field and left it to the 'Trots'.

In the Southwark Labour Party—to take one typical example—the old Labour hands claimed that they were being driven out by 'lunatics, Marxists, and Anarchists'.

There is, of course, another way at looking at all this. The Militants claim that they were doing only what needed to be done: revitalizing Constituency Parties which had grown obese, lazy, moribund, and dominated by the old. (Militants share Harry Truman's view that if you can't stand the heat, you should get out of the kitchen.)

Militant Tendency undoubtedly has thrown up a new breed of political activist in Britain—young, dedicated, puritanical, and, in the same sense that the word has been applied to Tony Benn, primitive.

Ironically, this minor revolution on the Left has been master-minded by some very old-style politicians. I went to a Militant Tendency meeting which was packed by the ardent young, but up on the platform the speakers were the editor of *Militant*, Peter Taaffe, and the father figure of the Tendency, Ted Grant, a South African who has been described as a 'revolutionary searching for a revolution'.

Both men claim to be radicals. But to me they sounded like old-fashioned Communist Party cadres preaching the doctrines of the Thirties, and I was astonished at the passionate response which they provoked from their young audience.

Obviously political idealism and political naivete repeat

themselves from generation to generation, and the old and cynical should perhaps be grateful for this. Militant Tendency does, indeed, put out some potent propaganda, tempting the young with the faint promise of political if not actual martyrdom. A militant pamphlet, *Where We Stand*, said:

> A socialist Britain...would undoubtedly trigger off similar movements to break capitalism throughout the whole of Europe. A socialist Britain would merely be the prelude to a movement to establish a socialist United States of Europe. It would shatter the grip not just of capitalism, but of the rotting Stalinist regimes in Eastern Europe and in Russia... A socialist and democratic Britain would give the final push to the Polish workers to overthrow the bureaucratic clique which is strangling Poland. This would detonate a movement of the working class throughout the whole of Eastern Europe and in Russia itself.
>
> No doubt the generals imagine that they could use the army in Britain to crush such a movement if it should prove necessary. However, such a movement would be paralysed by an appeal to the ordinary soldiers. They mostly come from the working class, very often from the most depressed areas of high unemployment in the north, Wales and in Scotland.
>
> At the same time, the mobilisation of the full power of the labour movement outside parliament would be a warning of the ferocious resistance which such an attempted coup would generate. The army of the Shah of Iran, one of the best equipped and largest armies in the world, disintegrated under the pressure of a colossal mass movement. This would be repeated only on a more gigantic scale in Britain, if the British generals attempted with the support of the capitalists to emulate their Iranian counterparts.

Heady stuff, generals and capitalists combining in Britain to send the tanks against the workers. It was not, however, this sort of appeal to juvenile romanticism that worried the Labour Party; rather it was the entryism not only into Constituency Parties but into local government and voluntary organizations, and it made action against Militant seem necessary.

The decision to move towards expulsion was made under the leadership of Michael Foot, and it was a particularly painful one for a man who had made a career out of being a rebel and an outsider. The orthodox Left of the Party was also deeply concerned, and there were many cries of 'witch-hunt'.

But a cataclysmic electoral defeat concentrates the mind wonderfully, and at the Labour Party conference in October 1983 the five members of the Militant editorial board, headed by Peter Taaffe and Ted Grant, were formally expelled. As Militant Tendency has no apparent structure, the five were regarded as the *de facto* leaders of the 'party within a party', or, as the official report put it, 'the central organising core'.

That left Militant with an estimated 4,250 supporters; and though the Labour Party has cut off five heads, the group has a solid understructure if it wants to rebuild.

*   *   *   *   *   *

If those who believed in the left-wing-conspiracy-to-take-over-Britain theory had a club, they might very well adopt the mole as their mascot. This industrious little animal crops up everywhere in the literature of the Eighties, burrowing away below the surface in the British intelligence services, or, more recently, gnawing away at the fabric of British industry.

The most famous mole hunt of 1983 took place at British Leyland, the state-owned giant, which has had a long record of industrial disturbance. In August 1983, BL management announced that it was sacking thirteen workers who had given false information on their application forms about their educational qualifications and previous employers. Or at least, that was the ostensible reason. The thirteen 'red moles' were also seen by Leyland and others as part of a Trotskyite plot to infiltrate the BL plant at Cowley, Oxford. According to this theory, a new kind of 'entryism' was under way.

Union leaders did not necessarily see it in that light. The thirteen workers were all members of the Transport and General Workers' Union, and the Union's district secretary, David Buckle, said that their sacking was an example of 'creeping McCarthyism' in Britain.

'I smell fascism in this country at the present time,' Buckle said. 'I am extremely worried, and I think anyone else in this country who believes in the right of people to hold political views—either in their home or in the work place—should get worried too.'

Fascism or not, the case of the red moles was a particular embarrassment for the unions. They are bracing themselves against the onslaught on their entrenched powers which the Thatcher government is determined to mount during its second term of office.

Thatcher and her former Employment Secretary, Norman Tebbit, have said that what they intend is the 'reform' of the trade union movement. The Labour Party says that they actually are planning the dismantling of the unions, as this will make the return of the nationalized industries to the private sector very much easier.

So though the TGWU felt obliged to support the Leyland Thirteen in word and deed (the dismissed employees unsuccessfully appealed) the whole of the trade union movement was dismayed by the affair.

The Right saw it as another example of the determination of the Left to destroy capitalism from within, and it gave Thatcher another club with which to beat the unions.

The Leyland moles were said to be members of the Socialist League, formerly known as the International Marxist Group. It has only about 1,000 members, but its newspaper, *Socialist Action*, has a readership of about 6,000.

Its members are mostly university graduates (Paul Johnson, the Right's most far-out voice, calls them 'the Visigoth intelligensia').

The Cowley moles, in their application forms, played down their educational qualifications, and gave themselves experience as manual workers which they did not have. They claim they did this because they were unemployed and needed the jobs, and BL would not have taken them on if it were known that they were political activists.

A report on the sackings in the *Daily Telegraph* gives the view of the whole affair taken by the right-wing Establishment. The Socialist League, the *Telegraph* said, had switched from confrontation (in the form of street demonstrations) to infiltration, with the leading trade unions as its target, as part of a new long-term strategy to gain control of the centres of power. The aim was to gain posts as shop stewards in key factories, which could eventually be used as bases from which to rally the workers against the government. BL plants were chosen because of the importance both of the car industry itself, and of the Transport and General Workers' Union, which organizes labour in the plants.

'Exposed! Tactics of the Red Wreckers', cried the *Daily Mail*, publishing a chilling interview with an ex-mole, who claimed that as an organizer for the Socialist Workers' Party, he had been involved in 're-educating' university graduates and turning them into workers on the shop floor.

All very meaty, this, but a soberer view was that the Right was suffering from another attack of the Reds under the bed disease. Even the employers' organization, the Confederation of British Industry, said the Leyland moles were a particular problem in a particular plant. 'If there were any more icebergs we would have seen them,' a CBI spokesman said.

'Mountains out of molehills', the *New Statesman* commented. It went on:

To have left wing beliefs and be discharged from a British car plant is far from being a unique event. The motor industry has a long record of enforcing such 'discipline'—though not

196

usually aided by mass recession and anti-union legislation. While political views have never been presented as the official reason for dismissal, sackings of this kind have invariably precipitated a more widespread employers' offensive against shopfloor organisation and representation. It is therefore not so much the fear of the few sensational 'red moles' which haunts BL management as the spectre of renewed shopfloor power.

The moles affair had one interesting sidelight. It revealed to the public at large the existence of a research organization called the Economic League which furnishes employers with information about militants. It is said to be the central reference point for the drawing up of blacklists.

The Labour Party research department says that in 1982 a total of 54 companies gave money to the Economic League for 'research'. These included the major banks, and a number of firms who are household words, but not BL, which stopped making donations in 1976.

The League itself says that it draws a distinction between legitimate trade union activity leading to industrial action, and the actions of extremists who seek to enhance their political influence by exploiting problems over pay and conditions.

Meanwhile, the employers continue to deny blandly that they keep blacklists. Whether this is true or not, the mid-Eighties do not look like a good time for industrial moles.

* * * * * *

The Conservative Party in Britain in the Eighties presents something of a paradox. It opposes the centralism and state control of socialism, but at the same time one of Thatcher's main targets in her second term is local authorities, which represent decentralized power.

Instead of giving local government greater autonomy, Thatcher and her ministers want to control it from Westminster by keeping a tight curb on rate increases. Among the government's manifesto promises was one to discipline high spending local authorities.

Within two years of the 1983 general election, the Thatcher government will also abolish the Greater London Council and six metropolitan county councils. Elections which are due in May 1985 will be cancelled and councils will be run by nominated members during their final year of life.

This interference from Westminster is likely to cause a few brave flags of revolt to be run up in the provinces, where it is already believed that anyone who lives north of Watford is a second-class citizen.

But some Labour-dominated councils have played into Thatcher's hands by their adventurism and their excursions into Loony Fringeland.

Ratepayers in Islington were not pleased, for example, when they discovered that Islington council in 1983 had sent fourteen unemployed black teenagers to Grenada for a six-weeks holiday (financed, naturally, out of the rates). The trip was arranged to coincide with the fourth anniversary of the coup which brought a Marxist-Leninist government to power in Grenada, and also the one hundredth anniversary of the death of Karl Marx.

Islington was 'twinned' with Grenada; and decided to also send it, as a fraternal gesture, its redundant dustcarts. The council's Labour members wear badges proclaiming themselves citizens of the 'Socialist Republic of Islington', and the Mayor has taken down the Queen's portrait from his office and replace it with the 'friendship document' with Grenada. (Security guards at the town hall have given the Queen's picture a home in their own office.) All this was, of course, before the US invasion.

Islington Council is also famous for having outlawed Irish jokes in the borough, though it has never revealed how it proposes to enforce this.

In 1983 two other London councils, Lewisham and Camden, sent groups of delinquent teenagers to the island of St Vincent in the Caribbean, to be rehabilitated at an experimental school. This also did not make their rate-payers very happy, especially as they later had to pay for council officials to go out and inspect the school.

On the far-out Left, however, it is the activities of the Greater London Council which have most shocked, titil-lated—or sometimes amused—the British since Labour took power at County Hall in 1981.

Among those *not* amused has been the Parliamentary Labour Party, ensconced across the river at Westminster, and constantly harassed by a group of Labour councillors who seem at times to be trying to set themselves up as an alternative (and much more radical) Parliament.

The Greater London Council has thrown up another political figure who (if he does not go into eclipse when Thatcher abolishes the GLC) will continue to be a thorn in the side of the orthodox Left. Ken Livingstone, County Hall's high flyer, is seen as a future frontbencher in the House of Commons.

Ken Livingstone is interesting not only in himself but because he is a leading member of the New Puritan school, headed by Tony Benn. Benn, though, has trouble with his image, as he is handicapped by his family connections, his rich wife, and his ineradicably posh accent.

Livingstone is the genuine article, in his present mani-festation at least, though increasing power has left its mark on him, and, like other puritans before him, he could be seduced by the good life.

Born in 1945, he is the youngest of the current gallery of important political figures of the Eighties, even younger than Neil Kinnock, or the Two Davids. A working-class lad with a south London accent worth its weight in gold, and no Oxbridge degree, he went to work at seventeen as an animal house technician in a cancer research laboratory, and entered politics at twenty-six as a councillor on Lambeth Borough Council.

His name was unknown to the world at large until he

emerged as Leader of the newly Labour-controlled GLC in 1981. Within a year, he was running neck and neck with Tony Benn as the most well-known left-wing figure in Britain.

Since 1981, Livingstone has ruled over an empire more populous and rich than many small countries: the GLC has seven million people in its area.

The man Livingstone displaced, the Tory Leader, Sir Horace Cutler, came to work in a chauffeur-driven car from his six-bedroom house in Buckinghamshire. But the new Leader was happy to be interviewed in his £20-a-week bed-sitter in one of the grottier parts of Maida Vale. Separated from his wife, he shares it only with a tankful of salamanders, creatures which were to become nearly as legendary as the Royal corgis.

Despite the wealth that he commands, Livingstone also announced that his only income would be his pay and allowances from the council. This amounts to £70 a week before tax, and in 1981, this was barely above poverty level. He declined to use the council's limousines, travelling by Tube or bicycle, or on foot.

Like Tony Benn, Livingstone quickly developed a symbiotic relationship with the media. He never lost an opportunity to belabour it as 'purveyors of filth', but television, radio and the press all cherished him, because even in the dog days 'Red Ken' could always be depended upon to explode a headline or two.

'Floats like a butterfly, stings like a bee' the *Times* said admiringly in a full page profile of him, though with his narrow-chested and weedy frame he makes an unlikely Muhammad Ali.

He is a card, exploiting with some wit the incongruity between his bedsitter rootlessness and the decorous solemnity of City Hall tradition, and turning back on themselves those early demonological insinuations that it was outrageously eccentric to iron one's own shirts and ride to work on the Tube, or that keeping salamanders as pets was evidence of a shared coldness of blood.

Meanwhile, there was never an idle moment at County Hall. Over its majestic pile a black banner now flew, giving the number of unemployed in London. Livingstone himself refused an invitation to attend the Prince of Wales' wedding, saying that he would be bored out of his mind if he went.

The Labour radicals on the council wanted to withdraw subsidies from the Royal Opera and the National Theatre and put on 'people's festivals' in the parks instead. This idea was mercifully thwarted, as was another to sell off the rich treasures of the Council-owned Kenwood House—a museum stuffed with Rembrandts, Vermeers, Reynolds and Gainsboroughs, and much visited by ordinary Londoners.

However, the Arts chairman of the council, Tony Banks, did succeed in shutting down the £2-a-glass champagne bar at the Royal Festival Hall. A champagne bar, he said, was silly, inappropriate and snobbish, and people who could afford to drink champagne should go and get it elsewhere. (The question was raised as to whether Banks had ever visited Moscow, where champagne is the main tipple at interval for patrons of the opera and the Bolshoi ballet.)

Ratepayers started complaining at the grants that the GLC was making to fringe groups like Babies Against the Bomb, the Southall Black Sisters' Association, the Irish Women's Group, and gay and lesbian organizations.

The official Labour Party itself intervened when the council tried to make a large grant to Troops Out, a movement which campaigns for the withdrawal of the British Army from Ulster. Michael Foot managed to persuade Livingstone that giving financial aid to Troops Out would be electorally damaging to Labour (then fighting a by-election in Bermondsey) and it was dropped.

However, Livingstone remains unrepentant about his

201

invitation in 1982 to Sinn Fein leaders to visit London. This was blocked by the Home Secretary under the Prevention of Terrorism Act. But there is an ironic twist in the tale, as one of the banned men, Gerry Adams, is now a Westminster MP and can visit Britain if and when he pleases, despite his alleged IRA connections.

The most popular move by the GLC under Livingstone was to cut Tube and bus fares in London to the bone, the deficit to be made up by higher rates. This was part of the council's deliberate Robin Hood policy of robbing the rich to help the poor, though it tended to overlook the fact that some travellers are also ratepayers.

The Establishment, seeing itself threatened by a move far more serious than giving grants to black lesbians, moved swiftly; and on an appeal by the stockbroker-belt, Bromley Council, Britain's five Law Lords in their majesty ruled that the GLC had no right to increase household rates to subsidize fares.

The activities of the GLC in the early Eighties were important not only to London ratepayers but to the country as a whole, because they represented a deliberate challenge by a radical body to the Thatcher government with its emphasis on self-help, on Victorian values, and on conventional morality.

The Council seemed to see itself at times as a *de facto* Opposition, having considered the Parliamentary Labour party as too right-wing or ineffectual to carry out this role. It also took its championship of the underdog—its red Robin Hoodery—very seriously indeed.

Despite its occasional forays into loonery, it struck a chord with the public. In 1982, the BBC ran a Man of the Year contest, inviting listeners to vote for their favourite characters. The Pope, who had made a successful tour of Britain that year, led all the rest, but Ken Livingstone was the close runner-up.

Livingstone came to the Foreign Press Association at the height of his popularity to talk to foreign correspondents, and he drew a full house. Seen in close-up, he is a very engaging, cool, funny man, who talks social revolution.

He told us that he did not really want to abolish the Royal Opera or the National Theatre. He merely wanted to bring the performing arts to the factory workers at lunch time and to housing estates in the evening.

He was more radical about the police, who (he claimed) are often right-wing Tories and nothing more than an arm of the British Establishment. In Livingstone's Britain, policemen would be brought out from behind their desks and taken away from monitoring their computers to walk the beat again. The GLC has actually drafted legislation to take over the Metropolitan and City of London Police, but now that it is threatened with its own abolition it is not likely to have the chance to put its ideas into practice.

Livingstone said that if the Thatcher government goes through with its plans to discipline local councils, councils should retaliate by 'buggering up' the Parliament. If the Thatcherites succeeded in their aim, the government would have more power over local councils in Britain than the Kremlin had in the Soviet Union, he added.

He has also been very caustic on the subject of the Law Lords, who disrupted the GLC's plan for cheap fares for bus and Tube travellers. 'Vandals in ermine' he calls them, or 'like Dr Who in their time machine'.

The election of June 1983 was a temporary setback for Livingstone. He had expected to run in a safe Labour seat and transfer over the river to Westminster. But he underestimated the strength of the feeling against him, and he will now have to wait until next time round. It is unlikely, however, that he will disappear from the political scene even if Thatcher succeeds in evicting the GLC from County Hall in 1986. 'Red Ken' looks to me like a survivor.

*   *   *   *   *   *

The hard Left and the loony Left in Britain are matched by

the hard Right and the loony Right, though in the early Eighties extremists of the Right managed to keep themselves more inside the closet.

The Tories were gleeful, in 1982 and 1983, about the Labour Party's troubles with Militant Tendency, but not so pleased when the Young Conservatives came out, on the eve of the 1983 Tory conference, with the accusation that there had been extensive entryism by extreme right-wing organizations into the Party.

The Young Conservatives presented Party headquarters with a report which had been drawn up with the approval of the then chairman, Cecil Parkinson. Even then, it might have been hushed up, had a copy not been leaked to the *Observer*—no doubt with the aim of avoiding its suppression.

The report said that there had been widespread infiltration of the party by the hard Right, mainly because of the falling off of open support for the National Front and other right-wing groups:

> With the collapse and fragmentation of the parties of the Far Right, some of their members clearly see infiltration of the Conservative Party as the best road to power and influence. After all, there is nowhere else for them to go.

The report warned that the infiltration would have to be stopped. If it were not:

> We shall have witnessed a political party harbouring fanatical racists, backed up by professional organisational support, and seeing open factionalism at its conference and within its constituency associations.

Apart from the reference to racism, it was a clear indication that a right-wing version of Militant Tendency was being seen as threatening the unity of the Tory Party. The report said that former members of the National Front and other extremist right-wing organizations had joined the

Conservative Party, and that some had stood as Tory candidates at national and local elections.

It gave specific cases, such as that of a Thomas Finnegan, the Conservative candidate for Stockton South in the June 1983 election. Finnegan concealed from his selection committee the fact that he had been a senior organizer for the National Front in Birmingham during the Seventies. Finnegan failed to win in Stockton, but only by 203 votes.

The report quoted an extract from a letter written by Richard Franklin, the Tory candidate in the Norwich council elections in 1983. The letter said:

> Those of us who have chosen to work quietly through the Conservative Party are not altering one iota of our basic ideology. Far from it. The new strategy merely represents a change of style.

Franklin was found to have been involved with the National Front and a wide variety of other extremist movements, and was expelled from the Conservative Party.

The Young Conservatives unearthed a whole range of other right-ring moles, and the BBC found in their archives an earlier interview with a Tory candidate who at that time was living in a house lavishly decorated with swastikas. He annually celebrated Hitler's birthday, and confidently told the cameras that the Führer would come to be seen as the great saviour of the white race.

The report also expressed uneasiness about the activities of a sitting Tory MP, Harvey Proctor, who appeared to be identifying himself with the anti-immigration group WISE (Welsh, Irish, Scottish and English). The problem, the Young Conservatives said, was that groups like WISE seemed to have been set up as a bridge between the Tory Party and the extremist organizations. This was not acceptable, and MPs who continued to have links with these groups should have the party whip withdrawn.

Harvey Proctor was unrepentant. He said that he was

proud to have been named in the Young Conservatives'
report. The committee which drew it up did not want him
to talk about or write about his views, but in fact his views
were those of the Conservative Party as a whole, as
expressed at successive general elections.

Thatcher herself said after Tom Finnegan had been
exposed in Stockton South that the Conservative Party did
not want National Front support, and would rather be
without it. But her earlier statement in a television interview that she could understand the feelings of British
people who felt that they were being 'swamped by an alien
culture' must have been seen by the extreme Right as an
open invitation to move closer to the Tory Party.

In recent years, there has been a decline in electoral
support for the National Front. In municipal elections in
1977, the NF was polling as high as 18.5 per cent of the
vote in some areas. In the general election of 1983, the
highest vote for a National Front candidate was 3.7 per
cent, and the average for all National Front candidates was
0.8 per cent.

One possible explanation is that a number of electors
who are opposed to letting in immigrants switched their
votes back to the Conservative Party because they felt that,
under Thatcher, much tougher lines would be taken. Or it
may be, as the Young Conservatives suggested in their
report, that part of the actual membership of the National
Front and other extremist bodies joined the Conservative
Party because 'they feel at home in it'.

Open support from the National Front is the last thing
the Conservative Party can afford, and one result of the
Young Conservatives' report has been better screening
procedures at constituency level.

But the racist strand in the Party remains as strong as
ever. At the Party conference in Blackpool in 1983, the
right-wing Monday Club was selling a book called 'It's a
Wog's Life' by 'Golly', and a group calling itself 'Choice'
was distributing a leaflet which demanded, among other

things, that the Prime Minister be moved to a new constituency 'where aliens pose no threat to British politics'.

The Conservative Party has not been the only target of British neo-fascists in recent years. In the early Eighties, fascist movements were recruiting among young people at punk rock concerts, particularly those featuring the 'Oi' sound.

'Oi' was the big sound of 1981, the most brutal manifestation of the rock scene. It has been described as 'populist punk, raucous, and rowdy and working class; the new face of rock and roll, the culture of youth on society's scrapheap'.

'Oi' turned out to be, mercifully, a passing phenomenon, but while it lasted it was taken seriously by sociologists who saw it as an expression of working-class unrest in a Britain then beginning to be hit by the worst recession since the Thirties.

The neo-fascists and neo-Nazis seized eagerly on 'Oi'. Decca released—and later had to withdraw—an LP called 'Strength Through Oi', on obvious echo of the Nazi slogan 'Strength Through Joy'. The record sleeve showed a skinhead kicking out with a huge boot which appeared to be coming straight at the beholder's face. He displayed on his left shoulder the insignia of the British Movement, a neo-Nazi organization, and the 'skin' was identified later as an organizer for the group.

The musical assault of 'Oi' suited the neo-fascists, who had found earlier groups like the Beatles too effete for their taste. The National Front magazine *Spearhead* once described John Lennon as a 'a multi-racialist exhibitionist junkie and professional peace creep'. The Beatles sound was, the magazine said, merely 'castrated tones emanating from weak faces, topping puny bodies prancing the stage in the manner of comic ballerinas'.

The Centre for Contemporary Studies, an independent research group, brought out in the early Eighties a report on the entryism of fascists into the rock scene. It said that the National Front and the British Movement had lost all hope of any significant victory at the polls, and had instead decided to conduct active recruiting drives among the young unemployed.

The 'Oi' sound obligingly supplied the groups with appropriate songs like 'Gang Warfare', 'Riot, Riot', 'Dead End Yobs', 'Blood on the Streets', and 'Running Riot'.

Some rock musicians were willing to go even further. At concerts held to launch a National Front campaign called 'Rock Against Communism' the songs were 'Kill the Reds', 'Master Race', and 'White Power'. At one concert given by a group called 'Bad Manners', the musicians finally had to stop playing because they could not make themselves heard above the shouts of 'Sieg Heil!'

Inevitably, there was a left-wing reaction. The Anti-Nazi League ran a campaign called 'Rock Against Race', and the more aggressive Socialist Worker Rockers was formed to 'put militant culture on the streets of London, and to be in the forefront of crushing Nazi gig violence'.

For a time, an ugly situation seemed to be developing, though the Centre for Contemporary Studies played down any fears that it would get out of hand. 'The young racists and the young thugs are a small, though active and vicious minority,' the Centre's report said. 'But this is a problem, disturbing though it is, with which the young majority can and will deal.'

As the Eighties go on, it begins to look as if this view is correct. The young unemployed have not proved as fertile a recruiting ground for the neo-fascist movements as their organizers had hoped: hence, perhaps the change of tactics to entryism into the Tory Party.

Towards the end of 1983, a survey of the unemployed young in the West Midlands and in Belgium, funded by the European Cultural Foundation, found that some white youths were being attracted to fascist activities because of a sense of alienation. 'This movement,' the report said, 'demonstrates the dangers of the frustration or disaffection that exists among the unemployed. These are unstable emotions and easily triggered into destructive reactions.'

However, the survey did not find the phenomenon to be widespread. There was no substantial sign of political rebellion, and though young people felt demoralized and isolated, their antagonism was mainly directed towards the official agencies with which they had to deal in their search for jobs or in getting the dole.

Extreme politics, whether of the Left or the Right, are generally regarded as peculiar to the young; but in 1983 the magazine *New Society* carried out a survey and found that the under-25s it talked to were more conservative than the generation above them, and that their views were more in line with those of the over-45s. It has been suggested that this is because the group in the mid-thirties to mid-forties may have become radicalized by the great 'protest' decade of the Sixties, and have tended to stay that way.

On both the Left and the Right, exponents of extremist views in recent years have certainly tended to be on the mature side. One of the finest examples of right-wing lunatic fringe activity in Britain came in 1983, when the press was full of stories about 'Major' Ian Souter-Clarence, who runs an organization called the 'Wessex Survival Services'. This was set up by the 'Major' (who in real life never rose higher than the rank of second lieutenant) to deal with the coming invasion of Britain by Communists and/or the consequences of a nuclear attack. The *Daily Express* said in its profile of Souter-Clarence:

Extreme views on the way Britain is run are well known in South-west England. The area is a retiring ground for many Army officers who from the peace and seclusion of their country retirement homes see a crumbling world around them, and mourn the old values. In wild talk over the sherry they talk of creating a new Britain by toughening young people by military training. There have also been plans to form a kind of underground, ready to go into action should the country by invaded by Russians or taken over by extreme left-wingers.

Ian Souter-Clarence went a little further than the rest of this circle of ageing men, still hankering after their active service days. He set up a military-style summer school at his home in Dorset, and he called it the 'Edelweiss School' after Hitler's favourite flower. One graduate of the school said that the training took place on the marshlands south of Poole, and concentrated.on the use of light marine craft and river ambushes. At the end of the course, the trainees were given an inscribed dagger, an echo of the SS.

Earlier, Souter-Clarence had organized a special army cadet force at Ringwood grammar school in Bournemouth. He called his elite group 'The Vikings', and took the boys on tough expeditions and commando assault courses. One man who knew him then said that he was 'a tough nut' with right-wing views who liked dressing up in uniform, and who had aspirations to greater forms of authority.

All this seemed fairly harmless until in 1983 armed police raided Souter-Clarence's house and seized two Germans alleged to be members of a para-military organization, and who were wanted in both West Germany and France on a variety of charges.

The two men, Walther Kexel and Ulrich Tillman, were alleged to be involved in bank raids, attempted murder, attacks on US military installations in West Germany, and a machine gun attack on a Jewish restaurant in Paris in 1982 where six people were killed. Souter-Clarence had been the men's host for two weeks.

Whether the miniscule 'secret armies' which surface from time to time in Britain are merely manifestations of eccentricity tolerated by the authorities, or whether they are more sinister organizations with links with terrorist groups in Europe, is a question which has not yet been answered.

* * * * * *

Not all right-wing groups in Britain belong, however, to the lunatic fringe. Some are pressure groups with impressive qualifications and with generous if somewhat obscure funding; and, in some cases, with ambitions to become think tanks advising Tory governments on matters of policy.

On the Left, the rise of these 'research' groups is seen as much more dangerous than the infiltration of a few neo-Nazis into the Conservative Party. In a brisk essay on the Big Sister State in late 1983, the editor of the *New Socialist*, James Curran, said:

> Far more frightening in many ways (than the neo-fascists) are the civilised and undeniably democratic members of the New Right, operating from such base camps as the Conservative Philosophy Group, the Social Affairs Unit, and the Centre for Policy Studies, for they do occupy places of influence in the heartland of the Conservative Party. A main thrust of their arguments, forcefully expressed within the elite echelons of their party, is that the role of the state needs to be strengthened rather than weakened in many areas of everyday life. As Maurice Cowley, an influential Conservative ideologue, argues in a seminal essay, "Authority should be the byword of freedom." The impact of these ideologues...can be seen in a number of recent developments as well as proposals for the next session of Parliament. Taken together, they represent a significant lurch towards an authoritarian state.

Curran's argument is that while the leadership of the Tory Party is preaching libertarianism, behind the scenes techniques or surveillance developed during the Ulster Troubles are being brought across the water to mainland Britain. The National Council for Civil Liberties claims to have evidence that the Special Branch is assembling dossiers on many law-abiding citizens who may, in the government's view, deviate from the norm—in that they oppose blood sports, have links with gay groups or work for multi-racial or peace organizations.

One notorious example of this sort of thing occurred in the autumn of 1983 and received wide media coverage.

Mrs Madeleine Haigh wrote a letter to her local paper objecting to the deployment of cruise missiles in Britain, and thereafter she received visits from two men who claimed to be investigating mail order fraud. When she checked with local police, they denied sending officers to see her, and the men were later disclosed to be Special Branch investigators. Mrs Haigh received an official apology, but she was not mollified.

The Campaign for Nuclear Disarmament has been a particular target of the Right. The government itself set up a special propaganda unit called DS 19 to counter it, but the unit was short-lived. It was closed down officially because, according to the Defence Secretary Michael Heseltine, CND was no longer a threat. More probably it was closed because the freelance anti-CND groups were doing what the government considered to be a more effective job, being unrestrained by any considerations of good taste.

When it comes to peace and anti-peace groups, the arguments rage on over who is funding what. The Right has always insisted that CND gets its money straight from Moscow; the Left says that the freelance anti-CND groups are funded by big business and the CIA.

There are nearly a dozen anti-CND organizations in Britain, coordinated by the Committee for Peace with Freedom, and chaired by the Tory MP, Winston Churchill. The most unlikely of them all is an anti-nuclear disarmament trade union group, funded by NATO. A right-wing trade union leader, Frank Chapple, is quoted in anti-CND pamphlets as talking about 'reactivated peace groups, manipulated by pro-Soviet apologists in one of the most brilliantly orchestrated propaganda offensives'. A cartoon shows a CND activist bearing some resemblance to Michael Foot wearing a 'KGB standard issue overcoat' and carrying an umbrella supplied by 'the Bulgarian secret service' while reading a copy of the *Guardian*.

Monsignor Bruce Kent, the secretary general of CND,

has offered to pay a substantial sum to charity if any of his opponents can supply proof that CND is funded from foreign sources. So far, he has had no takers. He says that he does not think the smears from the Right have damaged CND, except that they have made professional people more reluctant to become involved. He is concerned, however, with the effect that the mud-slinging has had on religious people; and he quotes one anguished correspondent who wrote asking how he, as a Roman Catholic priest, could link hands with 'Marxists, Lesbians, and Abortionists'.

The crudeness of the tactics of a number of right-wing groups makes it easy to dismiss them. The Left is watching with more anxiety the activities of the Adam Smith Institute, a group set up in 1978, but which only really began to impinge on public consciousness in 1983.

The Institute takes the general view that collectivism is dead, and, in the Eighties, that libertarianism is the name of the game. It sees its function as promoting monetarist doctrines, and finding 'non-governmental' solutions to economic problems. Founded by a couple of graduates of St Andrew's University, it started with a capital of only £1,000, but it is now said to have substantial funding from industry, business, and the City.

Obviously it is not short of finance, for it has embarked on its own grand design for Britain in the Eighties and Nineties. This is code-named the Omega Project.

The Project is being carried out by twenty working parties, dealing with every aspect of government activity from local councils to defence and calling on the services of one hundred experts, all dedicated to a free market economy.

The first group of Omegans produced a report on local government in October 1983. It calls for compulsory privatization of most council services, including garbage collection, road repairs, cleaning, school meals, and running of recreation centres. The list of candidates to be

213

handed over to the private sector is, said the report, almost endless.

Future recommendations from the Adam Smith Institute are likely to include the virtual dismantling of the National Health Service and the downgrading of the British Army of the Rhine. BAOR is to be largely supplanted by a rapid deployment force, available at short notice for use in trouble spots.

The Omega project reflects the thinking of the 'dry' wing of the Conservative Party, and the Adam Smith Institute maintains that its main objective is to short circuit the slow procedures of the civil service. If it continues along its present path, it is likely to find barriers thrown up against it along the whole length of Whitehall. The British civil service is famous for its ability to close ranks in the cause of self-protection.

CHAPTER ELEVEN

BRITAIN AND THE WORLD

This royal throne of Kings, this scepter'd isle
This earth of majesty, this seat of Mars
This other Eden, demi-paradise;
This fortress built by Nature for herself
Against infection and the hand of war;
This happy breed of men, this little world;
This precious stone set in the silver sea,
Which serves it in the office of a wall,
Or as a moat defensive to a house
Against the envy of less happier lands.

'Is it true,' a Korean asked Anthony Sampson when he was writing *The Changing Anatomy of Britain*, 'that Britain used to have an empire on which the sun never set?'

The memories of most people are not so short. For that large section of the population which is over (let us say) 45, the British Empire remains a perceived reality rather than a myth. It is probably true to say that Britain is still suffering from a post-imperial hangover. It has given away half the world, and has not yet found a new role for itself.

It was Winston Churchill's idea that Britain would continue to be an important centre of power, as it is at the intersection of three circles: Europe, America, and the Commonwealth.

That is one way of looking at it. Another view is that Britain is now living in the worst of all possible worlds. By entering Europe, it has seceded its sovereignty to the faceless bureaucrats of Brussels and so lost its dominant role in the Commonwealth. It has also, say the exponents of the scepterd' isle theory, become a lackey of the United States; or, in the cruellest gibe of all, Washington's poddle.

There are two main voices raised in support of these views—one on the Left, one on the Right. Tony Benn and Enoch Powell have little else in common, but on the need for Britain to regain its island sovereignty their hearts beat as one. Both men also play on a popular nerve. Though successive governments of both Left and Right have remained committed to membership of the EEC and the North Atlantic Alliance, a certain resentment at the role in which Britain now finds itself runs right through the national psyche.

As we have seen, public opinion polls taken in 1983 showed that a majority of Britons felt a great unease at the prospect of American-supplied cruise missiles being deployed in the United Kingdon. There is even more dismay over the fact that the British Government would not have any real control over their firing in the event of a nuclear war.

'The truth is,' said Tony Benn in the autumn of 1983, 'that there is hardly a single advance made by the people of Britain over many centuries that is not going to have to be defended again. Not since Julius Caesar's time has Britain been governed from Europe, by a constitution drafted in Rome; and not since 1066 have we had the armed forces of a foreign power—now American—permanently based in our country.'

Tony Benn's thesis is that Britain is now merely a colony in the new world order, and this less than forty years after London was the capital of the largest empire the world has ever seen. He argues that the United Kingdom is in triple bondage.

216

It is subject first to the imperialism of the International Monetary Fund (to which it has gone more than once as a supplicant for aid) and to the multinationals—global corporations now more powerful than nation states, which conduct their own business without caring for the economic consequences on their host countries.

Secondly, says Benn, Britain is in law and in practice a colony of an embryonic West European Federal State. In *Arguments For Democracy* he wrote:

> The most formal surrender of British sovereignty and parliamentary democracy that has ever occurred in our history took place in January 1972 when Mr Heath signed the Treaty of Accession which bound Britain to the Treaty of Rome and subordinated our key law-making and tax-gathering powers to the Common Market. The economic and industrial price we are paying for our abdication of sovereignty is now becoming apparent.

Thirdly, Benn says, the situation existing before 1876 has been reversed, and Britain is now a colony of the American empire. Because of atomic cooperation between the US and Britain, the United States is entitled to lay down the framework under which Britain's intelligence services operate and to have access to the material that they produce. Britain has had to seek American consent to go ahead with its own developments in atomic research.

> The expenditure on nuclear weapons and the programs for which they are designed are concealed from Cabinets as well as Parliament; and we have on our soil the armed forces of a foreign power, armed with weapons of mass destruction that can be fired without Parliament's approval. Those are, in effect, colonial arrangements under which, in a crucial area of government, we are part of an American world-wide military system.

Benn even foresees a 'national liberation struggle' ahead for Britain, similar to those carried out in many of its own former colonies in the post-World War II period.

This is dismissed by the Right wing of the Labour Party as yet another sign that Tony Benn has gone off into some cloud-cuckoo land of his own, but the idea is received with enthusiasm by the ardent Bennite young who see themselves as future Che Guevaras.

Benn's views on the colonization of Britain do, however, command support, even among those on the Left who regard calls for a 'national liberation struggle' as romantic nonsense. During the early Eighties, he was able to swing successive Party conferences to withdrawal from Europe and to unilateral disarmament. Both commitments were incorporated into the Labour manifesto in the 1983 election.

In 1984, the Party still remains pledged to unilateralism (which implies the removal of American bases from British soil) even if withdrawal from the EEC has been hurriedly swept under the carpet.

If Tony Benn has the backing of a sizeable body of Labour opinion, Enoch Powell—the former Conservative MP and minister and now the Official Unionist MP for the Ulster constitutency of South Down—continues to make his own lonely and idiosyncratic stand.

He is no longer a member of the Tory Party, but in recent years Powell has come increasingly to see himself as the conscience of British Conservatism. Though no link is acknowledged, he is also useful to the government for he is free to say what he believes, in a way that no minister or frontbencher can possibly be. It is a safe bet that public reaction to any speech by Enoch Powell is carefully monitored at the Conservative Central Office.

Like Tony Benn, Enoch Powell believes that Britain has sold its soul for an American mess of pottage, and/or that it is being led into serious error because of the government's ,fear—or purported fear—of the Soviet Union's aggressive intentions. In a speech in late 1983 which attracted a good deal of attention, Powell said he believed that British foreign policy was going through an exceptionally bad period:

There is a word, 'Finlandization'. It describes the process to which a state, nominally sovereign and independent, is subjected when it decides that in reality its actions must conform to those demanded or imposed by an irresistibly powerful neighbour.

I make no complaint against whatever courses the Finns may have thought it right to pursue. I do say that successive British governments down the last 30 years have Finlandized the United Kingdom in relation to the US without justification either of national interest or of *force majeure*.

The result has been to associate us with, and subordinate us to, the huge miscalculations and misconceptions which dominate American policy and which have led that country from one failure to another, failures mainly paid for by the inhabitants of those distant territories where the United States mistakenly sought its own interests by the attempt to coerce others into conformity with its invincibly erroneous preconceptions.

There has not even been compensation, if such it were, by finding ourselves on the winning side. In the last 30 years, whenever we have followed them as in Iran, or been tempted to follow them, as in Vietnam, the Americans have been the world's grand losers. We plaster the fact over in vain by telling us that, through it all, the United States has kept the Soviet Union at bay.

In his speech, Powell was objecting to the presence of a small British detachment in Lebanon, as part of a multinational peace-keeping force. It had been sent, he said, despite the fact that whoever held power in Beirut was a matter of total indifference to the United Kingdom:

In the absence of any such interest or commitment, we have no moral right by even the passive use of military force, let alone by killing or being killed, to attempt to determine the governance of Beirut.

How come we find ourselves in so absurd and unjustifiable a predicament? In order to dance, and to be seen to be dancing, to the American tune. We are delivering a token assent on our part to the intervention of the United States in the affairs of Lebanon.

Powell has also claimed for years, to the continuing

embarrassment of whatever government is in power, that the American State Department is involved with the British Foreign Office in a plot to (in his view) betray the Protestants of Ulster and hand the six provinces of Northern Island over to the government of the Irish Republic. The aim, he says, is to make Ireland a united island, so that it can be slotted more effectively into the framework of European defence.

This Powell theory is a fascinating one, involving as it does accusations of sinister dealings in the shady half-world hidden behind official government policies. He does not hesitate to call these dealings 'bloodstained', and because of the seriousness of his charges I will take a closer look at Powell's Ulster Conspiracy in a later chapter.

But while gaunt prophets like Powell and Benn are preaching the doctrine of disengagement, other voices are urging Britain to involve itself more and more with American policies.

The 'hands across the Atlantic' school would like to see active support for the United States stand in Central America as well as in the Middle East. One of Thatcher's think tank men, Sir Alfred Sherman, claimed in an article in the *Daily Telegraph* in October 1983 that the latest incursions of Communism in the Americas were a threat to Europe as well as to the United States.

The heading on the article was 'Why Britain's frontline lies in Central America', and it put forward a somewhat unexpected argument. Sherman said:

> Britain's future is inseparably linked with the Central American conflict. An extended Soviet bridgehead in the New World would outflank the old, and seriously undermine the American contribution to European defence. This in turn would be liable to reinforce neutralist tendencies in Europe.
>
> Now that our frontier is on the Rio San Juan—which divides Nicaragua from Costa Rica—much as it was once on the Rhine, can we afford to allow our thinking on Central America to be dominated by left-wing stereotypes?

Sherman argues that President Reagan's Central American policies are being sabotaged by Congress, and by hostile media campaigns, motivated by 'Marxism or masochism, playing heavily on Vietnamania'.

European support at this stage could therefore be crucial. European hostility, 'only barely mitigated by limited support in Britain, allows Reagan's opponents to argue that his policies are isolating America from its allies, while simultaneously providing fuel for neo-isolationists who would reduce America's commitments to Europe.'

The idea that Britain's frontier is now on the Rio San Juan raised some eyebrows even among the readers of the *Daily Telegraph*. Sherman's article, however, was not dismissed out of hand as it would have been in the early Eighties. He was a prominent member of the Number 10 Downing Street 'kitchen Cabinet', the group of independent, non-governmental advisers that Thatcher had gathered round her.

This made it all the more surprising, therefore, that the British Prime Minister fell out with the American Administration over the invasion of Grenada in October 1983. Up until then, Margaret Thatcher appeared firmly committed to the London-Washington axis, and she and Ronald Reagan had had a close personal relationship. No other western leader had ever been welcomed so warmly at the White House.

Not too long before the Grenada invasion, Thatcher had concluded yet another triumphal visit to the United States, where she is regarded with awe and respect because of the tough way in which she ran the Falklands war.

A senator from Nebraska jokingly told her that he was going to write in her name on his voting ticket, and the *Washington Post* said straight-faced that it had been informed by one of her aides that she had been offered the American presidency three times.

President Reagan compared her to Britannia and Churchill, and invented another title for her—'Defender of

221

the Realm'—which comes close to *lese-majeste*.

Back in London, even some sections of the Tory Party regarded this as going a bit over the top, and in the first personal attack on the Prime Minister for some time, the Conservative backbencher Julian Critchley (a former chairman of the Party's media committee) retaliated by describing Mrs Thatcher as 'a great she-elephant with Churchillian pretensions'.

Yet despite the Reagan-Thatcher mutual admiration society, the Prime Minister refused to back the Americans over Grenada on the grounds that a great power 'simply cannot walk into another country'. Military intervention by western countries could be justified only by 'overwhelming reasons', she said, which were lacking in this case.

In fact, Thatcher's reaction was compounded, partly as a result of her anger that Britain had not been consulted about US military action against a former British colony, and partly as a result of her anxiety over reaction at home, and how it would affect the government's defence policies.

The public was already touchy about the installation of US-supplied cruise missiles on British soil. The idea that these missiles were under the control of an American president and commander-in-chief who was capable of military adventurism in the Caribbean was not likely to reassure British voters.

The whole Grenada episode was an unhappy one for Thatcher. Not only was there a cooling in the relations between Whitehall and Washington, but Thatcher's stand alienated the gung-ho section of the Tory party.

A senior group of Tory backbenchers were among the signatories to an advertisement in the New York *Times* expressing British support for the invasion of Grenada, and, in effect, apologizing for the Prime Minister's stand.

Grenada also cost the Prime Minister the often-expressed admiration of the right-wing columnist Paul Johnson. This is not as trivial as it sounds, as Johnson is probably the most influential voice on the intellectual far Right in Britain today. His rejection of Thatcher was as dramatic and public as his previous adulation of her. He had, he wrote in a remarkable piece of soul-bearing in the *Observer*, given her a degree of loyalty and support that he had accorded no other politician. So her refusal to offer President Reagan whole-hearted backing over Grenada had, he feared, exposed her inadequacies as Prime Minister.

> What distresses me personally is that Mrs Thatcher's deepest instincts can play her false on a major issue of judgment, and above all, without her being aware of it. It is painful to hear her adopt the sanctimonious humbug of her progressive opponents and to see her slip so easily into the anti-American posture of the Far Left. Her courage and her sound instincts made her formidable. But if her judgment cannot be trusted, what is left? A very ordinary woman occupying a position where ordinary virtues are not enough. For me, I fear, it can never be 'glad confident morning' again.

* * * * * *

Though Grenada was a setback, Thatcher herself certainly believes that since her government came to office Britain has regained much of its stature as a world power. When the Argentines surrendered in Port Stanley in 1982, she told the crowds in Downing Street: 'Today has put the Great back into Britain.'

A Party election broadcast which ran before the election of 1983 began: 'Less than five years ago, we in Britain no longer believed we still had any right to think of ourselves as a world leader. But that has changed. Because of one woman...'

During the election campaign, I heard Thatcher suggest to a meeting of the Tory faithful in an unscripted aside that a Conservative victory in Britain would bring the Soviet Union to the negotiating table at the disarmament talks in Geneva. 'Mr Andropov won't negotiate on nuclear arms

223

until he knows a Conservative government with a good majority is back in this country,' she shouted, to rapturous applause. (She got her good majority, but Mr Andropov remained unmoved.)

Later, a great deal was to be written by political commentators about the dangers of a Churchillian posture, and indeed on the folly of encouraging Britain to see itself as a Great Power. There was considerable tut-tutting about Thatcher's regular outbursts against the Soviet Union, even if these were aimed at reassuring Washington.

'We are not in the same relation to the Soviet Union as the United States,' said David Watt, who until 1983 was the director of the Royal Institute of International Affairs. 'We lack the resources to accept the global responsibility of containing "Soviet expansion" even when we agree that "containment" is appropriate. We have regional interests in Europe which give us a different perspective from America's.'

Towards the end of 1983, however, it was noticeable that the Iron Lady seemed to be softening her anti-Moscow line. In a speech at the Conservative Party conference in the autumn, she said:

> Whatever we think of the Soviet Union, Soviet communism cannot be disinvented. We have to live together on the same planet. That is why, when the circumstances are right, we must be ready to talk to the Soviet leadership. That is why we should grasp every genuine opportunity for dialogue and keep that dialogue going in the interests of East and West alike.

This did not stop Britain accepting cruise missiles in late 1983, a step which made dialogue with the Soviets less likely. But the conference speech was a sign that Thatcher now sees herself as more of a world negotiator and less of a hard-line ideologue. In 1984, she visited Hungary, and went to Moscow for Andropov's funeral.

Whatever her ups and downs with Washington, she has undoubtedly raised Britain's standing in Europe. When she came to office in 1979, the Community was dominated by two arrogant, charismatic and powerful statesmen, Helmut Schmidt and Giscard d'Estaing. They ran an exclusive club, which was very reluctant to admit a pushy newcomer, and a woman at that.

Schmidt was to come round and form a working alliance with Thatcher, but Giscard remained disdainful. *'Je ne l'aime,'* he said, *'ni comme homme, ni comme femme.'* But the tide of history has swept away both Giscard and Schmidt, along with less notable European leaders. Thatcher, however, has survived, and in 1984, after Pierre Trudeau's retirement, she led the heads of the western power bloc in terms of political longevity.

She is now forging another Anglo-German alliance, this time with Chancellor Helmut Kohl, a conservative of her own radical kind. ('She is of such a charming brutality', one of Kohl's entourage has been quoted as saying after a visit by Thatcher to Germany, when she rode enthusiastically in a Chieftain tank.)

Thatcher's main problem with Europe is the same as that which has plagued other British leaders—namely the budgetary inequities which result in Britain and in West Germany bearing the main EEC financial burden and subsidizing inefficient or greedy farmers in other EEC countries.

Britain wants to put strict cash limits on the growth of EEC farm spending, to try to halt or to slow down the appalling over-production of food. It also wants to impose limits on any country's contribution to the EEC budget, based on its share of the Community's total wealth.

The Community itself is split over the Common Agricultural Policy. Britain, Germany and Holland—all highly efficient farming nations—are demanding a radical reform of the CAP. The French, the Italians and the Greeks are lobbying for the extension of CAP protection, and no doubt Portugal and Spain will follow suit when they join the Community.

The non-agricultural section of the Community is restive about the fact that as the butter mountains and wine lakes grow, so do subsidies to farmers. In Britain in 1982, farm incomes rose by 45 per cent; and farmers, who had cried poor for so long, began to emerge as among the top level of income earners. Even Tory MPs began to grumble about the huge amount of the agricultural subsidy, in 1983, running at about £1 billion a year.

The Common Market is rarely a laughing matter, but in the winter of 1983 there was one droll incident: the latter-day invasion of Britain by the Danes. The Danish parliament refused to accept the EEC fisheries policy which came into force early in January. The new policy made it an offence to fish inside the 19 km limit of member States, restricted boat numbers and size, and put restrictions on the type of fish caught.

Enoch Powell, always ready to make propaganda against the Market, seized on the announcement by the Danes that they would not abide by the new regulations as another sign that the Community was beginning to break down.

The Prime Minister, still fresh from her triumphs over the Argentines, made it plain that she would not tolerate a Danish invasion, and she sent the Royal Navy and the Royal Air Force to deal with any intruders.

The dark days of winter were greatly cheered for both the British and the Danes when Captain Kent Kirk, a Danish fishermen's leader and a Member of the European Parliament, sailed his fishing trawler into Britain's 19 km limit and was duly arrested.

Captain Kirk was accused by his critics of thinking of himself as a latter-day Errol Flynn, but the media loved him. He was everything a piratical skipper should be— handsome, exhibitionist, and endlessly articulate. Before he left port, he was presented with a Viking helmet; but he refused to wear it, much to the disappointment of the very seasick press accompanying him.

Everyone had high hopes that the fish comedy would

turn into a long-running farce. But it fizzled out when Denmark signed the fisheries agreement, and the European partners returned to their interminable arguments over the CAP.

If a referendum was held now, it is a safe guess that a majority of British people would stay in the Market, mainly because pulling out seems too extreme and troublesome a step. But the British still look with suspicion across the Channel at the inhabitants of less happier lands. A Gallup poll taken in 1983 showed that 27 per cent of those questioned thought that West Germany was Britain's best friend in Europe, with France (the old enemy) a poor second with nine per cent, and Holland third with eight per cent.

But the most interesting thing about the poll was that the 'don't knows' amounted to 50 per cent. The deduction drawn by political commentators from this was that Britons believed that belonging to the Market was buttering their bread, but that the old British insularity and suspicion of foreigners remained. Little has changed since Orwell wrote in the early Forties that the British had brought nothing back from World War I but their hatred of foreigners, except for the Germans whose courage they admired.

While Thatcher's main preoccupation in her second term of office is likely to be with Washington, she is also very anxious for Britain to play a part in sorting out the problems of the European Community.

She started her premiership as a very half-hearted European but she now has become a passionate one. According to her aides, she is not a federalist: she does not believe in a United States of Europe. She sees the European Community as demonstrating the force of independent nation states working together.

Those who think that Margaret Thatcher is being carried away by her Churchillian pretensions are not surprised by her ambition to enlarge what she calls 'the democratic mainland of Europe', seeing a bigger and stronger European

Community as a major force for world stability.

In 1983, she presided over the launching of an even more ambitious project, a world body called the International Democratic Union. The IDU is a development of the European Democrat Union set up in 1978 on a British initiative.

The EDU failed to achieve a great deal, but the idea seemed sufficiently attractive for a parallel body, the Pacific Democrat Union, to be set up in 1981. Both the EDU and the PDU are now combined under the umbrella of the International Democratic Union.

The launching of the IDU was described by Mrs Thatcher as a crusade for 'a great dominion of mind and spirit', and it says something for her personal pulling power that the event was attended by the West German Chancellor and the vice-president of the United States, as well as representatives of conservative Parties in such far-flung places as Australia, New Zealand and Japan.

The IDU has been useful to Thatcher, in that it appears to show Britain as leading a great international movement. In practice, it is likely to prove innocuous enough; though some hidden dangers may lurk in its expressed intention to help like-minded Parties in countries where they are a minority—or, as Thatcher might put it, to 'enlarge the democratic mainland'. The US already thinks it is doing that in Latin America.

* * * * * *

Being an Australian or a Canadian in Britain in the Eighties has some advantages. Citizens of the white Commonwealth cannot be slotted easily into the rigid British class system, and so they enjoy a certain social mobility. They are also seen as more energetic and more enterprising than the British (though this is also sometimes resented, as in the case of Rupert Murdoch, who is felt to be an over-achiever).

Sir James Goldsmith, the Anglo-French financier, has been quoted as saying: 'What is especially interesting is why the Canadians and Australians are so successful in Britain, because they are really ethnically the same, with the same origins and ethics as the English. A Canadian or an Australian who comes to England is outside the class system, doesn't have to be classified, and therefore can get on with everybody, whereas in England even today, the class system still has an influence, and is a container of energy. Everybody is desperate to be respectable in their own little group.'

As someone who has lived on and off for a long time in Britain (from the days when I needed no work permit to the tightly controlled situation of today), I still continue to be surprised, however, at the *disadvantage* of being an Australian, one which is not shared by Canadians or New Zealanders.

No one makes jokes about Canadians or New Zealanders. They are not thought of as funny. But Australians living in Britain begin, after a time, to feel as persecuted as the Irish. I have mentioned that the London borough of Islington officially banned Irish jokes; but, as I wrote at the time, the Irish, though usually portrayed as bumbling incompetents ('How many Irish does it take to change a light bulb?'), still did better than what one British commentator called 'the land of Foster's lager, blowflies, and the Vegemite sandwich'.

The image of the Awful Australian is so firmly engrained in British minds that the highest compliment an expatriate can be paid is: 'But you are not like an Australian at all!'

Who is to blame for all this would make a splendid subject for a PhD thesis. And for the benefit of anybody willing to undertake one, I will set down a selection of jokes and comments taken from a file built up over a three-year period:

There was, for example, during the 1983 Australian tour by

the Prince and Princess of Wales, a cover of *Punch* showing the Princess holding little Prince William in the back seat of a car, while the Prince says of his son:

> When he's not drinking, he's either throwing up or crawling round on all fours looking for his other shoe. No wonder the Australians love him!

In case the point is missed, a collection of drunken, flag-waving, singlet-wearing yobboes are glimpsed through the back window of the car.

From a jokey television show called 'Three of A Kind':

> Two hundred years ago [image of a sailing ship comes up on the screen] an event occurred which set back the human race 3,000 years. Australia was discovered!

From the *London Standard* television program guide:

> *CLIVE JAMES AT THE MOVIES*: Mr James, one of the world's few intelligent and erudite Australians, views the cinema serials of the forties and fifties.

From a television review in the *Standard*:

> Robert Hughes's antipodean accent in *The Shock of the New* has been polluting our air waves every weekend for quite some time now—or so it seems.

(The producer of Hughes' program wrote, in an indignant letter: 'If Bob Hughes were black or Jewish, the Race Relations Board would be on to Mr Grundy [the reviewer] in no time.')

From a review of a book of essays by Clive James (yes, again, but he is the best known Australian in Britain after Dame Edna Everage):

His failure to develop in the area of his choice has to do with the Australians' absolute horror of darkness, which is a fear of the Aboriginal, of the unknown, or—in a writer—of the eruption of the imagination, a perfectly reasonable fear. It produces a kind of aggressive congeniality which has nothing to do with cutting it in the arts, but is very nice indeed to have around after work.

(It seemed to me a curious verdict at the time on a country which has produced writers like Patrick White and Thomas Keneally and Christina Stead and Shirley Hazzard; or painters like Sidney Nolan or Brett Whiteley or Arthur Boyd.)

From a Fleet Street diary:

The bad taste crept into the catering, with only Australian wine and beer served. They can be quite nice, but this brand of red wine tasted like cranberry juice, and the white like pear nectar, both drawn from cardboard cartons.

From a column in the *Daily Mirror*:

I awoke at the moment Dame Joan Sutherland was giving a televised message from Sydney. Dressed in an enormous feathery hat and a lavish stage costume, the opera star, who speaks in the uninhibited strains of a Melbourne supermarket, was offering love and seasonal greetings. I quite genuinely thought it was Dame Edna Everage.

From the same columnist:

Ockers are hard-drinking, womanising, fist-swinging Australians who tend to crush a tube of Foster's lager in a bare hand in order to indicate their need for another.

From an article by John Mortimer:

Sydney is calculated to be the second 'gay' capital of the

world, a place where sun-kissed blonde girls lie on the psychiatrists' couches, sobbing for love.

From another Fleet Street diary:

Olivia Newton-John has been asked by the Australian Government to head a drive to attract tourists to the land of raw prawns and chateau chunder. Some hopes.

From a review of 'A Town Like Alice' on British television:

An Australian male is rather like a Victorian female. He remains true to his sexual stereotype even unto death...This is the fairy story of a very innocent or very peculiar people.

From the *Daily Mirror*:

I note from the snooty newspapers that the Australian High Commissioner, one Ransley [sic] Garland, is advertising for an English butler. Potential applicants should not be put off by the Barry Humphries creation, seen regularly on television, of cultural attache Sir Les Patterson. Not all Australian diplomats are covered with food and drink. Certainly not the smooth, urbane, impeccably mannered Ransley. So roll up.

From the *Times*:

The appearance of Sir Les Patterson, Barry Humphries's expostulating spoof Australian cultural attache, on last Sunday's BBC2 program, Time With Betjeman, has caused some confusion. The program's producer has received commiserations from several people who thought 'that Australian had had a bit too much to drink, hadn't he?' One man said: 'If that's their cultural attache, we should cut off relations at once.'

And so on. All this is hardly surprising, in view of the nature of Australia's cultural exports. For every hundred or so people who see one of the new wave of Australian films, millions see Barry Humphries or Paul Hogan or Norman

Gunston on television, and genuinely believe that this is the Australian stereotype. (I once caught a snatch of a woman saying on BBC radio: 'I used to believe Dame Edna Everage was overdone until I went to Melbourne.')

British comics like Kenny Everett even parody the parody. Everett invented an Australian called Bruce Droop (the British think all Australians are called Bruce) who appeared on television in a bush jacket, baggy shorts, a hat with corks and a belt with pouches for tubes of Fosters. Never one to shrink from bad taste, Kenny Everett completed his costume with an Aboriginal's head dangling on a string.

David Bowie came back from an Australian tour with a video allegedly showing Aborigines washing the streets by hand so that white Australians would not have to dirty the soles of their shoes. Bowie claims he joined the street washers. 'It was a gesture of sympathy,' he told a gullible British interviewer. 'I was trying to break a taboo which says Aborigines should wash the streets.' As temperatures soared into the hundreds, he said, he worked every day with the Aborigines, often from ten o'clock in the morning until ten o'clock at night.

Australians in Newport, Rhode Island, for the America's Cup did not help the image. British reporters there were able to reinforce their readers' prejudices by informing them that in elegant Newport, imported witchetty grub soup was on sale, as well as jars of liniment 'made from the Australian iguana'. Not to mention the 'shapely sun-tanned Australian blondes in upturned digger hats, flag tee-shirts, and exiguous shorts'.

Australians' passion for self-criticism adds to the image. On a trip to Australia, Michael Billington, the theatre critic of the *Guardian*, asked Patrick White what he disliked about his own country:

> The moral and material decay behind ordinary people's lives: the thing I have tried to put into my play, Signal Driver. I dislike the dishonesty and chicanery of public life. And in

private life, it's all grab, grab, grab—they're all grabbing as much as they can. Cars, yachts, consumer goods. What is supposed to be high society in Sydney is quite revolting. I suppose it happens everywhere now, but this is supposed to be pure, innocent Australia, and that is why I find it is so maddening.

And Germaine Greer, on the same subject:

Australia is a huge rest home where no unwelcome news is ever wafted on to the pages of the worst newspapers in the world. The vast mass of the population snoozes away roused only for a football match or a free beer.

Australia is a land of lotus eaters: to succumb to its lure is premature retirement, senility and death. If I and my fellow ex-pats sigh for the smell of eucalyptus and the call of the kurrawong, it's a sign we're growing old.

A huge rest home, a land of grab, grab, grab. Or, in a conversation I once overheard on a bus, 'like South Africa without the problems'.

The Royal Tour in 1983 added another curious ingredient to this mishmash: Australia as a land of seething republicanism.

British papers fondly labelled the new Prime Minister Bob Hawke as not only a republican, but 'the wild man of the Australian Left'. I had a call for help from a *Daily Mirror* reporter who wanted to include some Hawke 'republican' quotes in a story he was writing and couldn't find any in Hawke's file in the library.

'The Prince and Princess of Wales delivered a resounding body blow to Australia's "anti-Royalist" camp when over 200,000 people turned out to see them, jamming the centre of Melbourne, a supposed hotbed of republicanism,' wrote a *Daily Telegraph* reporter on the tour.

I will give the last word to a more sober summing up in the *Economist*, which said, in a survey of Bob Hawke's Australia:

One of the casualties of Britain's retraction into Europe over the past 20 years has been a dimming of British eyes to that cocky, abrasive half-Britain on the other side of the world. Americans and continental Europeans, also preoccupied with their economic troubles, and without even the fading imperial memories of the British, know even less about Australia. This is a pity. They are all missing something.

Australia is a place where the British temper and a European style of parliamentary government have been applied to an historical experience—the conquest of a continent—more like America's than anything Europe has known. The result is neither a reproduced Britain nor an American clone. The Australians have created a society different from both and in the past 17 years—since Sir Robert Menzies, 'British to my boot heels', relinquished his long Anglophile hold on power—they have gradually found the self-confidence to try their own solutions to the problems that harry us all. They may now have some lessons to teach.

CHAPTER TWELVE

BRITAIN'S CUBA?

In Belfast, two young soldiers of the Ulster Defence Regiment—one only twenty and the other twenty-one—stand in the dock and hear charges of murdering a Catholic man in Armagh read out against them.

A Belfast woman is blown to pieces and her child thrown through the window with his hair on fire when a bomb is planted in a cubicle in a women's dress shop.

Another bomb kills sixteen young soldiers and their girls in a disco in Ballykelly, and many months later, a 37-year-old woman and her pregnant 19-year-old daughter are charged with the deaths.

A 12-year-old child walking home from the shops with a carton of milk in her hand is killed by a plastic bullet fired by a British soldier. A 40-year-old man standing in his own kitchen in West Belfast dies when another British soldier fires a plastic bullet through the open window.

A mock 'tourist poster' in the Sinn Fein advice centre in Belfast shows a man with a machine gun and a woman and child with rifles leaning against a tree in a lush rural setting. It is captioned in gothic lettering: 'Guerilla Days in Ireland'.

In London's Hyde Park, a troop of the Household

Cavalry is blown up by an IRA bomb; and later in the morning, the pretty little bandstand in Regent's Park is a mass of bloody bone and flesh as an explosion rips through it while the band of the Royal Greenjackets is giving a lunchtime concert. The next year, a bomb kills Christmas shoppers at Harrods.

* * * * * *

Legacies of Ulster. Northern Ireland, in the Eighties, is a witches' cauldron of genuine nationalism, idealism, cynicism, cruelty, paranoia, fear, nervousness, and despair. It is a situation ripe for exploitation; and inevitably, the thugs, the racketeers, the petty criminals and—most dangerous of all—the psychopathic killers have moved in.

Whenever I go to Belfast, I feel as if I have walked onto the set of a surrealist film. The city's nightmare way of life is made all the more bizarre by the fact that its inhabitants have come to regard it as perfectly normal.

The main shopping area of the city is ringed with steel barriers which make it look like a concentration camp, even though the municipality, in an attempt to make them less menacing, has painted the steel grilles at the search areas in brilliant and garish colours. This, far from detracting from their frightfulness, adds to it.

Belfast's one surviving decent hotel in the central area, the Europa (now renamed the Forum in an attempt to take off the curse) is surrounded by a high wire fence, and guests must pass through a checkpoint and be searched every time they go in and out. Behind the bedroom doors are detailed instructions as to what to do if a bomb alert is called.

The railway station is invisible behind high walls, with a maze-like entrance: more searches here. Police stations in the more dangerous areas of the city have completely disappeared from view inside barricades of steel and barbed wire—so that they look like huge, untidily wrapped packages, creations of a deranged Christo.

Schools are fortified with fences and barbed wire. So are hospitals and children's playgrounds, though none of this, of course, stops the bombers. One of the main city hospitals has a hand-painted sign by an unknown graffitist: 'The Queen Victoria Hospital For Sick Provos', it says.

The Belfast press carries advertisements for anti-terrorist devices, and local inventers have come up with ingenious steel-spiked bomber repellants known as Dragons' Teeth.

It is in the main shopping area, however, that life in Belfast becomes, to the outsider, totally surreal.

Shoppers go calmly about their affairs in the fine grey drizzle that seems to be Belfast's normal weather. Their shopping bags are bulging; the shops are doing brisk business; the housewives chatter remorselessly; pensioners sit in sheltered spots in the shopping malls; teenagers come out of the takeaways with cartons of chips.

No one takes the slightest notice of the fact that an armoured personnel carrier has drawn up with a dramatic screech; or that soldiers with automatic rifles, in camouflage battle gear, are tumbling out and taking up crouching positions in doorways and at the corners of buildings, their guns swinging carefully to cover the crowd.

That is where the surrealism comes in. It is as though not one but two films are being shot: one an everyday story of shopping folk, one a war movie.

Nobody takes any notice either of the helicopter which buzzes overhead, keeping surveillance on the streets below; nor of the fact that a motorist driving in many areas of central Belfast will find himself covered at short range by the automatic rifle held by a soldier standing up in the turret of the smaller-version armoured personnel carrier (known locally as a 'pig') ahead of him. There are two men in the turret, one facing forward, the other facing back: the so-called Janus position. They swing their weapons constantly from side to side to give themselves a wide field of fire.

Other men with guns are on the streets. In a taxi going to West Belfast one day, we were stopped by a man who appeared to be a civilian, though he was wearing a dark blue flak jacket and carrying a small, stubby submachine gun. 'I shouldn't go this way if I were you, ma'am,' he said. 'They're hijacking cars just up the road.' I looked at the driver, he shrugged, and we went on.

Like hijacking, bombs are such an everyday part of life in Belfast that people appear almost indifferent to them.

Having lunch in the dining room of the Europa Hotel, I was surprised to see the waiters drawing the heavy velvet curtains, and asked why. 'There's a bomb next door,' the waitress said calmly. Sure enough, within two minutes, there was an almighty bang which rattled the cutlery and glassware, but everyone in the dining room went stolidly on with their meal.

I made a phone call in my room afterwards and as soon as I put the phone down, it rang again. 'Sorry to disturb you, ma'am,' the girl on the switch said politely, 'but would you mind closing the curtains and getting as far away from the windows as you can. We think there is a second bomb.'

As it happened, there wasn't. But when I rang a friend of mine at the BBC that night, he sounded preoccupied. 'Sorry,' he said when I commented on it, 'but there's a car bomb outside the building, and the Army are shooting at it to set it off. We can't get out to the pub until they have dealt with it.' I went to the window, and a few minutes later, I heard the explosion, a few streets away.

There are other bizarre aspects. The Ulster newspapers carry advertisements which say: 'If you know anything about terrorist activities—threats, murders or explosions—please speak now to the Confidential Telephone,' and give a Belfast number.

The Confidential Telephone is actually an answering machine, presumably on the principle that it may be easier to talk to a device about betrayal than a real live human being.

Belfast's Royal Victoria Hospital has now one of the best trauma and intensive care units in the world, because of the experience that its surgeons and nursing staff have gained during the Troubles. It has dealt with over 10,000 cases of civilians and combatants injured in the civil war; and one of its consultants, Mr Willoughby Wilson, has received the OBE for his work in the Hospital's surgical department. The Royal Victoria staff have become almost immune to mass horror. In one night alone, after the bombing of the Abercorn restaurant in Belfast in 1982, Willoughby Wilson and another surgeon amputated eleven limbs and removed seven eyes in a four-hour operating session.

The number of victims declined sharply in the late Seventies, but the Royal Victoria has still routinely to deal with kneecapping, the punishment for deviation from the strict rules of the Provisional IRA (PIRA) or the Irish National Liberation Army (INLA).

Kneecapping is carried out for unauthorized robberies or hijacking, and is normally done with a pistol, though for a time there was a vogue for using an electric drill. The punishment for offences involving sex, such as consorting with the wife of a comrade who has been 'lifted' by police or the Army is the removal of a testicle, or in extreme cases, both.

The nationalist organizations run very tight ships. A Protestant car fleet owner I knew in Belfast had good relations with the Provisionals because he was willing to ferry Catholics home at night, after late shift, in areas which other hire car owners would not risk entering.

He was outraged when one of his cars was hijacked, and made a complaint in an appropriate quarter. 'Within twelve hours I had my car back, washed and polished,' he said. 'They told me the kids who had taken it had been dealt with. That would be a kneecapping job.'

Despite all this, some people in Ulster will tell you that in the Eighties life is, if not exactly normal, at least not far off it. Claims are regularly made that there are places in the

Six Counties where people live an untroubled existence, hardly knowing that the Troubles have occurred. However, it is significant that this is entirely an Establishment, or Protestant, point of view. I know no Catholics who hold it.

But the Protestants are suffering during the present recession. With unemployment running overall at 21.5 per cent, and up to 40 per cent in some areas, economic hardship is no longer a burden which only Catholics must carry.

One major and intractable problem is the apparent collapse of the manufacturing sector in the province. In 1970, it employed 177,000 people; in 1983, no more than 95,000.

The desperate state of the Ulster economy has led to follies which in their turn make the situation even worse. The most notorious case was that of the British Government's backing of the ill-fated DeLorean sports car venture.

John DeLorean, an American, came with brilliant credentials. A highly respected automotive engineer, a former executive of General Motors, he sold Whitehall and the Northern Ireland Development Authority his plan to build his dream sports car in Belfast without any difficulty.

Less understandably, he also managed to persuade the government to put up most of the money while he retained his disastrous control of the enterprise. When the scheme turned sour and the dream car failed to sell, the British Government poured in more money.

In the end, the DeLorean project cost the British taxpayers £84 million pounds; and 2,500 workers at the DeLorean plant went back on to the dole, their fate all the more bitter because of the high spirit of optimism which DeLorean had managed to generate in his workforce.

Now John DeLorean is facing drug charges in California, entangled in legal processes that will have him in and out of the courts for years to come. In Ulster, his dream of bringing prosperity back to at least one sector of industry in Northern Ireland is now seen as a nightmare.

But there was a very good reason why the British Government gambled so heavily on John DeLorean. He was one of the very few overseas entrepreneurs willing to take the risk of setting up an expensive enterprise in the province.

The Northern Ireland Office has sent out missions to mainland Britain, to Western Europe and to the United States inviting investment on highly favourable terms, but there are few takers. The answer is always the same: when stability is restored to the six counties, potential investors will think again. At present, even British firms invest more heavily in the Irish Republic than in Ulster.

One sector of the economy is, however, picking up; and curiously enough it is tourism. Since the late Seventies, the number of visitors has been creeping steadily upwards, though there was a sharp dip in 1981, because of the drawn-out hunger strike by IRA prisoners in the Maze, which ended with the deaths of ten young men.

But in 1982, the rise in tourist numbers was 21 per cent, bringing it to a creditable 712,000, compared to the 1.2 million visitors a year before the Troubles. Room occupancy in 1983 was up to 45 per cent, the highest figure since the late Sixties, and Tourist Board officials were predicting that the total of visitors for the year would reach the three-quarters of a million mark.

Most of these visitors are, however, from south of the border and a number of them are day trippers. The Northern Ireland Tourist Board wants to attract overseas tourists, particularly those from prosperous countries with money to spend.

It plans to target in on countries like Australia, which have traditional links with Ulster. The Board says that 25 per cent of Australians have Irish connections; and that 850,000 have specific links with Northern Ireland.

It is obviously not easy to persuade potential visitors, however, that Ulster is a desirable tourist destination. The image in most people's minds is of bombings, dying hunger strikers, the rattle of gunfire at IRA funerals, carnage and desolation.

During 1983, in an attempt to overcome this difficulty, the Tourist Board took a number of foreign correspondents on tours of the rural areas. A German travel writer who was a guest on one of these trips wrote afterwards: 'To walk between trains round the four corners of Frankfurt railway station courts more dangers than a drive along the hundreds of kilometres of Northern Ireland's coastline.'

That is going a bit far, but it true that the Northern Ireland countryside is beautiful, peaceful, and empty. A tourist bus is stopped at an occasional roadblock, and even country pubs have rock barriers outside to prevent cars loaded with explosive being driven up to their walls; but these small ominous signs apart, it is easy, in rural Ulster, to believe that the Troubles have never happened.

(And yet, a week after we had been driven through the town of Dungannon and been assured that it was thoroughly pacified, there was a shootout at noon in the main street between police and gunmen and two men were killed.)

Ironically, one of the main charms of the Ulster countryside is that it *is* so empty—even at the height of summer when sweating motorists sit in their cars, bumper to bumper on European highways, and once-beautiful resort towns become hells of seething bodies. Ulster's traffic-free roads, its uncrowded pubs and its damp tranquility make it a lost paradise in a world of mass tourism, and the Tourist Board is pushing this line.

Coming back to Belfast from this journey through the other Ulster produces a profound feeling of disorientation. West Belfast still remains the ugliest of scars on the fact of Britain, a religious and economic ghetto, an area of shattered buildings and ruined hopes, where hate grows and festers in some of the most frightul slums in Europe.

When I was in New York in late 1983, I went up to Harlem, and walked through areas where the arsonists and the wreckers had been at work, leaving a trail of wanton damage behind them. It was a nightmare scene. But parts of West Belfast are worse, with overcrowded, squalid, graffiti-scrawled blocks of flats interspersed with piles of rubble resembling bomb sites. Factories and offices are protected by barbed wire barricades and dragons' teeth.

The notorious Divis flats, built in the late Sixties to rehouse 900 or so inhabitants of Belfast slums, epitomize the hopelessness of Catholic West Belfast. The flats themselves have turned into a massive slum, with windows boarded up with plywood and walls scorched by arson attempts. The flat blocks are hopelessly overcrowded, with an estimated population of between 3,000 and 4,000 (many of them squatters). At least 65 per cent of the occupants are unemployed, and arrears of rents are seven times the national average.

Coming face to face with a soldier, with an automatic rifle at the ready, no longer surprises anyone: the Army regularly patrols the corridors of the Divis flats.

The first killings in the Divis occurred in 1969 when the Royal Ulster Constabulary shot a young man and a 9-year-old child, after claiming that they had come under fire from the flats. There have been a number of deaths since, some of them of soldiers and police, some of residents, some of children. The British Army and the RUC know that gunmen or bombers may be waiting for them in the dark galleries, and they tend to shoot first and ask questions afterwards.

It is hardly surprising that the Sinn Fein candidate for West Belfast, Gerry Adams, concentrated on housing settlements like the Divis flats when he campaigned in the 1983 general election. It was votes from the Divis which helped to send him to Westminster—in theory, anyway, for he has never taken his seat there.

* * * * * *

The unhappy Cabinet minister who carries the burden of

the civil war is the Secretary of State for Northern Ireland, James Prior. The former Employment Secretary was banished across the water because of his 'wetness' and because of his implicit criticism of Mrs Thatcher's economic policies.

Prior is a rotund, comfortable man, intended by nature to be an optimist. But as time goes on, and his initiatives fail, he is clearly growing despairing over peace prospects in the Province.

In theory, there is cause for optimism. For in 1982 and 1983, there were signs that the Provisional Sinn Fein (the political wing of the Provisional IRA) was moving into a new phase and was becoming as interested in the electoral process as in waging guerilla war. The slogan became: 'The Armalite in one hand, the ballot paper in the other'. This at least was better than the complete rejection of the ballot for the bullet.

But the Northern Ireland Office saw this as a sinister rather than a hopeful portent. It was concerned that the change in attitude could eventually mean that a 'respectable' Sinn Fein could replace the moderate Catholic political party, the Social Democratic and Labour Party (SDLP), as the main party which would attract Catholic votes.

Voters have already put three Sinn Feiners into the House of Commons. The first was Bobby Sands. Sands was elected as MP for Fermanagh and South Tyrone even though he was a long-term prisoner in the Maze, and he became the first of the H-block hunger strikers to die.

The second was Owen Carron, who stood as an H-block candidate in the by-election after Sands' death. Carron did not take his seat at Westminster, though, unlike his predecessor, he was free to do so. He was ousted in the 1983 general election.

The third is Gerry Adams, a controversial and highly interesting politician still in his thirties—and, since November 1983, the official Leader of the Sinn Fein Party as well as MP for West Belfast. He achieved further status in 1984 when he survived an assassination attempt.

I went round the Belfast slums with Adams one day during the 1983 election and found him cool, wary and soft-spoken. Tall, with gold-rimmed glasses, he looks like a lecturer at a redbrick university; but he is an unrepentant revolutionary and supporter of the IRA.

The British have long believed that Adams is an active IRA member. This view was supported by an IRA renegade, Peter McMullen, who appeared on a Granada television program in December 1983. McMullen alleged that Adams had served as a brigade commander of the PIRA in Belfast, and that he was also responsible for attacks in mainland Britain.

In a grisly little vignette, he added that Adams had watched when, in 1972, two of his men held down a 'prisoner' while a third shot him in the back of the neck.

When Adams was invited to London by the Greater London Council in 1982, he was banned by the Home Secretary under the Prevention of Terrorism Act. However, the Home Office had never had any direct evidence against Adams, and though he was interned at one time, they were forced to release him. Now he is an MP. He can no longer be kept out of Britain, and he can take his seat in the Commons when he chooses.

Adams appears, in fact, to be following the traditional path taken by many of the leaders of Britain's former colonies, who started off as 'freedom fighters' or 'terrorists' —depending on your point of view—and ended up as Prime Ministers.

This is what is worrying the Secretary of State. At a meeting of the Conservative backbench committee late in 1983—it was a private meeting but its proceedings were leaked to the press—Jim Prior was very pessimistic about the chances of the SDLP halting Sinn Fein's advance.

He said that the task of governing the Province would become virtually impossible if Sinn Fein continued to capture parliamentary seats and superseded the SDLP.

The latter is showing signs of weakness and of division. If that happened, Prior said, Ulster would become Britain's Cuba.

Prior presumably also sees Adams in the role of Fidel Castro, for he told the backbenchers that the Member for West Belfast had the capacity and style to become a totalitarian dictator.

Certainly there was naught for the Northern Ireland Office's comfort in the annual conference of Sinn Fein in Dublin in November 1983, when Gerry Adams took over the leadership of the Irish republican movement. He made a tentative approach to the Protestant faction in Ulster when he said that Sinn Fein sought 'the unity of all our people in an independent Irish democracy shaped by all its citizens'.

But Adams has never made any secret of the fact that, like Mao Tse-tung, he believes that political power grows out of the barrel of a gun; and being a Member of Parliament has not changed his views. He made this declaration to the conference:

> There are those who tell us that the British Government will not be moved by armed struggle. The history of Ireland and of British colonial involvement throughout the world tell us that they will not be moved by anything else.
>
> I am glad of the opportunity to pay tribute to the freedom fighters, the men and women volunteers of the IRA.

There are those, however, who think all these platform and parliamentary dramatics are simply camouflage for something much deeper and sinister, and that the two sides are more united than they appear to be.

The chief exponent of this school is the Ulster Unionist MP for South Down, Enoch Powell, an obsessive man who has long since abandoned his race-war theories for his attempts to uncover the Great Ulster Conspiracy.

Powell is certainly an eccentric in the grand English style, but it would be a mistake to take him lightly because of that. He is, in his own way, both honourable and honest; and he is ready, unlike most politicians, to put the unpalatable into blunt words, at whatever cost to himself. He has, to a large extent, sacrificed his own career by doing this.

It could be argued that his attitudes on race have done the cause of racial harmony in Britain some service, by bringing ugly prejudices into the open where they can more easily be examined and fought.

In any case, Powell, loyal to the Ulster Unionist Party which took him in when he was politically homeless (though he remains a High Tory at heart), is now no longer as concerned with racial issues as he is with the fate of his adopted province.

We had all heard rumours of the Powellite conspiracy theory. But members of the Foreign Press Association had the luck to be given a full exposition of it by Powell himself, when he came to the FPA in Carlton House Terrace for a routine briefing.

Staring from the television screen, Powell is formidable enough. Seen in person, he is utterly compelling—the Ancient Mariner of Westminster, fixing his listeners with his glistening eye, and daring them to let their attention waver.

Foreign correspondents are a cynical and impatient lot, but no one moved as Powell, speaking without pause and without notes, but with a wealth of erudite verbal embroidery, outlined for ninety minutes or so his Great Ulster Sell-out theory.

Basically, Powell believes, it all stems back to NATO and the wish of the Western Alliance to have the island of Ireland united, so that it can play its proper strategic role in the region instead of being (as it is now) a weak link. For years, he says, undisclosed forces have been working towards this end, and it has only recently been revealed that they have been practising deception and falsehood on the people of Ulster and on the whole British nation.

The behind-the-scenes actors have been the government

of the Irish Republic, the United States Administration and the British Government, with the British Foreign Office as the most guilty of all. The IRA and INLA have been used as 'sub-contractors'.

Enoch Powell actually made a speech on this subject to his own constituents in County Down, and it would be a pity not to quote directly from it. Successive British governments, Powell said, were primarily responsible for the situation that came to a head in Northern Ireland in 1968, and not the government at Stormont Castle:

> What, then, was the object of those British governments? A united Ireland. Who were their allies? The State Department, with its eyes upon Ireland as a strategic position, and the Irish Republic, with its eyes upon the proclaimed aspiration of the country.
>
> What was their instrument? the IRA and international terrorism. What were their methods? Outrage, murder and assassination. Who were the victims? The people of Ulster, the people of Britain, the successive generations of British politicians.

Powell hedges slightly when he is asked how far past and present Prime Ministers and Secretaries of State for Northern Ireland have been privy to the plot. However, he says, James Prior and his predecessor Humphrey Atkins are 'just the latest in a series of guilty ministers—guilty either by deliberate intention or guilty by wilful purblindness and stupidity'.

Some time in 1982, Powell said, Mrs Thatcher's eyes were finally opened to the villainy of which she had been made the unintentional accomplice. Unlike other Prime Ministers, she had to some extent backed away from what he calls 'the bloodstained machinations' of the unification lobbyists, but her position is not firm enough to please him, and he never ceases urging her not to sell out.

The accusation that it is secretly trying to hand over the six Counties to the Irish Republic and is conniving with killings as part of the deal understandably irritates the Foreign Office.

When he was talking to us at the Foreign Press Association, Powell asked ominously who was responsible for the murder in March 1979 of Airey Neave, Thatcher's close friend and adviser, who was expected to become the Northern Ireland Secretary in the first Thatcher government.

In January, 1984 he went further and suggested publicly that the murder of Earl Mountbatten in August 1979 was 'a very high level job not unconnected with the nuclear strategy of the United States'.

The government itself and a number of responsible people in Northern Ireland regard Powell's conspiracy theory as ravings, but it would be folly to dismiss the idea that serious moves to reunite the six Counties of the north with the 26 of the south will not be made in the next decade. The Protestants of the north certainly believe that the British government would be glad to disembarrass itself of Ulster, and they will fight to the death to prevent this.

There is no doubt, either, that there is an American interest in unification, official or unofficial.

Noraid, the New York-based Northern Aid Committee which is made up of American sympathizers for the Republican cause, is believed to have sent £2 million (or possibly much more) to the Province over the past ten years. At least some of this has been used by the Republicans to buy arms, though ostensibly it is subscribed for welfare for prisoners in British jails and for their families.

Noraid sent a delegation to Ulster in 1983, and the Northern Ireland Office had to grit its teeth and watch while the visitors toured the Province and praised the 'courage and daring' of the IRA at crowded meetings.

Noraid's spokesman on the tour, Martin Galvin, is frank enough about the organization's position. 'The IRA is fighting a legitimate war against the British Army and the RUC,' he said. 'Every nation has a right to defend its soil. I would expect the people of England to do the same if they had Russian troops on their soil.'

Life in Ulster often has a touch of the lunatic, but even by Northern Ireland standards, the Noraid visit to the 'bandit country' round Crossmaglen was bizarre.

The IRA staged a fake hold-up on the road for the visitors, with hooded men leaping from the bushes to block the coach's path, waving rifles and a machine gun. Far from being alarmed, the visitors cheered and took movies of the event. A little further on, at the approach to Crossmaglen, the cameras came out again, to take a picture of a large slogan saying 'Brits' graveyard' on a wall.

Noraid and the Irish National Caucus, a Washington pressure group, are immensely useful to the Republicans, and the trade across the Atlantic is two-way.

While the American groups are sending funds, the Republicans reciprocate with propaganda material and with a regular supply of speakers who will catch the attention of the media.

During one of my visits to Belfast, a young Sinn Fein official told me that speakers were chosen for their human interest value. 'We send relatives of prisoners, blanket men, families of hunger strikers, people who have suffered directly at the hands of the British,' he said. 'If we present the human side of the struggle, people are prepared to listen to what we have to say about the results of British imperialism in Ireland.'

The Republican propaganda machine is very effective. During the hunger strike in the Maze prison, millions of Americans saw and heard 10-year-old Bernardette McDonnell talking about the Ulster tragedy at a time when her father, Joe, lay dying in jail, in the last stages of starvation.

The propaganda campaign was run in the Seventies and early Eighties from the Republican Information Centre in the Falls Road. The Northern Ireland Office has frequently complained angrily that the media devotes too much coverage to the Republican cause, but it continues to ignore the fact that one reason for this is the IRA's accessibility.

Any journalist who wants to visit the Northern Ireland Office must make an appointment in advance, take the long taxi ride out to Stormont Castle, and stand in the rain behind a wire fence while guards check credentials and furious guard dogs bark nearby.

But I could always see a Republican spokesman by simply walking into the Falls Road building off the street—past, it is true, a car bomb barrier, and, quite often, the guns of an Army patrol outside. It is a dramatic place. The walls are hung with photographs of dead hunger strikers, the offices haunted by ardent pale young men with beards and battered old survivors straight out of an O'Casey play.

This shabby building has been for years the nerve centre of the IRA's propaganda effort, though its effectiveness has tailed off since the hunger strike of 1981. The ten deaths failed to move the Thatcher government, and the leaders of Sinn Fein made the decision to start wooing voters instead of sacrificing lives.

The Republican Information Centre is a physical symbol of the difficulties which can be experienced, in a democratic system, when dealing with a determined nationalist uprising. The Northern Ireland Office would undoubtedly have dearly liked to silence the Centre, which it considered was séducing and misleading journalists. But whatever the young men who staff it during the day may be doing at night, it has no official connection with the IRA; and any attempt to close it down would cause an uproar.

The British Government had a very considerable problem with its image on the world scene during the period of the hunger strikes and the so-called 'dirty' protest.

Even though both these protests were called off they are still not forgotten. They are commemorated in street art, which is one of the most remarkable features of Belfast today. I remember two huge murals, painted on house ends: one of a larger-than-life dying hunger striker, his face dominated by enormous eyes, looking upward as a smiling Jesus bends down to lift him in his arms; the other of a nearly naked prisoner on the 'dirty' protest, on his hands and knees, like an animal in his filthy cell, watched compassionately from above by the Sacred Heart.

Men who are prepared to starve themselves to death or to live wrapped in blankets, in cells thickly smeared with their own excrement, provide powerful images for their cause. The impact of the hunger strike in particular was expected to be very great.

When it started, Seamus Mallon, a leading Roman Catholic politician (and a moderate) said to me that the hunger strike was a highly emotive weapon in Ireland, and that he feared that as soon as the first coffin came out of the Maze prison there would be a bloody upheaval.

Surprisingly, that didn't happen; and one reason why the protest had eventually to be called off was the effort which the Northern Ireland Office put in so as to appear humane in its treatment of the dying prisoners.

Relatives, priests, British politicians, and even MPs from the Irish Republic were allowed access to the men. 'All glittering eyes and no flesh', the Irish visitors said of Bobby Sands (who, at 27, became Britain's youngest—and shortest-lived—MP) when they saw him in the fiftieth day of his fast.

When the men were close to death and were sent to the prison hospital, the medical staff went to extraordinary lengths to make them comfortable. They slept on either fleece blankets or on water beds, and it was the boast of the hospital that not one of the ten ever had a bedsore before their deaths.

Nurses rubbed liniment into their dry skins (which was cracked by vitamin deficiencies) and bandaged their elbows and knees so that the sharp bones would not pierce the skin and cause bleeding.

Because the men found it hard to swallow ordinary water, special consignments of spring water were flown in from the Scottish highlands. (While all this was going on, an enterprising British correspondent stationed in Moscow went out on the streets and asked Russians what they thought of this sort of treatment for political prisoners. Most declined to believe it.)

The Northern Ireland Office even allowed the men to watch television; and, as they lay dying, they were able to see the funerals of those who had preceded them. Those funerals were themselves media events, with the police and Army standing to one side as masked gunmen fired volleys of shots over the coffins.

It was, all in all, an amazing performance—and the fact that it had so little effect on the British Government was a big, if temporary, blow to the Republican movement. The one single factor which the IRA had not reckoned on was the inflexibility of the Prime Minister. Thatcher made it clear from the beginning that she regarded the hunger strikers not as political prisoners but as violent criminals; and the slow death of ten young men moved her not at all. In public matters she is not a sentimental woman.

* * * * * *

Is Thatcher right, when she claims that the Provos and their counterparts on the Protestant side—fewer in numbers than the IRA but equally murderous—are not patriots but common criminals?

It would be foolish to try to downgrade the genuine passion on one side for unity with the Irish Republic, and on the other for keeping Ulster part of the United Kingdom. The continuing high level of the murder rate in Northern Ireland shows how strong those feelings are.

But it is also true that terrorists inevitably become involved in crime as a means of raising funds for their organizations.

An academic at the University of Aberdeen, William Boyes, has carried out a study of what he calls 'the unholy alliance of crime and terror', and his findings were published in 1983 in *Contemporary Affairs Briefing* Vol. 2 No. 7 by the Centre for Contemporary Studies, an independent research institute.

Boyes says that in Northern Ireland the paramilitaries on both sides of the religious war dominate the criminal underworld. They 'license' selected criminals, taking a percentage of the profits of crime. As we have already seen, petty criminals who step out of line are punished by kangaroo courts.

The Provos' paper *Republican News* claimed in 1982 that the British Government was attempting to strike back by setting up its own force of small-time criminals, with the aim of undermining support for the PIRA.

The republican movement receives, as mentioned earlier, a proportion of its funds from overseas groups like Noraid; but it has been estimated that in the peak year of its recent activities, 1980-81, overall expenses were £4 million—so the money had to be found from other sources as well.

In 1982, according to the *Sunday Times*, the Provisional IRA received £1.3 million in protection money and other rackets connected with the building industry. Boyes says that the Protestant paramilitaries, the Ulster Defence Association, receives a substantial income from massage parlours and drinking clubs under its protection.

The main speciality of the Provisionals, however, is armed robbery. £1.3 million was stolen in the recent peak year, 1982, and the figure for most years of the Troubles is over half a million. In a single train robbery in 1978, the Provos are believed to have netted a quarter of a million pounds for their funds.

Boyes claims that paramilitaries on both sides are now involved in a drugs-for-guns racket, though use of drugs by their own members is not permitted and is brutally punished. Northern Ireland, he claims, is now becoming one of the major centres for drug trafficking in Western Europe. Thefts of drugs from chemist shops and other sources have become routine. The drugs are exported, and the profits are used to buy weapons.

One of the great dreads of the Northern Ireland Office is that kidnapping will become an established way of raising money, as it has become in Western Europe. There have been one or two cases of kidnapping, though it is not clear whether these were officially sponsored or whether they were private énterprise activities undertaken by local branches of PIRA or INLA. It has been suggested that the unsolved disappearance of the racehorse Shergar in 1983 was a kidnap attempt which went wrong.

Thus, as the Eighties march inexorably on, Jim Prior's warning that Ulster will become Britain's Cuba seems less far-fetched. True, the level of violence is far below that of the dreadful years of the mid-Seventies, when the annual death rate was up to nearly 500, and the rate of injuries to civilians, soldiers and police ran into many thousands. The British Army now has between 9,000 and 10,000 troops in Ulster (less than half the number at the height of the Troubles) and far more of the burden of enforcing security is being taken by the Ulster Defence Regiment and the RUC.

Yet the atrocious killings and maimings still continue. No week goes by without one. In the last fourteen years, the British Army and the UDR between them have had more than 500 men killed and about 4,000 wounded.

Civilians too continue to die. Some are killed by the paramilitaries, others by the hated 'Brits'. A survey by the National Council for Civil Liberties in 1982 showed that in a ten-year period, fourteen people were killed by rubber and plastic bullets fired by the security forces. Seven of those killed were children aged between ten and fifteen years. In one year alone—1981—30,000 plastic bullets, all of them potentially lethal, were fired by security forces.

'There have been hundreds of injuries, including blindness and brain damage,' the Council's survey says. 'A report by four surgeons, suppressed for many years, on 90

Belfast victims of rubber bullets in 1970-72, listed one death, two cases of total blindness, seven of blindness in one eye, five of severe loss of vision, four of facial disfigurement. The normal plastic bullet is a cylinder $3\frac{1}{4}$ inches long and $1\frac{1}{2}$ inches in diameter. But sharpened versions, and encased torch batteries, have been picked up and fired by Royal Marine Commandos in 1981.'

One of those killed by a plastic bullet was a 12-year-old girl, Carol Anne Kelly, of Belfast. She was struck while walking home from the shops with a carton of milk in her hand. Another was Peter Doherty, forty, killed in his own kitchen in West Belfast by a bullet which came through the window.

Plastic bullets (or—as the Army calls them—baton rounds) are now in the armoury of police forces on the mainland, despite protests from many quarters.

In 1983, republican sources claimed that one reason for the improved security statistics was that the British Army and the RUC were pursuing a shoot-to-kill policy and gunning down suspected terrorists on sight. This claim was supported by the moderate Catholic party, the SDLP, and by the Roman Catholic Church itself.

John Hume, the president of the SDLP, said that what was happening was 'legalized murder'. In two months, seven Republican supporters were shot dead and two others wounded at police roadblocks, in what were officially called stake-outs. In only one case were the dead men found to be carrying arms—and even then, the rifles were unloaded.

The head of the Roman Catholic Church in Ireland, Cardinal Tomas O'Fiaich, said that two of the seven men had been threatened with death by the security forces beforehand.

The shoot-to-kill order was officially denied, and Thatcher described the accusation as rubbish. But after the protests the number of incidents of this kind dwindled abruptly; and later in the year, when a young unarmed man was shot dead in a Roman Catholic area of Belfast, the soldier who killed him was officially charged with murder. The soldier himself was only eighteen.

The other controversial reason for the improved security situation is the use of what the Northern Ireland Office calls converted terrorists, what the media calls super-grasses, and what the Republicans call informers. This is the most hated word in the Irish vocabulary.

Supergrasses have provided the security authorities with some spectacular successes. They have gone at least some way towards crippling the military strike capacity of the PIRA.

In a trial which ended in August 1983 in Belfast Crown Court, twenty-two members of the city's Provo network received jail sentences totalling more than 4,000 years. Patrick Teer, one of the Republican leaders, was jailed for 747 years for attempted murder, conspiracy to murder, possession of guns and membership the IRA. Kevin Mulgrew was sentenced to 963 years on charges ranging from conspiracy to murder to membership of the IRA. He is already serving a life sentence for murder, and like Teer, he will presumably live and die in prison.

All the men and women—the oldest being a 71-year-old woman who was convicted of letting her home be used by gunmen—remained totally unrepentant. They were convicted on the evidence of supergrass Christopher Black, who testified against his former comrades for immunity, for money, and for the chance of a new life abroad.

The use of informers—especially when they are paid large sums of money—has aroused deep unease in both Ulster and Britain. Lawyers are unhappy about convictions obtained on uncorroborated evidence, particularly in courts that are already made dubious by the absence of a jury. (In the Christopher Black case, the verdicts were reached and the sentences passed by one judge alone, Mr Justice Kelly, who wore a bullet-proof vest and was protected by police marksmen. Trial judges in Ulster hear cases at the risk of their lives.)

By the end of 1983, the supergrass pheonomenon seemed to have passed its peak, threats of retribution and the actual kidnapping of close relatives having discouraged a number of potential informers. At leat six are known to have withdrawn evidence previously volunteered and to have refused to take part in court cases.

* * * * * *

Even if the peak of the Troubles seems to have passed, the threat of isolated atrocities still remains; and there is no way of guarding against it. A single bombing can blow the search for a political solution sky high.

The bomb which reduced the Droppin Well pub disco in Ballykelly to ruins in December 1982 also destroyed a number of careful initiatives launched by the Thatcher government. Sixteen people—soldiers and civilians, among them young girls—died in the blast. The scale of the disaster forced the British Army to confine the 10,000 Army personnel serving in the Province to barracks when they were off duty.

This was a big step backwards, for the recent policy had been to encourage soldiers to bring their wives and children to Ulster during their two-year tour of duty, and for the families to mingle and make friends with the local community. The bombing of the Ballykelly pub disco put an end to that, and the families spent Christmas behind barbed wire.

The ability of the bombers to strike with impunity in mainland Britain is also a nightmare for the government. Security authorities have been completely unable to stop Republican active service teams from moving into British cities and striking against any target they choose.

The bombers are not squeamish. Devices used in the

early Eighties have been packed with six-inch nails, which mutilate their victims and produce frightful and lasting injuries to those who survive the blast.

The double bombing in London in July 1982, which killed nine people and injured fifty-three, was, however, a tactical mistake. Two bombs went off—one when a troop of Blues and Royals of the Royal Horseguards was riding through Hyde Park; the other in Regent's Park, during a concert given by the Royal Green Jackets' band.

The Regent's Park bomb was set off under the bandstand, and the dead and injured included Londoners, office workers sitting peacefully in deckchairs and eating their lunchtime sandwiches.

The brutality of the bombers' work stunned Britain, but it was the attack against the Household Cavalry which caused national outrage. Seven horses of the Blues and Royals' troop were mutilated by the blast and had to be destroyed. Pictures of their bodies piled up in Hyde Park dominated the television screens during the night news bulletins.

Nothing could have caused more anger in a country with an obsessive devotion to animals, and where the horse is a kind of god.

The summer bombings provided a propaganda weapon for the government—one which it did not hesitate to use, letting the media have all the access it wanted to the survivors, both human and animal.

The atrocity created a new national hero. This was the horse Sefton. The animal had been so atrociously gashed open by the nails which the bomb contained that it seemed impossible that it should ever go back on duty. Day by day the media monitored Sefton's progress, and the television cameras moved in for close-ups of its gaping, livid wounds. Admirers all over the nation sent get-well cards and even parcels of food from Harrods.

Sefton did survive, to have a book written about him, to have his portrait painted, to receive an animal bravery medal, and finally to take his place again as a mount in the Household Cavalry, which provides the sovereign's escort.

After the bombing, the troopers of the Horseguards continued to ride through Hyde Park over the traditional route. The first time the Blues and Royals rode through the park after the incident, the standard bearer defiantly carried not a new colour but the tattered and bloodstained one which had survived the blast. It was an irresistible bit of heroics, of the kind in which the British excel; and it hardened still more feeling throughout the nation against the Republican cause, as did the 1983 Christmas bombing at Harrods.

But if the government sometimes scores a propaganda victory by default, the intractable problem of the divided community still remains.

There is a bitter joke made by Ulster people themselves which says that if a solution to 'the Irish problem' was found, the Irish would then immediately invent a new one. This may be more true than a joke. Whatever moves the governments of Britain and of the Irish Republic make towards a political settlement are usually wrecked by the savage tribal and religious loyalties of the people of Ulster.

The Northern Ireland Office always tells visitors that most of the injustices inflicted by the Protestant majority on the Catholic minority have now been remedied. This seems to be so on the surface, but in fact discrimination remains inbuilt and systemic. The prosperous Protestant areas breed prosperous and law-abiding citizens; the festering slums of West Belfast breed hopelessness and violence.

There is even some questioning now about the size of the Protestant majority, which is always cited as a reason for Ulster remaining in the United Kingdom. In late 1983, the Belfast *Sunday News* commissioned a study which suggested that 42.7 per cent of Ulster's population of 1.56 million are Catholics, and not 31.1 per cent as officially estimated by the government. (The 1981 census gave a figure of only 28 per cent, but this was because the census was taken during the Maze hunger strikes and many Catholics boycotted it as a form of protest.)

The implications of the *Sunday News* study are obvious. The government's case for retaining Ulster within the United Kingdom becomes progressively weaker as the Catholic population rises. With the higher Catholic birthrate, soon almost half the people of the six counties will be in favour of union with the south.

Even moderate Catholics, who want no part in IRA activities, are no longer quiescent about the discrimination which is practised against them. They have learned the advantage of pushing 'the Irish problem' onto the world stage. In 1983, a group of trade union officials and Roman Catholic schoolteachers had talks with a visiting US Congressman, Richard Ottinger, about the difficulties which Catholics experience in getting jobs.

At the end of his stay, Ottinger told a press conference that he had found evidence of systematic discrimination against Roman Catholics by American companies in Ulster. He said that he intended to press ahead with legislation which he had introduced in the American House of Representatives and which aimed at imposing economic sanctions on firms guilty of discrimination.

He will be backed by the Irish National Caucus, the anti-British pressure group, which has made attempts of its own to stop American deals going to Ulster firms which have been reluctant to recruit Catholics for their workforces.

When the European Parliament announced in 1983 that it was planning to send an investigator to Northern Ireland to report on the political and economic difficulties of the Province, MPs on both sides of the House of Commons were infuriated.

It was obvious that the Catholic side would make full use of the opportunities of such an investigation, though the MPs based their objections on the threat to Britain's sovereignty. One Tory MP, Tony Marlow, said furiously that the 'inadequately employed itinerants of the Brussels travelling circus' were trying to take over the powers of the Commons.

It must be said, however, that in a region of high unemployment, both sides on the religious divide sometimes practise economic suicide. In July 1983, 80 workers at an Ulster meat plant lost their jobs because of a dispute over the flying of the Union Jack.

Flag flying is important in Northern Ireland because it proclaims allegiances. Even in country areas Union Jacks flapping over the roofs of private houses indicate a loyalist majority in a village, while the Republican flag flies in the predominantly Catholic areas.

The Moy meat plant in County Armagh had an integrated workforce. But every time the Union Jack was flown, the Catholics walked off the job; and when it was taken down, the Protestants went on strike. In disgust, the management closed down the plant and paid off the men, telling them that they would not be re-employed unless and until they found some way of reconciling their ideological differences.

The British Government's main move towards a political solution in the early Eighties was to hold elections for the setting up of a Northern Ireland Assembly. This was intended to return at least some semblance of self-rule to the Province; to break down direct rule imposed with the help of the Army, and thrust on Ulster men and women, whether they liked it or not, a mild form of devolution.

The Assembly was to have 78 members, both Protestant and Catholic, who would form themselves into a number of committees which would oversee and advise on the work of government departments.

James Prior and the Northern Ireland Office pinned their hopes on this new body. It was seen as providing an opportunity to back alienated Catholic opinion in the Province.

That gaunt and lonely prophet of disaster, Enoch Powell, saw it of course as fitting neatly into his conspiracy theory.

For him, it was another move in the Foreign Office's under-hand game of handing over the six Counties to the Catholic south.

In the event, the voters obediently turned out—but the results left a bitter taste in the government's mouth. Sinn Fein, pursuing its 'Armalite in one hand, ballot paper in the other' policy, entered the electoral process, and so split the Catholic vote.

The Assembly was dominated by the two Protestant Parties—the official Unionist Party, and Ian Paisley's Democratic Unionists—while the moderate Catholic party, the SDLP, lost ground; and while Sinn Fein took five seats. This meant that the Northern Ireland Office had from then on to deal with a Party representing the IRA, whose motto was 'Smash the British Connection'.

During its first year of life, the Assembly was hardly more than a talking shop for the Protestant side, neither the SDLP nor the Sinn Fein members having taken their seats.

The British Government continued to insist that it had considerable value, because of the work which went on behind the scenes and in committees.

However, like most Ulster initiatives, the Assembly's chances of survival—already meagre—were sabotaged by violence and terror. In November 1983 gunmen attacked a little Pentecostal Church in County Armagh and killed three of the Church elders. Seven others were wounded when the attackers sprayed the Church hall with bullets, ignoring the fact that twenty-four young children were in the congregation. Responsibility was claimed by a group (previously unknown) which called itself the 'Catholic Reaction Force'.

As a result, the official Unionist Party boycotted the Northern Assembly, leaving it to Ian Paisley's Democratic Unionist Party and the tiny Alliance Party.

Most people agree that the Assembly has so far per-formed one useful function. It has absorbed a considerable amount of the surplus energies of the Reverend Ian

Paisley, who is also a Westminster MP, a Member of the European Parliament, and Moderator of the Free Presbyterian Church.

Fifteen years after the Troubles began, Paisley still dominates the Ulster scene. He is a huge, demagogic figure, a hero to his supporters (who see him as the one man who can save them from being devoured by the Papists in Dublin) but he is evil personified to Catholics.

Two years ago Paisley's nuisance value to the Northern Ireland authorities reached its peak when he threatened to step out of his churchly role and become a war leader.

He announced himself to be, in effect, the reincarnation of Lord Carson (who had founded the 1912 Ulster Volunteer Force) and virtually kidnapped a number of journalists to witness a midnight parade of his followers on a hillside somewhere in Ulster. The reporters, who had been taken there in closed vans, watched in astonishment as 500 Paisley men marched up and down, waving, in lieu of actual guns, their firearms certificates.

Later in the year Paisley announced that he was planning to raise a private army of 100,000 men and women under the sign of the Red Hand. To show that he was in earnest, he paraded the nucleus of this Third Force at Newtownards near Belfast.

Groups of men in paramilitary uniform, some hooded or masked, filed in formation before their commander-in-chief. No guns were visible, but some carried cudgels. They wore armbands with the traditional Ulster sign of the Red Hand, and the legend 'God for Ulster'.

It was the biggest display of paramilitary strength in the Province for many years. Paisley rallied the crowd with a fighting speech, calling Mrs Thatcher a liar and a traitor, and urging Protestant men and women to follow him in a fight to the death for the total extermination of the IRA.

Paisley said afterwards that his Third Force would mount vigilante patrols and hunt down terrorists. He urged the British Army to conduct 'snatch' operations in the IRA-held border areas to bring out wanted men.

All this, of course, delighted the IRA, which saw the possibility of the festering situation in the Province turning into open civil war. The British Government was appalled, watching itself being dragged deeper and deeper into a hopeless involvement.

But for reasons not explained, the Third Force never came into being, and the reincarnation of Lord Carson turned back into the familiar hulking figure of Ian Paisley, though in a milder and more moderate version. Paisley threw himself into the work of the Assembly with extraordinary enthusiasm, and his voice was heard more often in the Stormont chamber rather than bellowing invitations to death or glory in market squares.

These are those who believe, however, that he has not really changed, and that the old hard man is still there behind the present, relatively conciliatory, mask. He is simply biding his time, his enemies say.

But biding his time for what?

In Ulster, questions are always being asked, but answers are never provided. The latest body which has been created to try to wrestle with the future of Ulster is the New Ireland Forum. It is headed by the Irish Taoiseach, Dr Garret FitzGerald; his coalition partner, the Labour Party Leader Dick Spring; the opposition Leader, Charles Haughey; and the Leader of the SDLP, John Hume.

The New Ireland Forum gives the Catholics their talking shop, just as the Northern Ireland Assembly provides one for the Protestants.

So far the ideas which the Forum has considered are joint sovereignty over the six Counties by London and Dublin (a concept which seems to an outsider to be a sure recipe for disaster); a new all-Ireland state with a liberalized constitution; and some kind of confederation, with regional parliaments in Belfast and Dublin.

In the meantime, Sinn Fein is going quietly about its task of making itself electorally respectable. With members at

Westminster and in the Northern Ireland Assembly (in principle at least), its next target is the European Parliament. This would provide a very important platform for Republican members, for it would take their cause squarely onto the world stage. A victory in the European elections for Sinn Fein would also mean defeat and humiliation for the SDLP, and would be a sign that Sinn Fein was winning the battle for the minds of Ulster Catholics.

Sinn Fein's enemies say that its present tactics are only a prelude to the unveiling of its grand plan, which is the overthrow of the elected government in Dublin and the setting up of a Marxist state.

Sinn Feiners dismiss this as Establishment propaganda. In any case, whatever their grand plan may be, its implementation must lie far in the future.

The primary task for both sides is to find a way of stopping the slow self-destruction of the tortured province.

CHAPTER THIRTEEN

BLACK AND WHITE BRITAIN

In 1949, the black and Asian population of Britain was about 25,000, students included. It was mainly concentrated in two communities, the dock area of Cardiff (locally known as Tiger Bay) and the South End of Liverpool. These two ghettoes held three-fifths of Britain's non-whites, so it was largely a case of out of sight, out of mind.

Immigrants complained at that time, however, that there was considerable colour prejudice, and that blacks found it hard to get jobs or decent lodgings, or sometimes even to be served in restaurants. 'On the curb of a Liverpool pavement, a coloured British Subject expresses the indignation of his people,' said the caption of a picture in *Picture Post* in July 1949. The article was titled: 'Is There A Colour Bar in Britain?'

The coloured British Subject was Mr Nathaniel Ajayi, a former British prisoner-of-war in Germany. He had lived in five European countries, but he said he knew of nowhere else in Europe where the coloured man was treated with more unofficial contempt than in Britain.

In the Early Eighties, however, isolated cases of colour prejudice are no longer the issue. Blacks and Asians (or, in official Whitehall terminology, people from the New

Commonwealth and from Pakistan) are now a formidable 2.2 million, or four per cent of the population. They still to some extent live in ghettoes, but the ghettoes are spread along the length and breadth of the country. Many of their children speak no longer in the accents of their parents' homelands, but the purest Cockney, or Scouse, or Glaswegian.

According to the statisticians, by the year 2000 the black and Asian population of Britain will be 3.3 million, and after that it will stabilize at six per cent of the population. The stabilization will occur because by that time tighter immigration laws will mean that most of those eligible to enter from the New Commonwealth will have already arrived, and because the present difference in family size will have disappeared as blacks and Asians conform to British ideas of limiting fecundity.

So whether the conservative element likes it or not, Britain is already a multi-racial society, and will become more so, though the colour prejudice which Nathaniel Ajayi complained of thirty years ago still exists and has become more systematized. With a four per cent immigration population, there is no non-white MP in the House of Commons, and only two black life peers in the Lords. A few token blacks and Asians appear at the conferences of the major political parties.

However, it is also fair to say that for a country which has had a large and mainly unpopular influx of immigrants of different skin colour and lifestyle, Britain is doing a better (or less worse) job of assimilation than most other nations. The glaring cases of racial discrimination can be balanced by some success stories, and at least Britain has never practised the legal segregation of the races which made the civil rights struggle in the United States so inevitably violent. No non-white in Britain has had to sit at the back of a bus, or had police dogs turned on him when he tried to enter a whites-only restaurant.

Nevertheless, blacks and Asians in Britain today still

269

have legitimate cause for anger. In 1983, a Sikh teacher, Mrs Harvinder Suthar, was awarded £500 compensation after she had complained to the Council for Racial Equality about racial abuse in a school staffroom.

'Here comes the foreigner,' a male colleague said. 'Wogs, Pakis, coons, they are all foreigners. All foreigners should go back to wogland!' The responsible local authority, Avon County Council, gave Mrs Suthar compensation for her wounded feelings, and ordered the male teacher involved to attend a 'racism awareness' course.

A BBC television Panorama program in 1983 caused an uproar when extracts from essays written by young police cadets were read out. The cadets, the police officers of the future, were set 'Blacks in Britain' as a subject. When the essays were handed in, the head of the college, Commander Richard Wells, said that he thought he was being made the victim of a bad joke, as the racial attitudes revealed were so appalling. However, he had made certain investigations, and the cadets appeared to be completely sincere.

One extract: 'Blacks are a pest. I don't have any liking for wogs, nig-nogs, or Pakis. They come over here from some tinpot country and take up residence in our over-crowded country. It makes me cringe when I see a black bloke out with a white woman. Putting it bluntly—keep them out.' Other essays were similarly openly racist.

Panorama also interviewed the chairman of the Police Federation, Leslie Curtis. He appeared undismayed by the fledgling policemen's attitudes. He jovially likened a policeman calling a black a 'nigger' to an Australian calling an Englishman a 'pommy'. He would not himself, he said, use the phrase 'black bastard' but 'that's a common phrase which is used throughout the land'.

'If a police officer calls a black man a "nigger", shouldn't he be dismissed?' the interviewer asked. 'No, no, indeed not,' Curtis said. 'It's like anything else. Why should he be dismissed for calling him a "nigger"? If somebody all his life has used the phrase "nigger" and he doesn't do it detrimentally, he recognizes a black man by that particular phrase the same as I recognize "cockney" by that particular phrase or any other walk of life, then it's a matter of how the recipient receives it.'

The fact that police officers were so frank about their attitudes caused a great deal of surprise because of the criticism of 'hard' policing methods in immigrant areas and of the general loss of confidence in black communities in the police following the urban riots of 1981.

The undeclared war between sections of the police force and the immigrant community is possibly the greatest present obstacle to the creation of a harmonious multi-racial society in Britain. The police continue to deny that such a war exists, but examples of it can be seen on the streets of any British city.

For three years, I lived in London's Notting Hill Gate, an area with a heavy black population. It was commonplace for police to stop young blacks, to push them up against police cars and give them a quick search. I saw a black teenager almost in tears one day as he tried to convince a policewoman that he was the owner of a cheap little transistor radio which she had found in his jeans' pocket.

I also had some illuminating conversation about police tactics with Joe, a black handyman who did some work at my Notting Hill flat. I asked Joe if he would take his tools home with him at night instead of leaving them in my living room, but he said that he would rather not: any black man leaving a white apartment building with a bag or a bundle after dark stood the chance of being picked up by a cruising police car and taken to the station for a search.

This had happened to him twice, Joe said, so he no longer took the risk. Joe was not at all bitter about this. An immigrant from Grenada, he was almost illiterate, but a handyman of great and diverse talent. He could turn his hand to anything, and he was making a fortune and salting it away largely tax free, for he preferred to be paid in cash.

Joe is doing very well in Britain, and regards occasional police harassment as a minor irritant, nothing more.

Others feel differently, and have good reason to do so. The main reason for the Brixton riots of April 1981 (which looked, for a while, like the start of a race war) was the atrocious relations between the black community and the police.

It is ironic that the trigger for the rioting was an incident in which white police were trying to help a young black man who had been stabbed by other blacks. Blood was welling from the wound in the man's back and the police were attempting to keep him immobile on the seat of a car until the arrival of an ambulance. A hostile crowd gathered and assumed that some sort of harassment was going on. It snatched the boy away. Later, rumours spread that he had died, and that the police were responsible.

Despite this incident, Brixton police continued with an idiotically tactless stop-and-search operation which they had begun (it was even more tactlessly code-named 'Operation Swamp'), and the result was inevitable. It has been described by Lord Scarman, the commissioner who was appointed by the government to investigate the ensuing riots:

> During the weekend of 10-12 April, the British people watched with horror and incredulity an instant audiovisual presentation on their television sets of scenes of violence and disorder in their capital city, the like of which had not previously been seen in this century in Britain. In the centre of Brixton, a few hundred young people—most, but not all of them black—attacked the police on the streets with stones, bricks, iron bars and petrol bombs, demonstrating to millions of their fellow citizens the fragile nature of the Queen's peace.
>
> The disturbances were at their worst on Saturday evening. For some hours, the police could do no more than contain them... The toll of human injury and property damage was such that one observer described the scene as comparable with the aftermath of an air raid. Fortunately, no one was killed: but on that Saturday evening 279 policemen were injured, 45

members of the public are known to have been injured (the number is almost certainly greater), a large number of police and other vehicles were damaged or destroyed (some by fire) and 28 buildings were damaged or destroyed by fire.

The scenes in Brixton were to be repeated elsewhere during that anguished summer of 1981—in London's Southall, in Liverpool's Toxteth, in Manchester's Moss Side, in Handsworth, Wolverhampton, Smethwick and Birmingham. In the nation's living rooms, millions of Britons watched with increasing anxiety the violent confrontations taking place between black (and white) youths and police, and scenes of arson, wrecking and looting. It looked for a time as if the experience of American cities in the late Sixties was to be repeated in Britain.

Some commentators saw in it a reflection of the long running saga of violence and despair in Northern Ireland. 'The similarity was neither superficial nor coincidental,' said a report on 'Copy Cat Hooligans' by the Centre for Contemporary Studies. 'The wearing of balaclavas, and plastic bags to conceal identity, the firing of dustbins, the commandeering of milk floats, the petrol bombs, the looting—all this was a clear reflection of the picture of life in Northern Ireland as we see it on our television screens, torn from the total context of Northern Ireland, in which the majority of people abhor the violence as much as any mainlander, and carry on their day to day lives as normally as possible, and where many people work quietly behind the scenes to bring peace and reconciliation.'

But it was not to be, after all, a replay of Northern Ireland. Just as extremism does not flourish under an English heaven, the climate also appears to be wrong for prolonged rioting. Perhaps the traditional damp and drizzle of a British summer have a discouraging effect. The government's rapid decision to turn the traditional British bobby into the helmeted Martian figure familiar on the continent, and to equip the police with plastic bullets, CS gas and water cannon, may also have had something to do with it.

The police themselves suffered so many casualties in the early days of the rioting that they became more aggressive. On some occasions they advanced on the crowds drumming with their nightsticks on their riot shields in the manner of Zulu warriors.

In July 1981, a police raiding party went to Railton Road, Brixton, in the early hours of the morning and broke into fourteen houses with axes and crowbars, giving as their reason that they were looking for a petrol bomb factory.

In sixty minutes of systematic destruction, the police smashed windows, broke down doors, pulled out fireplaces, ripped up carpets, slashed chair covers, broke mirrors, overturned television sets and refrigerators, pulled doors off cupboards, and scattered belongings everywhere. No petrol bombs were found, and the only arrests were of seven men in a squat.

Railton Road is known in Brixton as 'The Front Line', a phrase which originally meant to the black community a place where people gathered to chat. But after the riots and the police raid, the term took on another context. I walked along Railton Road the morning after the July raid, and the houses were being guarded by muscular men, some of them with German Shepherd dogs on leashes. It would have been a brave policeman who would have gone to the 'Front Line' that day.

The government somewhat belatedly did what it could to dampen down the situation by sending task forces into the inner cities, and by providing infusions of considerable funds to alleviate some of the worst symptoms of urban decay.

Tougher policing methods (and the threat of worse), plus some at least token interest by the government in improving conditions for both blacks and whites in the inner cities, has gradually eased the general situation. There has been, so far, no repetition of the violence of 1981.

But there are still few signs that the police have changed their attitudes or their policies.

An extraordinary survey published in November 1983 showed that racial prejudice and racialist talk was pervasive in London's Metropolitan Police. The tone for racist jibes was often set by senior officers, and, on the whole, racism in the Met was 'expected, accepted, and even fashionable'.

I have called the survey 'extraordinary'. This is because it was commissioned by the police themselves (though by a former commissioner, Sir David McNee, and not by the present Commissioner, Sir Kenneth Newman, who was clearly unhappy about it). It was carried out by the Policy Studies Institute, an independent but highly respectable research group, with Establishment heavies on its board. One of the researchers, Stephen Small, was himself black. He worked undercover in black communities and personally experienced rough police handling and meaningless arrest.

The survey showed that young men of West Indian origin have the highest chance of being stopped and questioned by police, though in 70 per cent of cases the outcome of these contacts is negative. In lay language, this means that seven times out of ten, the police have had no reason for the stop-and-search. The figure for 'negative' confrontations in the white population was only 14 per cent.

Even among young whites, the survey found that there was a dangerous lack of confidence in the police. But among young West Indians, the situation was described as disastrous. Among blacks, 62 per cent thought that police used threats and unreasonable pressure in questioning; 53 per cent thought that excessive force was used on arrest; 56 per cent believed that there was unjustifiable violence at police stations; 43 per cent were of the opinion that police often fabricated evidence, and 41 per cent believed that police made false records of interviews.

A study of whites aged between 15 and 24 showed that only one-third thought police used threats or unreasonable pressure in questioning, and only one-fifth thought that they used excessive force on arrests and that they unjustifiably used force on people held at police stations.

The Policy Studies Institute found, however, that blacks were just as ready as whites to make use of the police in time of need, and that they reported crimes just as often. 'By and large, therefore, the views of young West Indians are not anarchic,' the report says. 'They want a police force, and in practice, they make use of its services like everybody else, while being highly criticial of it in some respects.'

Curiously enough, the team of researchers found that police moved faster and more efficiently to investigate a crime when the victim was West Indian than when he or she was white or Asian. This is probably because they are under close scrutiny these days by black community leaders and police supervisory committees of Labour councils—but it is still a sign of grace that they move faster.

The report also suggested that verbal racism in the police force does not always influence performance; rather, it is a sign that the police themselves feel they are under attack. This fits in with the frequent charges by the Right that racial unrest is being deliberately fomented in black and Asian communities in Britain by *agents provocateurs* of the far Left.

In his report on the Brixton riots, Lord Scarman said that the evidence suggested that 'a sinister contribution' to the riots was made by strangers. 'Clear and credible evidence was given to me in private session by two witnesses who reside in streets adjacent to Railton Road that they saw white men making, stacking and distributing petrol bombs,' Lord Scarman said. He added that, 'without the guidance and help of certain white people' young blacks would probably not have used petrol bombs against the police.

The Left itself has admitted its interest in racial conflict. The Young Socialists said after the Brixton Riots that they had moved into the area 'to give political direction', and a group from Militant Tendency and other Left fringe parties offered 'political aid' in Liverpool.

The far Right, of course, is also busy. In a study after the disorders of 1981, the Centre for Contemporary Studies said:

Those who are familiar with the race relations situation in Britain will realise the extent to which disadvantaged white youngsters are being manipulated by the extreme Right into blaming their unemployment and poverty on ethnic minorities and committing violence against these minorities.

The Metropolitan Police Commissioner, Sir Kenneth Newman, blames both the Left and the Right, and claims that there is an undertone of criminality. 'Activitist groups trawl for issues which provide a cloak for drug trading and movement of stolen goods,' he said in his report on crime in the metropolis for 1982. The groups sought, in their own interests, to represent practically any police intervention as harassment.

There has certainly been in the Early Eighties, more than one case of exploitation of personal tragedy for political ends. The most notorious was the Deptford fire of 1981, when thirteen black teenagers were burned to death during an all-night party in a private house.

It was a monstrous disaster, and probably not an accidental one. The forensic evidence showed from the beginning that the fire had started inside the house, a theory that later and harder evidence was to confirm. But while the bodies were still being pulled out of the house, stories began to circulate that white arsonists had been seen throwing a firebomb through the window; and distraught parents were ready to believe it, seizing at anything which would take the blame away from the people present at the party.

Professional protest groups moved in to help set up the New Cross Parents' Massacre Committee. Demonstrations were organized against what was openly labelled a deliberate racist attack on young blacks, and there were repeated clashes with the police. Lord Scarman named the Deptford fire tragedy as one cause of tension on the streets of Brixton before the riots.

Yet by the end of 1983, the chairman of the Parents' Massacre Committee George Francis (whose son died in the fire), was saying that he and other parents were now satisfied that the key to the tragedy lay inside the house and that there was no racial motive.

The *cause celebre* in the black community in 1983 was the death of Colin Roach, a 21-year-old black youth who walked into the entrance of Stoke Newington police station in North London and killed himself with a shotgun blast on January 12.

Later that year, an inquest jury returned a verdict of suicide. There was evidence that the boy was disturbed and believed himself to be under a curse. It is possible that he chose the entrance to a police station to shoot himself as a protest over police tactics against blacks, but he left no manifesto behind him.

The Roach family was desperately unhappy with the way the police treated them, and there is a long history of mistrust and resentment between police and blacks in the area. The whole thing might have been quickly forgotten by all but the relatives, however, had not an instant Colin Roach Family Support Committee materialized, with grants from the Greater London Council and Hackney Council.

Roach's parents had already had a second post-mortem carried out on their son's body by a private pathologist, only to be told that the findings supported the suicide verdict. But despite this, they were encouraged by the Support Committee to call for yet another inquiry, and to try to have the case brought before the European Parliament.

No evidence has ever been found to suggest that Stoke

Newington police were involved in Roach's death, yet repeated anti-police demonstrations were held, in which a huge blow-up photograph of the boy was carried in procession. Before the fuss died down, as it inevitably did, leaving the parents to pick up the pieces, ninety people had been arrested, and relations between the police and the black community had reached a new low.

The far Left has not such a long and consistent history as the National Front and the fascist Right in stirring up racial trouble, but it is an area into which it is increasingly moving in the Eighties.

One solution frequently offered to the problem of confrontations between the police and the non-white communities is the recruitment of more black and Asian police.

The number of Blacks and Asians which the police have been able to recruit remains pitiably small. A head count in 1982 showed that there were 160 non-white police officers in the Metropolitan force, and 226 in other forces in England and Wales. This means that only one police officer in 400 throughout the country is a member of Britain's ethnic minorities.

Some blacks and Asians are known to have some difficulties with entrance tests for the force; but the government has, probably sensibly, rejected suggestions that the standards should be lowered on the grounds that this would unofficially create first-and second-class policemen.

The main barrier, however, is the attitudes of the young blacks and Asians themselves. When Sir Kenneth Newman talked to a group of us one day at the Foreign Press Association, he said that black boys and girls were unwilling to enter the force because of peer pressure in the black community. People with whom they had grown up tended to regard any black man who became a policeman as a race traitor, an Uncle Tom.

'As for the Asians,' Newman said with an ironic smile, 'we simply aren't good enough for them.' Asian parents, usually hardworking and ambitious, had far greater plans for their children (their sons in particular) than allowing them to become police constables.

* * * * * *

Even though massive problems remain, there are some signs of progress towards the acceptance of a black and white Britain. If you still see slogans like 'Wogs go home' scrawled on walls over Britain, areas exist where blacks and whites have found some sort of *modus vivendi*. One of these areas is Notting Hill Gate, a name which was once synonymous with racial disturbances.

I have already said that black residents of Notting Hill have to endure some harassment from the police; but on the whole, it is a peaceful area of astonishing racial diversity. Arabs and Pakistanis run most of the small shops, though a Polish-owned delicatessen which stays open until nearly midnight seven days a week is mainly staffed by Vietnamese refugees and Hong Kong Chinese.

Greeks, Italians, Indians and Chinese own the restaurants; and a Japanese corner shop sells kimonos, rice bowls, chopsticks and paper lanterns.

Blacks and whites tend to live in separate areas, though a number of Irish have moved into the black ghetto, as have some whites bent on gentrification. But if the races are still rather wary of actually living next door to each other, they at least shop together, use the same doctors and hospitals, go to the same cinemas, and send their children to the same schools.

It is an area where almost any eccentricity is tolerated. The Rastafarians, who worship the Emperor Haile Selassie and wear their hair in dreadlocks mingle in the Portobello Road market on Saturday mornings with punks with green and red and silver hair and faces painted the dead white of geishas. There is a certain amount of cross-cultural exchange: dreadlocks caught on for a while among the young whites, though the finer texture of European hair cannot produce the same spectacular effect.

Notting Hill may not be an ideal community, but it is an area where familiarity, on a day-to-day basis, has bred out fear; and it shows that a multi-racial society of moderate harmony is not, as the far Right claims, an impossible ideal.

Notting Hill reaches the peak of its achievement during the Carnival, which is held on the Bank Holiday weekend at the end of August each year. The Carnival used to be, in the bad old days, a trigger for racial violence. Now it has become the annual celebration of a marriage of cultures.

It is the biggest street carnival in Europe and probably the most flamboyant. Steel bands mounted on floats parade through the streets, reggae music belts out from giant speakers on every street corner, the costumes each year grow more gaudy and gorgeous. In 1983, the theme was Roman Times; and more than a quarter of a million people, white and black, turned out to watch the parade. It was made up of Roman centurions with brave red plumes, of glittering winged birds seven feet tall, of mysterious gods and voodoo dancers—none of whom seemed to have much to do with Ancient Rome, but nobody cared.

The Rastafarians pasted up pictures of the dead Emperor, Haile Selassie, on walls along the processional route, and stalls sold goat curry and dumplings, fried fish, and all varieties of soul food. Even all black All Saint's Road, the main trouble spot in the area, was on its best behaviour, and the drug pushers took a holiday and joined the procession. Among the whites who followed the steel bands were many family groups, young couples with one or two children, and the black and the white kids danced together.

Tall policemen did their yearly duty for the photographers and embraced pretty black girls, or swapped hats with obese housewives in slippers. The cynics say that the Carnival is merely window-dressing, a camouflage for the racial divisiveness which still exists, but I am not so sure that this is true. Every year, the mingling seems more genuine, and the camaraderie less artificial, the atmosphere softer and more relaxed. The Notting Hill carnival is about what communities all over Britain will increasingly have to learn: how to live with each other.

There are other positive signs: if there are no non-white MPs in the House of Commons, blacks and Asians are now chosen as candidates; and the *Times* was able, before the elections of June 1983, to run a feature on 'The blacks most likely to get to Westminster'. In the event, none of them did, but it is a safe bet that one or more will be there after the next election, even possibly on the Tory benches.

London had its first Asian mayor in 1979, in the Borough of Hounslow. Brent and Hackney and several provincial towns followed. There are about 100 black councillors in local government, and increasing numbers of blacks are becoming shop stewards and union officials. A Sikh barrister, Mr Mota Singh, has gone up to the bench. As in other countries, blacks who find most avenues closed to them have gone into sport, and are heavily represented in professional football.

Unemployment still remains a greater problem for the ethnic communities than for whites. A survey in 1981, the year of the riots, showed that unemployment in Liverpool among young blacks was running at 50 per cent. In Brixton in the same year, it was 55 per cent for blacks under nineteen.

Two years later, the situation was worse. The Commission for Racial Equality found in July 1983 that unemployment among black teenagers in some inner-city areas had reached 60 per cent. Half the country's employers still discriminate against black job applicants, the Commission said in its annual report, and this occurs despite all the legal safeguards. Black workers also found it harder to be promoted.

Even if the long-promised upturn in the economy takes place, it will not greatly benefit the ethnic minorities, for the majority of them were originally employed in manufacturing, a sector which will never regain its old vitality.

It is noticeable that, in some ways, Asians do better than West Indians. They are entrepreneurs by nature, buying small shops and businesses where they work long hours, using family members as inexpensive labour. They are taking over the vacuum left by the English small shop-keeper, who survives in country areas but is a dying breed in the cities. A few of the traditional sweets-and-tobacco or grocery shops still exist in the inner areas, but they are an increasingly rare sight; and the ancient men and women who run them are disappearing one by one, to be replaced by exotic delis or Indian newsagents.

The Asians also have the advantage of a very disciplined family structure which binds parents, children, and kinsmen together, and which allows them to operate as a unit. Their main disadvantage is that in a society which is at least theoretically Christian, they are Moslems. This immediately sets them apart and creates social and employment difficulties.

The Moslem attitudes on women have also caused serious problems in some areas. The city of Bradford, for example, has already a non-white school population of 25 per cent, and most of these are Moslems. By 1990, because of its high proportion of young Asians, Bradford City Council forecasts that 35,000 of its 86,000 school children will be from ethnic minorities.

Bradford's Moslem parents are not happy about sending their daughters to co-educational schools, and late in 1983, they were keeping their girls at home in protest against a proposal by the City Council to merge the last two single-sex schools in the inner-city area.

The possibility of a large-scale and permanent boycott had to be balanced by the Council's educational committee against its dislike of segregating the sexes. In the end, Islam won. Separate schools for boys and girls in the 13 to 18 age-group were retained.

Moslem parents in Bradford have also succeeded in

having Halal (ritually slaughtered) meat served at school meals. (The Council then found itself under attack from animal rights campaigners who object to the cruelty of the methods used.) The Moslem parents also demanded separate shower cubicles so that their daughters did not have to strip before other girls. In 1983, the Moslem girls were taking showers with their clothes on.

The Asian community also differs from both whites and West Indians in that Moslem women often stay at home. There is no difference in any of the three groups in the number of male job seekers. But a government survey in 1982 showed that while 60 per cent of all women in Britain were in the labour force, only 40 per cent of Indian and Pakistani women worked. This compares to 80 per cent of West Indian women. Indian and Pakistani children, both boys and girls, now continue their education longer than either whites or West Indians, so it is likely that this situation will soon start to change.

The fact that such a high proportion of West Indian women work in turn creates special difficulties for the black community, and here again I quote the invaluable and often percipient Lord Scarman. In Caribbean society, he said in his report on the Brixton riots, it was the custom for women—mothers, grandmothers and aunts—to hold the family together, disciplining the children and offering security to the old and disabled:

> The role of the man was at best supportive, but seldom dominant. At worst he was an absentee of little or no significance. It is no cause for surprise that the impact of British social conditions on the matriachal extended family structure of the West Indian immigrants has proved to be severe. Mothers who in the West Indies formed the focus of the family became, in many cases, wage earners who were absent from the family home.

Black immigrants to Britain had suffered 'destructive changes' in their family lives, Scarman said; and as a consequence, there was an abnormal number of single-parent families in the black community, a higher than average proportion of children in care, and (in the Brixton area alone) hundreds of young black people were homeless, sleeping rough, or living in squats.

* * * * * *

The major political parties have all accepted, with differing degrees of resignation, the concept of a multi-racial Britain. The Conservatives are by far the most reluctant to do so, however, and a sizeable segment on the Right of the Party is in favour of stopping immigration or even of repatriating blacks and Asians already on British soil.

As an early warning signal that the days of tolerated immigration have come to an end, the Thatcher government in 1981 introduced and forced through the British Nationality Act.

This Act creates three classes of British citizenship, two of which are almost meaningless. The Act makes it clear that, in future, only people actually living in Britain as of right (by birth or by naturalization) are the genuine article. Automatic citizenship will no longer be conferred on children born in Britain, however, if their parents are not citizens.

The other two categories are 'citizenship of British dependent territories' and 'British overseas citizenship', both of which offer the nominal protection of the British government, but not the right to enter and live in Britain.

The main purpose of the Act is unstated but obvious. The government wants to safeguard against any further incidents such as the big intake of Asians in 1972, when Idi Amin threw businessmen and shopkeepers out of Uganda.

It is also looking ahead to 1997, when the People's Republic of China is almost certain to repossess the territory of Hong Kong. Five million Chinese in Hong Kong are already worrying about their future, and any time from now on, trickles of immigration could start which would eventually become a flood. Britain, under the Thatcher government, has already erected its own high barriers against this possible Asian influx.

In its 1983 election manifesto, the Thatcher government pledged itself to continue what it described as 'policies which are strict but fair'. It also pointed out that from the time that Mrs Thatcher had come to office in 1979, immigration had dropped to its lowest level ever since a system of controls began twenty years before. In 1981, there was a drop of almost 20 per cent on the 1978 figure, and there was a further decrease of 8.5 per cent in 1982.

It was obvious from the beginning that the Tories under Thatcher were determined to take a tough stand on immigration, but it is equally obvious that neither the Labour Party nor the SDP-Liberal Alliance are enthusiastic about a further influx of migrants from the New Commonwealth.

Labour opposes the British Nationality Act. It calls the Act 'racist' and promises to replace it with a more liberal version when it returns to power. The Labour Party says that as it is clear that large-scale immigration to Britain is ending, it would honour any existing major commitments towards would-be immigrants.

The Alliance also opposes the Nationality Act, which it says is offensive and discriminatory. It would like to see the passing of a Bill of Rights for immigrants, to be administered by a United Kingdom Commission on Human Rights.

Both Labour and the Alliance have shown more interest than the Conservatives in improving race relations, a concept to which the Tories pay only lip service. The new Leader of the Labour Party, Neil Kinnock, has committed Labour to what he calls an 'offensive against racial inequality'. He has advocated ethnic monitoring as a way of eliminating discrimination against non-whites in the work force, backed up by economic sanctions against firms who refuse to cooperate.

Kinnock did not actually spell this out, but it has since been suggested that a future Labour Government could withhold government contracts from firms found guilty of discrimination, with devastating effect.

* * * * * *

In the early Eighties there were still heard, however, the voices of those echoing Enoch Powell's notorious 'rivers of blood' speech of decades before. At the Conservative Party conference of 1983, a motion for the repatriation of blacks from Britain was actually debated. The Prime Minister prudently stayed away from the session on immigration, and the party leadership breathed a sigh of relief when the motion was defeated on a show of hands. Party conferences tend to be a great deal further to the Right than the Parliamentary Party, and a close vote would have been embarrassing.

The television reporting of the debate was embarrassing enough anyway, with some of the most unruly scenes for years, and the voice of unabashed racism speaking loudly from the conference floor.

The rejection by the conference did not stop the Tory right-wing Monday Club from circulating a 'fact card' on Britain's non-white population, which included statistics on the proportion of crimes committed by blacks and Asians. Launching it, the Tory MP for Billericay, Harvey Proctor—one of the main anti-immigration voices on the Right—advocated stopping wives and children of immigrant men settled in Britain from joining their husbands, and introducing a system of cash incentives for migrants who want to leave Britain.

In the background, however, ideas are stirring which are much more interesting than the grandstanding at Party conferences. Some voices on the Right are speaking with a more persuasive subtle tone than those who scream 'Go home!' at public meetings or even than Enoch Powell himself in his prophetic days.

A glimpse into this sort of far-Right thinking came in a talk given by the Conservative Philosophy Group in 1982, and later reprinted in the *Salisbury Review*, which describes itself as a magazine of Conservative thought. The speaker was John Casey, a Fellow and Tutor of Gonville and Caius College, Cambridge, and a university lecturer in English.

Casey puts forward a view which, stripped of its erudite decorations, is basically one of the inbuilt inferiority of blacks to whites. Among West Indians, he says ('and above all those actually born in this country'), there is a structural inability to fit into English civilization. This is demonstrated, particularly among Jamaicans, in an extraordinary resentment towards all forms of authority—including police, teachers, and Underground guards. The black community, Casey says, has also a different family structure, educational standards lower than any other group, and a record of involvement in a disproportionate amount of violent crime.

'I believe that the great majority of people are actually or potentially hostile to the multi-racial society which all decent people are supposed to accept,' Casey told his audience. However, he said, this majority had been intimidated by the media into accepting that their attitudes ('absolutely normal thirty years ago') were disreputable. So they came to believe that nothing could be done to prevent the evolution of such a society.

Casey then went coolly on to examine what he thought *could* be done.

One idea, originally put forward by the right-wing columnist Peregrine Worsthorne in the *Sunday Telegraph*, was of the breaking up of large concentrations of immigrants, so that British cities would not become too 'foreign'.

This is desirable, Casey said, but difficult to enforce. It entails direction of labour, and a system of internal passports (South African style!) to make sure that black workers do not return illictly to their original homes. Even for the far Right, this seemed to be going too far.

Voluntary, assisted repatriation? Yes, said Casey, a possibility, and probably the most humane method of keeping down the numbers. There was nothing wrong in principle with repatriation, he said, instancing the return of *colons* from Algeria to metropolitan France, the exodus of Portuguese from Africa, and of white Rhodesians from Zimbabwe. However, the drawbacks were that such a policy would cost thousands of millions of pounds and would offend 'liberals' (not a word of commendation in Casey's vocabulary).

His own preferred solution, he said, would be one now considered unthinkable in polite society: gradually to alter the status of black people in Britain so that they became guest workers, like the Turks in West Germany. Eventually they would return to their country of origin, with property, a pension, and possibly some compensation from public funds.

Casey overlooks the fact that such a scheme might also imply coercion, and he paints a sunny picture.

> They would be like the *perioeci* in ancient Greece; or perhaps like Plato's poets—crowned with olives, annointed with oil, provided with a capital sum, and sent away from the city. After such a measure had been enacted, it would still be possible for Britain to decide upon a proportion of the immigrant community to consider for naturalisation—being guided by numbers, special skills and requirements—much in the same way that, say, Australia, selects its potential immigrants.

Some West Indian community leaders are encouraging the ambition of the far Right to start a scheme of assisted repatriation. One told a meeting of the Monday Club in October 1983 that about a quarter of a million of Britain's West Indians would leave if funds were available. This claim is obviously unrealistic, but it is true that the number going back to the West Indies is growing slowly year by year. This is probably because the recession in Britain is destroying any idea that it is a land of opportunity. A sharp economic upturn, however, would quickly stop the exodus, which was estimated at about 18,000 people in 1983.

* * * * * *

Despite John Casey and the others who think like him, it seems to an outside observer that a majority of people in Britain have accepted the idea that they live in a multi-racial society, even though they may not like it.

A few optimists like Lord Scarman believe that the riots of 1981 performed a useful function in bringing matters to a head, and forcing the nation to look deep into the hearts of its own inner cities. At a Commonwealth Law Conference in Hong Kong in 1983, Scarman said that the riots had been 'a superb and healthy catalyst for the British people'. He went on: 'We are cleaner. We are healthier, and we are much wiser.'

CHAPTER FOURTEEN

THE POLITICS OF CLASS

Anthony Crosland, who died in office in 1977 as Labour Foreign Secretary, is often mourned on the Left as one of the great gurus of modern socialism. In the mid-Sixties, he was Education Secretary. Introducing the idea of comprehensive schools, he said:

> All schools will more and more be socially mixed; all will provide routes to the universities, and to every type of occupation from the highest to the lowest. Then, very slowly, Britain may cease to be the most class-ridden country in the world.

Has the process of breaking down the class system really started, nearly twenty years on, with 90 per cent of children in the state educational system attending comprehensives, and only a handful of old-style grammar schools left?

The answer is probably yes, though not all in the way which Crosland meant. The old secure heights of privilege remain unstormed, the public schools and Oxbridge keep their dominant role, but several important themes have emerged.

One is the *embourgeoisement* of the traditional working

291

class, sizeable numbers of whom have turned into house owners, car drivers, and Conservative voters. Another is the emergence of a new kind of labour market aristocracy (it could almost be called a new priestly class): those who speak in the language of high tech. In another ten or twenty years, computer literacy may be an indispensable requirement for upward mobility.

But on the actual question of social class, it is useful to look backwards as well as forwards, and I want to turn to George Orwell, as I have several times before in this book. (In 1984, the temptation is irresistible, for there are few better guides than Orwell to some aspects of England Past.) Orwell was obsessed by class in the same way that other writers are obsessed by sex. His feelings about the working class seem to have produced in him a guilt of almost a sexual nature, probably because so many of his reactions were physical rather than mental. It is very likely that this guilt, as much as ideological conviction, was his main reason for becoming a socialist.

He claims, however, that his feelings on class were common among middle-class people (he called himself 'lower upper middle class', though this seems a bit uppish for the son of a minor colonial civil servant) before World War I. He was conscious of them from the age of six onwards, when he was told to stop playing with the plumber's children. He later saw this as a common defence mechanism by middle-class parents to stop their children acquiring 'vulgar' accents, but it had dangerous results.

In *The Road to Wigan Pier*, Orwell wrote:

> So, very early, the working class ceased to be a race of wonderful and friendly beings, and became a race of enemies. We realised that they hated us, but we could never understand why, and naturally we set it down to pure, vicious malignity. To me, in my early boyhood, to nearly all children of families like mine, 'common' people seemed almost sub-human. They had coarse faces, hideous accents, and gross manners, they hated everyone who was not like themselves, and if they got

half a chance, they would insult you in brutal ways. That was our view of them, and though it was false, it was understandable. For one must remember that before the war, there was much more *overt* class hatred in England than there is now.

Orwell insists that there was a physical reason for this: the middle classes were taught from childhood that the lower classes smelled. He quotes, in support of his theory, Somerset Maugham writing in *On A Chinese Screen*: 'I do not blame the working man because he stinks,' Maugham said, 'but stink he does. It makes social intercourse difficult to persons of sensitive nostril.'

Orwell cannot leave the subject alone. He talks of seeing in childhood 'a great sweaty navvy' in layers of greasy clothes, with, underneath them, an unwashed body, brown all over (so imagined the young Eric Blair, not yet then George Orwell), 'with its strong, bacon-like reek'.

Even servants, though known to be clean, were unappetizing, their skin texture and sweat different from the middle classes. Blair/Orwell describes in *The Road to Wigan Pier* how, when he was in Burma in his early twenties, he was attached for a short time to a British regiment:

In the hot mornings, when the company marched down the road, myself in the rear with one of the junior subalterns, the steam of those hundred sweating bodies in front made my stomach turn. And this, you observe, was pure prejudice. For a soldier is probably as inoffensive, physically, as it is possible for a male white person to be. He is generally young, he is nearly always healthy from fresh air and exercise, and a rigorous discipline compels him to be clean. But I could not see it like that. All I knew was that it was *lower class* sweat that I was smelling, and the thought of it made me sick.

In 1984, it is inconceivable that any author would write like that, or that his publisher would print it if he did. Probably the nearest you would get today would be some of the racist 'hate' literature I have received in the streets in

Britain, which tends to dwell on physical characteristics, smell, and a tendency to spread disease as reasons for disliking minority groups.

The class war, in the way that Orwell and other socialists saw it, is largely over. This is proved by the constant failure of the Left to drag the working class to the barricades at election time. Even as passionate a leader as the president of the National Union of Mineworkers, Arthur Scargill, cannot manage it. Miners, who in Orwell's day had existences which were nasty, brutish and short, have moved up to second place among the nation's top 20 wage earners, and more and more of them own their semi-detached houses instead of living in squalid back-to-backs.

In the election of June 1983, two of the dozen British constituencies with the highest concentration of mineworkers returned Tories. In another two the Labour candidate had a narrow victory; in six the Labour vote was under 50 per cent; and in none of the twelve was the Labour vote over 60 per cent. (All this doesn't necessarily make them socially acceptable. Miners in Yorkshire, earning £15,000 a year, were blackballed in 1983 when they tried to join a local country club, even though they could easily afford the £250 a year membership fees. 'We are not encouraging miners to come here,' said one of the directors. 'We do not want ferret racing and pigeon clubs—and that's the sort of thing they do.')

It is true, however, that a solid working-class ethos still remains. George Orwell, when he was not being disgusted by the lower orders, tended to wonder whether their home life was not more 'sane and comely' than that of their betters. He did not think that it was really possible to be intimate with the working class; but, in his more optimistic moments, he admired the 'perfect symmetry of a working class interior at its best'. In *The Road to Wigan Pier*, he said:

Especially on winter evenings after tea, when the fire glows in the open range and dances mirrored in the steel fender, when Father in shirt sleeves sits in the rocking chair at one side of the fire reading the racing finals, and Mother sits on the other with her sewing, and the children are happy with a pennorth of mint humbugs, and the dog lolls roasting himself on the rag mat it is a good place to be in, provided that you can be not only in it but sufficiently of it to be taken for granted.

Seen from the viewpoint of 1984, Orwell's working-class interior looks mawkish, patronizing and unreal; but even fifty years on, the idea of the *cosiness* of working-class life still has its attractions. Apart from 'The Archers', a story of a farming family which has been going for so long on radio that its origins are shrouded in antiquity, the most popular and longest-running serial in Britain is television's 'Coronation Street', which has kept millions compulsively switching on their sets for more than two decades.

Coronation Street has been sold all over the world; it is even seen with Chinese sub-titles in Hong Kong. The Poet Laureate, Sir John Betjeman, has publicly acclaimed it. It is set in a working-class community in Lancashire, and stays largely within that community. In 1983, a television critic pointed out that only the Street is 'safe'; when its inhabitants leave the enclave, they tend to become subject to disasters like coach accidents or abduction.

In the Seventies, a producer who thought the series should be more socially relevant started opening up the Street to the world outside, and introducing 'significant' political and social themes. It slumped disastrously in the ratings, and any attempt at social relevance was thereafter abandoned.

In the Eighties, Coronation Street remains month after month, year after year, at the top of the popularity listings. It is the program which more Britons watch than any other, while all the more trendy sitcoms about working-class life drop one after the other out of public view. It offers viewers a sense of security, a reassurance that familiar, neighbourhood values still exist in a world which is changing with bewildering speed. It is stable and old-fashioned, the antithesis of the world of Monty Python, which the Eighties sometimes seem to resemble.

Class differences are one of the main staples of the British entertainment industry. A most classic example is 'Dad's Army', now, alas, defunct, like its two principal characters. Its cleverest ploy was the persistent class skirmishing between Captain Mainwaring, played by Arthur Lowe, and his sergeant, the greatly treasured actor John le Mesurier, who died at the end of 1983.

Mainwaring, as well as being a captain was a bank manager; and Sgt Wilson, his clerk, called him 'Sir' in both capacities with delicate mockery. For Captain Mainwaring knew, his platoon knew, and all the millions of viewers in Britain knew that although he might be an officer he was not a gentleman. He was ineradicably lower middle class, while his clerk and sergeant was a public-school man, and therefore forever his social superior, however fallen on hard times.

The class war may be over but class nuances remain. They are of absorbing interest to everybody, from sociologists to foreign observers of British life and manners.

It can also be argued that class still plays a more important role than first appears, and that one end result of centuries of rigid social stratification is precisely the 'British disease' of the Eighties: the lack of initiative, the stifling of the creative genius of the race, and the suicidal demarcation practices of the trade unions. When I was making a survey in 1983 of Japanese firms in Britain, I found it fascinating that, though at Japanese insistence such demarcation practices had been got rid of by bringing all employees into a single union, yet the workforce had accepted with alacrity the equally rigid and ritualistic practices imported from Japan, such as morning assembly and the wearing of uniforms. It is as though the British have a *need* to be compartmentalized and identified by groups.

One of the main exponents of the view that class has,

even in the Eighties, a strangulating effect in Britain is Dr James Bellini, formerly Head of Political Studies at the Hudson Institute's Paris headquarters, and more recently an author and presenter of economics programs on television.

Bellini says that there has been no real revolution in Britain, and that this has resulted in the ossification of class structures. This is a view which I have heard from other economists, who have also seen the lack of a violent revolutionary upheaval as a bad thing for Britain.

In his book *Rule Britannia: a Progress Report for Domesday 1986*, Bellini argues that a feudal system still exists in Britain, and that it is upheld by an informal apartheid based on social rank rather than on race. While Asia, the United States and Western Europe will form a high tech constellation in the not-too-distant future, according to Bellini Britain will remain feudal, splitting into two nations.

The rich man will still be in his castle, even if wealth now will come from information and technology rather than land. The poor man will not be at the gate but well outside it.

> There will be a small, closed world, where knowledge is God, and the altars are tended by a monastic order of information brokers. And there will be a vast backwater economy around it, where unemployment, menial work, crafts, moonlighting, barter and brigandry are the standard features of everyday life.

Curiously enough, this theme is echoed in one of Peregrine Worsthorne's essays in the *Sunday Telegraph*, though the two authors could not be more dissimilar. Bellini is racing onwards to the high tech, computerized world of the twenty-first century, while Worsthorne is looking nostalgically back to the past.

Worsthorne is a little like Enoch Powell. Both of them can be counted on to put forward a point of view so outrageously conservative that it appears to become wildly radical. I have already quoted Worsthorne as lamenting the demise of the 'knights of the shires' as a political force, and regretting even more the emergence of the Thatcherite Tories, the 'thrusting, ambitious, tough-minded and short-sighted' New Men, whose view of the world is that from the windows of suburbia.

Worsthorne later returned to the subject from a different angle, when he put forward a case for the resurgence of feudalism.

The lower classes (his term) are growing so vulnerable and pitiable in Britain today, he says, that nothing can save them but the old feudal remedy: the protection and patronage of those in high places.

> So we are back to square one; to a society where the best, indeed the only hope for the weak lies in the generosity of the strong, in the existence among the strong of a tradition of *noblesse oblige*. No wonder, therefore, the aristocratic principle is once again returning into fashion, not so much in response to the demands of the strong as to the needs of the weak.

Worsthorne clearly does not expect too much in the way of patronage and compassion from the New Tories—the meritocratic politicians who, having got to the top by their own efforts, think that everyone else can do the same. (Though he does not cite her, Thatcher is the most outstanding example.) On the contrary, Worsthorne says, Britain should be turning its mind to 'cherishing and strengthening all those aspects of the old order which helped to make the English gentleman such a model for the world'. He is deeply regretful that William Whitelaw, made a viscount by Thatcher, has no heirs and so will be the first and last of his line.

> If only there were a second Lord Whitelaw waiting to succeed, and many generations of further Viscounts, as yet unborn,

stretching the line long into the future! For who can doubt that hereditary privilege is a very small price to pay to preserve so valuable a species, than which none will have a more beneficient rule to lay in the grim years that lie ahead.

There is some sort of odd logic in what Worsthorne says. The present economic situation, and the likelihood of many dark days to come, do look like producing an increasing need for paternalism. It is more likely, though, to come from the State than from some new breed of feudal lords, or from the twentieth-century equivalent of the mediaeval monasteries.

In the Eighties the working class is splitting itself into two rather in the manner of an amoeba. The larger section is moving up into the lower middle class, with aspirations towards home ownership and holidays on the Costa Brava. The smaller section—the unemployed, the chronically under-privileged, and parts of the immigrant population—is sinking further down.

We have seen in an earlier chapter that Paul Johnson doubted the theory of the *embourgeoisement* of the working class, suggesting that instead the middle class was picking up nasty lower-class habits. But it is happening just the same. The sociologists are busy inventing new terms for this upwardly mobile group, such as the 'midway' class, or the 'first-generation lower middle class'.

The way up the ladder is now rather different from what it was when (say) Margaret Thatcher was a schoolgirl. At that time, clever children started their climb by winning scholarships to grammar school, then to university. Nowadays the upward movement is much broader, and is largely based on earning capacity.

Some political analysts believe that the working class, in the sense that the term was once understood, has now abolished itself. The 'working man' is no longer part of a class struggle, but is an individual interested mainly in improving his own economic and social standing.

According to the findings of the 1971 census, 36.5 per cent of the British people were defined as middle class. In the early Eighties, the figure is 48.7 per cent. By the Nineties, non-manual workers will be in the majority in Britain.

Analysis of the results after the last general election seemed to show that house ownership is the key to movement from one class to another, and that this strikingly coincides with a change in voting patterns. (This is the main reason, of course, why the Tories are so anxious to sell council houses to tenants.)

A MORI poll taken after the election showed that among working-class home owners, 47 per cent had voted Conservative and 26 per cent Labour. Of working-class council tenants, 49 per cent had voted Labour and 24 per cent Tory. About 25 per cent of each group voted for the Alliance. Suburbia rules, OK?

Labour has been criticized from both inside and outside the Party for ignoring these changes in class structure, and certainly its failure to take them into account was a factor in its defeat at the last election.

Labour's critics say that the Party is still kneeling before a fallen idol, or chasing a phantom which no longer exists. The new Labour Leader Neil Kinnock, though himself by instinct an old-fashioned romantic socialist, has tacitly acknowledged that a major Party target in the next four years must be the first-generation middle-class voter.

Analyzing the election disaster late in 1983, he said that one reason why it had occurred was that Labour had over-concentrated on appealing to the poor, to the unemployed and to the minorities:

> The harsh electoral reality dictates that if we are to be of real use to the deprived and insecure we must have the support of those in more secure social circumstances—the home owner as well as the homeless, the stable family as well as the single parent, the confidently employed as well as the unemployed, the majority as well as the minorities.

The hard Left, still clinging to ideas of class war and to the belief that revolution is better than evolution, is not happy about this change in thinking at the top. Even the soft Left is concerned, particularly about the selfishness and lack of sympathy for those left behind which, it claims, accompanies upward social movement. According to this view, once class solidarity is lost, all is lost.

It is true that a survey commissioned by London Weekend Television in 1983 for a series called 'Breadline Britain' showed that the gap between the 'midway' and the working class was rapidly rising as the economic recession dragged on.

The 'midway' class has suffered a great deal less than the working class during the recession. An analysis of the 'Breadline Britain' survey showed that only 22 per cent of working-class home owners felt that unemployment was a problem for their family, affecting one or more members. The figure for council-house tenants was twice that, 44 per cent. At the time the survey was taken, 33 per cent of council tenants had had to borrow money from friends or relatives for day-to-day needs in the last year, while only 10 per cent of the 'midway' class had to borrow. A quarter of all council-house tenants declared that they felt they were poor on a permanent basis, while only six per cent of the 'midway' class complained of 'poverty'.

However, the 'midway' class was far ahead of either the middle class or the working class in suffering fears about possible unemployment, or about the job prospects of their children. I found the same phenomenon when I talked to a selection of people who were migrating to Australia. Most were in the skilled-worker category, and all had secure and relatively well-paid jobs. Nearly all were house owners. But all of them gave feelings of insecurity as a reason for leaving Britain.

Curiously enough, with all this discussion of the infusion of new working-class blood into the lower middle class, there is not very much heard of (the heartfelt cry of a few years ago) by the established middle class that they were on the verge of being wiped out by high taxation and inflation. Middle-class families in Britain today, provided they have not (and many have) been hit by unemployment, are doing quite nicely. Taxes are higher than ever, but inflation is below the level of salary increases; and the middle class make judicious use of the health and education facilities of the welfare state for their basic needs, 'going private' if they want something special.

A sub-class of the middle class is, however, not doing so well: the people on fixed (often Service) pensions. Where else but in Britain would you still find a charity called 'The Distressed Gentlefolks' Aid Association', which is under the patronage of the Queen Mother? 'Could this be *you* in a few years' time—remembering the joint you used to buy?' asks an advertisement, featuring a photograph of a handsome silver-haired couple ('The times when they used to entertain family and friends—now just a fading memory of happier days') looking wistfully at joints of meat hanging in a butcher's shop window. One suspects that the 'Distressed Gentlefolks' Aid Association' is not attracting too much support in the present economic climate. Distress is a common commodity in Britain in the Eighties, and it is not confined to gentlefolk.

Matching the phenomenon of the upward-moving 'midway' class is the creation of a sub-stratum of the working class which now or in the future may come to be called the non-working class.

The bright hopes of the early Fabians that universal education would prove the cure to everything considerably pre-dated Tony Crosland's prediction about the comprehensive schools. Both have proved to be over-optimistic.

In 1983, a survey was made by the Adult Literacy and Basic Skills Unit which showed that two million adults in Britain were functionally illiterate. This means that they had difficulties with reading and writing to an extent that their daily lives were affected. Their numeracy skills were also poor. Yet only one in ten men and one in twenty women interviewed had tried to improve their reading by going to classes. Only one in ten men and one in forty women had sought help with number problems.

Functional illiteracy creates unemployment, for people with below average reading and numeracy skills have less chance than others of applying for, getting and holding jobs. If, by the end of the decade, computer literacy is a necessity for many jobs, it is also obvious that a new pool of near-unemployables is being created.

'We are seeing the creation of a workless class which is growing up illiterate and innumerate,' said Clive Jenkins, the chairman of the TUC education committee, during a trade-union debate on education in 1983.

In the past, the illiterate and innumerate could at least be absorbed in unskilled jobs. With mechanization taking these over and with robots promising to wipe out yet another section of the working class, the semi-skilled—a large group of chronically poor—class becomes inevitable. The 1983 study entitled 'Parents and Children' by Professor A. B. Atkinson of the London School of Economics and Mr A. K. Maynard of the University of York showed that poverty is inherited in much the same way as physical height, and that a child of poor parents has only a 50 per cent chance of escaping from the poverty cycle in normal times. In times which are abnormal, the chances must naturally decrease.

The gap between the hopes of the educational reformers and reality can be easily illustrated. In 1981, 71 per cent of undergraduates in British universities came from middle- and upper-class homes. One in three undergraduates come from public schools, though they educate only one in seventeen of British school children. In the first (autumn) term of 1983, 47 per cent of the intake at Oxford came from independent schools.

In the Eighties, Britain is far from being Disraeli's 'one nation'. It is split and fragmented between the employed and the unemployed, between black and white, between the crumbling inner cities and the affluent suburbs, between workers and management—and not least, between North and South.

The North-South divide can be illustrated by unemployment percentages, taken from a table for August 1983. In the prosperous South-East, 9.3 per cent of the population was on the dole, and in the South-West 10.6 per cent. But the formerly prosperous West Midlands had 15.3 per cent unemployment; the North-West 15.4 per cent; and the North overall 16.6 per cent. The unemployment rate in Wales was 15.3 per cent; and in Scotland 14.7 per cent.

In major cities, the figures were in some cases even higher. Liverpool had 19 per cent of its workforce out of jobs in 1983; Glasgow 16.5 per cent; Birmingham 16.7 per cent and Manchester 13.5 per cent. These cities are in the industrial heartlands, where manufacturing industry has been hardest hit.

The economic discrepancies between North and South are already having some tangible effects. A survey carried out in 1983 by the Central Statistical Office on regional trends showed:

- Earnings in the south were higher than elsewhere. In London and the Home Counties, after-tax per capita income was £3,741 in 1981, compared with the national average of £3,100. In the West Midlands, the figure was £2,815.
- More new mortgages were granted in the South-East than anywhere else in Britain. The highest home ownership in Britain (65 per cent) is in the South-West. The lowest is in Scotland (37 per cent).
- The best schools are in the South-East, and the area has the highest proportion of boys and girls leaving school with at least one A-level. The North had the poorest record of educational achievement.

The North-South differences are also reflected in voting patterns. After the June 1983 elections, Labour had no seats south of a line from London to Bristol, and only 30 out of 260 in a line drawn from the Severn to the Wash. Yet in 1945 more than a third of Labour's seats were in the south. In less than ten years, between 1974 and 1983, Labour has lost 62 per cent of its seats in southern England, compared with a loss of 25 per cent elsewhere. It is in danger of becoming a Party of the poor, of the dispossessed, of the powerless and of the North—while the South, where the power lies, remains stolidly Tory.

CHAPTER FIFTEEN

GENTLEMEN AND TRAITORS

Class permeates every aspect of British life. In its own mysterious way, the class factor is even at work in the looking-glass world of espionage. No country other than Britain has produced such a talented collection of gentlemen spies.

This may very well be linked to another obsessive British characteristic: the passion for secrecy and for camouflage. Voluble and extroverted foreigners coming to Britain are baffled by the impenetrable surface which British society presents to them. It takes a long time to understand that beneath that cool, detached, and often deliberately distancing exterior, strong and often curious passions are stirring.

The Americans do not make good spies. They have an overpowering need to explain their motivations and to confess their misdeeds to the world. Any journalist who has worked in Washington knows how damagingly frank the State Department desk officers can be, compared to the chill and ironic mandarins of the Foreign Office.

The Americans openly locate the Central Intelligence Agency, the headquarters of their spying operation, in Langley, Virginia, and list it in the phone book. A foreign correspondent may ring up and ask to speak to a press officer, though whether he or she will get an answer to a query is another matter.

The British pretend that the domestic and foreign intelligence services, MI5 and MI6, do not exist, by disguising the location of their headquarters and attempting, though not usually successfully, to hide the identity of the Secret Intelligence Service chiefs. Instead of operating from a large modern centre crammed with the latest in technology, like Langley, the two services seem to prefer shabby buildings in London, suburban 'safe houses' or country estates. It all fits in with the slightly amateurish, upper-class image.

Even the operations centre, which carries out high-level high tech communications surveillance as part of a global link-up, hides behind the non-commital name of Government Communications Headquarters. And it is located, ironically enough, at the spa town of Cheltenham—an elegant and well-kept relic of the days when society came there to take the waters, which is still full of retired army officers and their ladies, who fill in their empty years writing letters to the *Daily Telegraph*.

Centres like GCHQ are removing the human factor from spying as, in the jargon of the trade, SIGINT (signals intelligence) takes over more and more from HUMINT (field agents).

But from the Fifties onwards, the British intelligence establishment has been battered by a series of scandals in which the human factor has played a major role. They have ranged from indiscretions in high places to outright treachery. Even a small selection shows why Britain has gained a special notoriety in the world intelligence community.

A government minister, John Profumo, was found in the Fifties to be sharing a mistress (and a high-class prostitute at that) with a Soviet diplomat.

Two Foreign Office high-flyers, Guy Burgess and Donald

Maclean, defected to the Soviet Union, for which they had worked for years as agents.

The 'Third Man', Kim Philby, was discovered to have been working for British intelligence and the KGB simultaneously.

Sir Anthony Blunt, eminent art historian and art adviser to the Queen, was revealed to be a former Soviet agent.

The Labour peer Lord Bradfield, better known as Tom Driberg, is alleged to have worked for the Czechs or for the Russians or for both as well as for MI5, though the British intelligence services knew what he was doing. (Driberg was a well-known and cheerfully unabashed homosexual, and his elevation to a life peerage has always been something of a mystery.)

In the Eighties, Britain's former ambassador to Moscow, Sir Geoffrey Harrison, confessed to sleeping with a Soviet chambermaid who was probably a KGB operative.

A former British High Commissioner to Canada, Sir Peter Hayman, was shown to be a member of a paedophile group, and to have sexual preoccupations which would have made him subject to blackmail.

The British spymaster, Sir Roger Hollis, head of MI5 from 1956 to 1965, has come in recent years under suspicion of being a long-time KGB agent. The accusation was made by Britain's veteran spywatcher, the journalist Chapman Pincher, and it is based on in-house investigations of Hollis' career, both before and after his death in 1973. The allegations have neither been proved or disproved, and remain a subject for perennial argument.

The British public finds all these scandals in high places irresistible. They are far more glamorous than the occasional cases which surface of hard-up young clerks or Army corporals selling secrets for money.

During the early Eighties, one of the most successful and long-running plays in the West End was Julian Mitchell's 'Another Country', which, though it used other names, did not attempt to disguise the fact it was a fictional account of the public-school days of Guy Burgess, and an attempt to explain the reasons why Burgess became a traitor. (Mitchell suggests that Burgess even in his late teens realized that, while the other boys who experimented with homosexuality at their public schools would turn in adulthood into respectable husbands and fathers, he would always be an outsider. This made it easy to seduce him into the trade of treachery.)

Even the millions in the provinces who never go to the theatre in London became instant experts in espionage through the television versions of John le Carre's 'Tinker, Tailor, Soldier, Spy,' and its sequel, 'Smiley's People'. These series were compulsive viewing for the nation, and terms like 'safe house' and 'postman' and 'vicar' passed into everyday language.

Le Carre has always exploited the class element in his espionage novels, and television turned the class aspect to rich use, with a background of clubland and country houses contrasting sharply with the seedy world of the field agents. The original George Smiley (before television metamorphosed him into Alec Guiness), was short, fat and unimpressive, but still unmistakeably with the right sort of background; and his wife, the elusive Lady Ann Smiley, was a peer's daughter.

Even though two of the protagonists are dead, the Burgess-Maclean-Philby affair still remains a valuable lode to be mined. At the end of 1983, it yielded up an odd little gem, the film 'An Englishman Abroad', based on a real-life encounter in Moscow a quarter of a century ago between Guy Burgess and the Australian actress Coral Browne.

Miss Browne met Burgess willy-nilly when he burst into her dressing room (she was in the Soviet Union with a touring company) and, being drunk as usual, threw up in the washbasin. Surprisingly undeterred by this, Browne accepted an invitation to luncheon with Burgess at his flat, only to find that he had an ulterior motive. The spy who had gone out into the cold could not bear to wear Moscow tailoring, and wanted to be measured up for some Saville Row suits. 'What did I do in Moscow?' Coral Browne was to say later. 'I measured Guy Burgess' inside trouser leg.'

Another visitor to Moscow found Burgess living in a well-kept flat full of his own furniture. This had been shipped out to him by the Foreign Office, presumably at taxpayers' expense. 'They've been awfully decent about some things' Burgess said, adding cheerfully that another advantage of Moscow was that there was no servant problem.

Even after death, the spies continued to haunt the British imagination. When Donald Maclean died in Moscow, his ashes were sent back to Britain and buried after dark, by lantern light, in the family plot, with the local vicar presiding—though not, one supposes, with much enthusiasm.

Anthony Blunt, stripped of his knighthood, followed the other two, but with more dignity. He died quietly in his London flat over breakfast in 1983. A religious service preceded his cremation, and flowers covered his coffin. His brother Wilfred, as respected a writer in Britain as Anthony Blunt had been as an art historian, was at the funeral. He, as well as many of Blunt's friends, had remained close to him, and was highly defensive of his reputation.

'When this scandal is finally pushed into a small corner of history, and there are other scandals to take its place, my brother will be remembered as a great art historian,' Wilfred Blunt said. 'His name will live on.' This was too much for the Fleet Street columnist Geoffrey Levy, who wrote angrily:

> There was a time when a traitor's head would be impaled on Traitor's Gate, and the populace would jeer and cavort in front of it. [But] the traitor Anthony Blunt was despatched from this England with the reverence and dignity befitting a saint.

Blunt's case was probably the most interesting of the group

of spies who were recruited at Cambridge in the Thirties. He himself became in his turn a recruiter, and how many 'moles' remained burrowing away even after Blunt was no longer active is a question which continues to obsess the spywatchers.

Blunt is said to have told his interrogators that he ceased to work as an agent after 1945, but the indefatigable Chapman Pincher claims that he was a much more durable and dangerous operator than he ever admitted. Chapman, who has good contacts within the intelligence community, says that Blunt carried out, after 1945, at least such routine work as finding safe houses, organizing 'letter boxes', and picking up money for more active agents.

In 1945, Blunt became surveyor of the Queen's Pictures; and in 1964 when, after years of suspicion and fruitless interrogations, he at last cracked, he was granted unconditional immunity from prosecution and left in place in the Royal Household.

This generosity must have astonished Blunt as much as it was later to stagger the nation. He continued to lecture and to write as well as to carry out his Royal tasks, and at the same time he worked with MI5 filling in at least some of the pieces of the jigsaw (only he knows how many were left out) of espionage operations in Britain since the Thirties. The Prime Minister of the day, Sir Alex Douglas-Home (later Lord Home), was not consulted, nor even told, of Blunt's confession. This is believed to have been because Home would have sacrificed pragmatism to propriety, and refused to allow a traitor to work in the Queen's household.

Some Prime Ministers, in any case, dislike having spies thrust under their noses, as illustrated by the famous remark of Harold Macmillan, when he was told of the arrest of the spy William Vassall. 'Oh, that's very bad news,' he said, 'very bad news. You know, you should never catch a spy. Discover him and then control him, but never catch him. A spy causes far more trouble when he is caught.'

It is believed Prime Minister Harold Wilson was not told about Blunt until 1967, when, presumably, it seemed sensible to leave well alone.

Even more interesting is the Queen's attitude. In his book *Their Trade is Treachery*, Chapman Pincher says that he knows beyond doubt that she was told by her private secretary, Sir Michael Adeane, that her Surveyor of Pictures was a confessed Soviet agent. She agreed, however, that he should be kept on in the national interest.

'Presumably the Queen experienced some distaste, but she rarely had occasion to meet Blunt,' Pincher says. 'This was perhaps just as well, considering that the regime to which he had been dedicated had murdered her relatives [the Russian Royal Family] and detested monarchs on principle.'

The Queen, who has a knack of distancing herself from the more squalid side of everyday life, seems to have done it successfully all through the long years of spy revelations. The late Richard Crossman, in his diaries, says that he once tried to discuss the Philby affair with her, at a time when the papers were full of it, and that she replied simply that she did not 'read that sort of thing'.

Blunt was finally uncovered by the writer on espionage Andrew Boyle, who became convinced that he was the 'Fourth Man' in the Cambridge spy network, just as Kim Philby had been the 'Third Man'. Fearing a libel suit he named him only as 'Maurice' in his book *The Climate of Treason*.

It was then that Blunt made the mistake which was to result in his ruin. Instead of leaving well alone, he took fright when he heard about the references to 'Maurice', and asked the distinguished libel lawyer, Michael Rubenstein, to contact Boyle's publishers in an attempt to see a copy of the book.

The correspondence between the publishers and Rubenstein was leaked to *Private Eye*, which in those days did not worry too much about libel suits—not having amassed as many as they have today. The *Eye* first published the correspondence, then took a bold leap forward and named Blunt as the 'Fourth Man'.

From then on, Blunt was lost. The Labour MP for Hartlepool, Edward Leadbitter, tabled a question in the House. And Margaret Thatcher, then only a few months in office, faced up to it squarely, to make her statement that one of the most famous art historians in Europe, and a long-time servant of the Royal Household, was indeed a former Soviet agent.

The Palace announced the same day that Blunt had been stripped of his knighthood. He became the first man to suffer this indignity since the Irish patriot Sir Roger Casement in 1916—though he, of course, lost his life as well. There was no suggestion, however, that Blunt should be prosecuted, Thatcher saying in her statement that 'having regard to the immunity granted in order to obtain [his] confession, which has always been and still is the only firm evidence against Blunt, there are no grounds on which criminal proceedings could be instituted.'

The velvet-glove handling of Blunt, a member of the Establishment and a part of the 'old boy' network, makes an interesting contrast with that handed out to the other notorious Soviet agent uncovered in the last five years. Geoffrey Prime, who betrayed the secrets of the Government Communication Headquarters at Cheltenham, was given a sentence of 38 years in prison, and, as he is already middle-aged he is unlikely to emerge alive. But then, of course, he is not a gentleman.

Andrew Boyle has some interesting theories on why the Cambridge spy ring, the group of what he calls 'ruling-class radicals' remained undetected for decades.

Well-travelled Soviet leaders like Maxim Litvinov, he says, realized after World War I that the British class system with its 'tightly enmeshed web of trusting relationships' was in one way the country's strength, and in another its greatest weakness. The privileged sons of the ruling

313

class, if they could be recruited, would make effective and very dangerous agents, because no one would suspect them. Once in place in the Establishment, they would be almost untouchable, for who would dare suggest that someone so indubitably 'one of us' was a traitor?

This theory is borne out by the fact that the Cambridge group did indeed move into the heart of the Establishment—Burgess and Maclean into the Foreign Office, Blunt as an eminent academic and Philby as an intelligence section chief—and by the fact that even their weaknesses (Burgess was a notorious drunk and Blunt a homosexual) were overlooked and condoned.

What nobody really has explained satisfactorily is why the best and brightest of the generation were so easily subverted. Idealistic notions about righting the inequities of the world is one thing, working actively for a foreign power is another (though Philby and Burgess seemed to have both enjoyed the excitement of playing a dangerous double role).

If Blunt had carried through the intention which he had occasionally expressed of writing his autobiography, he might have been the one to strip away the mask and show what lay behind it. But he is dead, as are Burgess and Maclean. Only Colonel Philby, KGB, remains alive in Moscow.

Blunt died, no doubt to many of his old associates' relief, without leaving behind any writings or any significant papers. His disgrace had obviously not harmed him financially. His estate was a handsome £850,000, and as a last gesture he offered a painting by Poussin, Rebecca at the Well, to the nation in lieu of tax.

* * * * * *

If Blunt is the classic example of upper-class Soviet recruitment, Geoffrey Arthur Prime, now serving his 38-year sentence, illustrates the more sordid side of real-life espionage. Blunt and his circle may, to a certain extent, have been play-acting; Prime was in deadly earnest.

Prime, a Russian-speaking linguist at Government Communications Headquarters, had been spying for the Soviet Union from 1968 until he resigned in 1977, and possibly even after that. He said that he was leaving because of pressure of work and of personal problems, and so unsuspecting were his superiors at GCHQ that they pressed him to stay on.

But Prime insisted on going, and became a minicab driver. Even so, when he was arrested in 1982, part of his espionage kit was still in his possession; and he is known to have had a meeting with his Soviet controllers in Potsdam in 1981, at which he was paid £4,000. This has always aroused suspicions that though Prime may have been on the outside after 1977, yet he continued to have contacts with other undetected agents on the inside.

The Prime case deeply alarmed the Americans because GCHQ partners the US National Security Agency (as well as similar agencies in Canada, Australia, New Zealand and the NATO countries) in a global network of electronic surveillance. Military, diplomatic, and commercial traffic by radio, telex, telephone and satellite are all monitored.

The National Security Agency subjects potential employees to a month's long process of security clearance. This involves background checking, psychological grilling, and polygraph (or lie detector) tests, which include a number of embarrassing questions intended to show up personality weaknesses. The Prime case thus illustrated once again the famous British habit of muddling through, as well as the astonishingly amateurish nature of security checks. Although it could also be said that this is in fact rather admirable, and that it shows how impossible it would be for Britain to become a police state, nevertheless it sent the 'cousins' in Washington into near-apoplexy.

Britain relies on a system called 'positive vetting'. When Prime was arrested it was shown up to be a long way from foolproof. For one thing it relies in a rather touching way on the integrity of the interviewee, who is asked to fill in a long questionnaire on his background, lifestyle and habits.

Obviously an experienced agent could use such a questionnaire to create any sort of an impression he wanted, while avoiding outright lies which could easily be exposed. The person being vetted is also asked to provide two referees, and inquiries made after the Prime arrest showed that though sometimes these referees were visited and grilled, in other instances they were never approached.

The full tragi-comedy of the Prime affair was underlined when one of Prime's referees (a woman called Dorothea Barsby, who was at the time a friend of his wife) admitted that she knew he claimed to be a Soviet agent even before she vouched for him during 'positive vetting' in 1973.

She was severely criticized for this during a hearing by the Security Commission into the failure of the vetting process; but Barsby, who in 1983 was running a mobile hot-dog stand on the A2, called a press conference at her solicitor's office (the same Michael Rubenstein who acted for Anthony Blunt) to say that she was just being made a scapegoat for MI5.

She said that she had only acted as a referee for Prime because his first wife, Helena, had asked her to do so. She did not even know what job he was holding. 'If anyone had told me that Prime held a position of high trust in government service, I would have said that the government were off their heads,' Barsby said with feeling.

Helena, who later split with her husband, told her that Prime had confessed he was a spy when there was 'a blazing row' over a packet of money she had found in his pocket. Barsby said that Helena had not believed it, and neither had she. It was just another excuse, one of many which Prime gave for having mysterious quantities of money.

'Nothing he ever said or did gave me any reason to believe that he was doing anything else but fantasize about himself, to conceal from himself that he was a rotten husband and a dismal failure as a human being. People like that don't do secret service work, or do they?' Barsby said.

But Prime was concealing something much more damaging than unexplained sums of money from both his wives (he married again after his divorce from Helena). This man, who was in a position of high-level trust in a security establishment, was also a molester of young girls.

He was both obsessive and methodical: police found in his belongings lists containing thousands of names of girls, gathered from such sources as lists of school results in local newspapers or reports of any event in which female school-children had featured.

Prime was eventually caught because of an attack on a 14-year-old girl named by police only as Jacqueline. He called at the family's house when she was alone, threatened her with the blade of a bottle opener, ordered her to lower her knickers, then masturbated in front of her.

When this was reported to Worcester police, the incident checked with a number of others which involved a voyeur who used threats. The man had vanished without trace. But this time Prime made a mistake. He had driven up to the house in a two-tone bronze Ford Cortina with an 'S' registration. A computer scan came up with the names of 426 owners in the region, a largeish but not impossible number to check out.

In April 1982 police arrived at Prime's cottage in Cheltenham, explained their business, and asked politely to take his fingerprints. The police officers thought that this latest Cortina owner resembled the description which Jacequeline had given them, but they decided to do nothing until his fingerprints had been checked.

That night, Prime confessed his guilt for the sexual attacks to his wife Rhona, and also told her that he was involved in espionage. The next morning, he telephoned police and told them that he was the man they were looking for.

Ludicrously enough, the police still knew nothing about Prime's activities as an agent, and even when their former employee appeared in court on assault charges, GCHQ and the security agencies did nothing.

This left Rhona Prime in an almost impossible position. It took her three weeks to make up her mind, and she asked for advice from her priest, her doctor and her solicitor. No one knows what they told her, but eventually she went to the police, reported to them that her husband was involved in espionage, and that she had found what appeared to be a spy's kit in a carrier bag under a bed.

Even then, the security authorities refused to intervene. They left the investigation and the preparation of the case against Prime to the West Mercia police.

At the Old Bailey, Prime was sentenced to thirty-five years for espionage and three years for sexual assault. The severity of the sentence must have staggered him, for by then the interrogators had moved in and he was co-operating fully.

The case was seen in Britain as the worst since Philby's defection, though no one outside GCHQ and the intelligence services knows exactly what information Prime sold to the Soviet Union. When a sketchy account was given at the Old Bailey, the evidence was heard *in camera*.

According to the results of an investigation carried out by the *Sunday Times*, Prime gave the Russians details of a top secret project code-named Argus, which is run jointly by the National Security Agency and GCHQ. Argus is reported to be a satellite which can monitor voice transmissions, thus at least theoretically making it possible for British and American intelligence to listen in to telephone conversations (say) between members of the Soviet Politburo, or between military headquarters and forces in the fields. This has not been confirmed or denied, but the Lord Chief Justice must have taken the damage done by Prime into account when sentencing him at the Old Bailey. The spy Anthony Blunt was made a knight for services to the Royal Household. The spy Geoffrey Prime was jailed for thirty-eight years.

Apart from the litter of wrecked lives and wrecked reputations, the spy scene in Britain in the Eighties sometimes has a charming air of farce about it. There was, for example, the case of Captain Anatoly Zotov—the naval attache at the Soviet Embassy, who was expelled from Britain in December 1982 for conduct unbecoming to a diplomat.

The Blunts and the Primes may have gone undetected, but Special Branch agents were industrious in following Captain Zotov on a holiday visit to Portsmouth and Plymouth in the summer of 1982.

Zotov and the Soviet air attache Serge Smirnov, dressed in casual clothes and carrying cameras (sinister, that!), joined a pleasure boat which takes trippers round the Devonport dockyard to look at warships at anchor. At Plymouth public library, Zotov asked for any books on submarines, and he photocopied an article from the Naval Review. He told the librarian that he was the Soviet naval attache; and in Torquay, when he talked to two drinkers in the Wig and Pen Club, he identified himself in the same way.

The two drinkers, Mike Tullis and Glen Aris, were later visited by Special Branch and questioned about the conversation. They were told that Zotov had been on a recruiting mission, and had they expressed any wish to become Soviet agents, he would have made them an offer. Aris was sceptical. 'If this was a Russian spy operation, it was nothing like Smiley's People,' he said thoughtfully.

In diplomatic and defence circles in London, Zotov's expulsion was regarded with dismay. He was a gregarious man, good at his job, and with a fine, trained tenor voice. At dinner parties, according to his acquaintances, Mrs Zotov would announce: 'I think my husband would like to sing,' and he would burst into 'It's a Long Vay to Tipperary'. 'It almost blew the windows out,' said one of his fellow guests.

Another Soviet diplomat expelled in 1983, Colonel Guennadi Primakov, shared Zotov's liking for consulting public libraries. This is a simple and straightforward method of doing things—a long way from the tortuous techniques of spy fiction.

Colonel Primakov used the public library at Cambridge. He asked to see anything which was available on civil defence, and gave his address as Kensington Palace Gardens. The librarian remembered that the Soviet Embassy was located there, and made a joking note in his office diary: 'Civil defence file consulted by "Russian spy"'. Another library official was not amused, and told the Cambridge police, who showed little interest. There the matter rested, but the story emerged when newspapers carried reports of Colonel Primakov's expulsion.

Both sides seem equally disingenuous. Lance Corporal Philip Aldridge of the Intelligence Corps Field Unit, who had been positively vetted for security work, decided in 1982 to sell some secrets to the Russians so that he could buy a car.

His technique was as simple as that of the Soviet diplomats paying visits to public libraries. He simply rang up the Soviet Embassy, and asked to speak to the 'intelligence diplomat'. When the telephone call became too complicated, he photocopied the file cover of a document dealing with Exocet missiles, and sent it to the embassy with a covering note: 'If this appeals to you, insert a notice in the personal column of the *Daily Telegraph* on September 4, 1982—"Spider we like you, love Mum".'

This did indeed appeal to the Russians. They inserted the advertisement, though even there they got it wrong and it emerged as: 'I love you, Spider. Love Mum'.

Nothing really came of all this, and there is some doubt that Aldridge ever met any Soviet agents or handed over any documents. Nevertheless, at his trial in 1983, he pleaded guilty to offences under the Official Secrets Act and was jailed for four years.

Then there was the middle-aged Irish couple, Tony and Margaret Hayde, who received in the mail an entry form in a competition for a free holiday in Spain run by a company called Casuro. Mrs Hayde filled it in; and in July 1983, the Haydes were notified they had won third prize, a week at a hotel in Torremolinos. When they arrived, they were contacted by a man claiming to be a tourist courier, who invited them to lunch with the second prizewinners in the competition.

Over lunch at Granada, the 'courier' and the 'second prizewinners' confessed that things were not as they seemed. All three were members of British Intelligence, and they offered the Haydes £10,000 to provide 'a bit of security' for their son Rory, then only ten.

Why this interest in the Haydes? They were members of the Irish Republican Socialist Party, and had met Dominic McGlinchey, chief of staff of the Irish National Liberation Army and the most 'wanted' man in both Ulster and the Irish Republic.

What the British agents were looking for from the Haydes was information about people, places and meetings—anything, in fact, to do with republican activities.

The Haydes refused indignantly, checked out of their hotel, and returned home. Claiming that they had nothing to do with terrorists, they blew the story to the press, supplying a copy of the letterhead of Casuro, the travel firm offering the holiday. Alas, this was not of much help as the address given, 'Albemarle Way, EC1', turned out to be a rent-a-mail-box company, guaranteeing 'complete discretion and confidentiality'. The telephone number was answered only by a recorded voice asking the caller to leave a message.

In April, 1984, absurdity reached its peak when an Old

Bailey jury was told an MI-5 man called Michael Bettaney had spent months trying to give the Soviet Union top-secret information, without success.

Bettaney's repeated efforts to enrol himself as a double agent were treated by the Russians as a clumsy attempt to infiltrate their network, and according to some reports, it was the Soviet Embassy which actually tipped off the British Secret Intelligence Service that there was a cuckoo in the nest. Bettaney was sentenced to 23 years in prison.

* * * * * *

It is the combination of tragedy and 'Carry On Spying' farce which makes the intelligence world irresistibly fascinating. The early Eighties were vintage years for spy-watchers, and with assorted experts claiming that there are still anything from thirteen to thirty moles still in high places—some of them knights of the realm—there are chapters of the long-running spy serial which have yet to be written.

CHAPTER SIXTEEN

THE FOURTH ESTATE

In October 1983, at the beginning of the first term of the university year, Jesus College, Cambridge, came under siege by the battle-hardened corps of photographers, reporters and television cameramen, whose main job is now to keep up a non-stop surveillance of members of the Royal Family.

The reason? The Queen's fourth son, Prince Edward, had just entered the college as an undergraduate. A new instalment of what its critics call 'The Royal Soap Opera' was about to begin. Fleet Street had high hopes that the young Prince, sharing his staircase at Jesus with women students, would provide some titillating moments for its readers in the months to come, though it was too much to expect that he would match the ratings of 'The Prince and the Actress', the drama (or farce) in which his elder brother had starred earlier.

Even before Prince Edward arrived at Cambridge, his admission caused a minor upset, for his educational achievements hardly seemed to entitle him to a place in what is still a highly elitist institution. However, the grumblings were soon forgotten, and Buckingham Palace and the Central Office of Information had consultations about the next hurdle—the Prince's first days as a student.

It was decided that the best way to handle it was to hold an open day for the press, and to let the cameras poke into the students' rooms in the college, and to interview the college head porter, often as impressive a figure as the Master himself. The supposition was that once the press had done all this, it would pack up its cameras and tape recorders and go away.

On the contrary, one brief glimpse only stimulated media appetites, and the press camped outside the college for three days, attempting from time to time to infiltrate one of its members inside in disguise. Women students who were to share the Prince's staircase were traced in advance to their home addresses and lovingly described. The *Sunday People*'s prize find was 'lissom Liz Underwood, a keep fit fan from Brighton who exercises in a leopard-skin leotard'. She was to be, it said gravely, the Prince's 'sizzling neighbour'. The Jesus College siege was bad news for the Royal Family, whose attempts to discipline the press, or at least to persuade it to behave in a more mannerly fashion, have met with decreasing success, year by year, over the last decade.

The media presents the Palace with a major dilemma, for it knows that without the press royalty might very well not survive. Prince Charles has been quoted as saying: 'If the photographers *weren't* interested, that would be the time to start worrying.' But what the Royal Family wants is something that, in the Eighties, it apparently cannot have: tasteful, discreet, controlled coverage, always favourable.

There is nothing new about the public appetite for gossip about royalty, or about scandalous reporting of the sexual conduct of members of the Royal Family. The cartoons published on the amours of the Prince Regent, for example, would raise eyebrows even today.

But after Queen Victoria introduced the era of the Virtuous Monarch, scandal in high places became more interesting, because it was rarer. The most remarkable aspect of the affair between the future King Edward VIII and Mrs Wallis Simpson was the fact any mention of it was kept out of the British press for so long, even at a time when American papers were openly speculating that Mrs Simpson's coming divorce might result in the King of England being cited as co-respondent.

It is impossible to imagine present-day newspaper editors (not only in Britain but in the Dominions) agreeing to a self-imposed news blackout on anything relating to the King's relationship with a married woman. This extraordinary fact was organized by Lord Beaverbrook, and it held up until the gravity of the constitutional crisis made it impossible to maintain any longer.

In the Eighties, not only do the popular papers cover every conceivable nuance of Prince Andrew's dalliance with the actress Koo Stark, but they run polls among their readership to test popular opinion on the subject. (The overall verdict is that a young war hero fresh from the South Atlantic had every right to take a glamorous lady on holidays, soft-porn queen or not.)

The Queen obviously finds it hardest of all to come to terms with the present situation, for even earlier in her own reign the Crown retained a certain amount of its mystical significance. She could ensure that her own personal privacy was respected, and indeed she largely still manages it to this day. (That is why the intrusion of Michael Fagan into her bedroom in the summer of 1982, and the flood of cartoons of her sitting up in bed in her nightgown and hair curlers must have been a bitter and humiliating experience for her.)

The change in the coverage of the Royal Family has been in a large degree due to technology. The unwinking eye of the television camera keeps a non-stop vigil; and small, powerful cameras with zoom lenses have made the paparazzi and their British equivalents very mobile. The old-style press photographer with his heavy gear and his need for an assistant to stand on a chair holding the flash is gone, replaced by a photographic guerilla, capable of operating anywhere, at any time. One outstanding example of this in the early Eighties was the *Sun* photographer who crawled through the low, jungly undergrowth of a tropical island to take a picture of the very pregnant young Princess of Wales in—or mainly out of—a bikini. Few photographs have caused the Royal Family more shock and anguish, and the outcry was such that the tabloids agreed to a stand-off, but only for a while.

Another factor which influences saturation coverage is that the press, as opposed to the electronic media, has found the Royal Family a circulation booster almost as rewarding as bingo.

Radio has to some extent mastered the art of gossip, though the enormity of actually *saying* (rather than writing) something which will be heard by millions tends to blunt the sharpest tongue; television has little to do with gossip, it only records events.

So gossip and speculation about the Royal Family is largely left to the papers. It provides an invaluable weapon in their fight against the inroads made by television into their circulation. The Fleet Street diarists in particular (a grand name for gossip columnists) keep alive on snippets about 'the Royals' and are often surprisingly accurate in predicting future events.

The Royal Family, while angrily protesting about what it regards as non-stop intrusion into its private lives, is still not above using the media when suitable. The Palace made no move to rescue Lady Diana Spencer, then a helper at a Kensington kindergarten, when she was harassed day and night by cameramen and reporters during the period of her courtship by Prince Charles. It was widely believed at the time that the Royal Family was allowing this 19-year-old girl to go through trial by fire in order to see how she would stand up to media attention. If she broke down under the strain, she would not be able to tolerate the rigours of Royal life, and would therefore be an unsuitable candidate for the job of Princess of Wales.

Diana Spencer endured the persecution of the paparazzi surprisingly well for so young and apparently shy a girl. But the harassment had a cumulative effect, and after her marriage she was seen to be suffering from a complaint diagnosed (by the press at least) as 'media claustrophobia'.

There were, indeed, stories that even before the wedding she was having serious emotional problems, and an enterprising theatrical management made capital out of this by promoting, in the West End, a 'quickie' play called 'Her Royal Highness?' This suggested that during the engagement Lady Diana had actually had a minor nervous breakdown, and that her place had been taken on public occasions by a look-alike, a young Sydney barmaid whom Prince Charles had noticed on an Australian tour.

The humour of the play centred round the efforts made by the Royal household to turn a rough Sydney girl with a ripe line in expletives into a fake Lady Diana, but the result was so excruciating that audiences fell away to disaster level. In an attempt to save the piece, the promoters planned a television advertising campaign using actors in the roles of the Queen, the Queen Mother, and Prince Charles and Lady Diana. The Palace did not overtly intervene, but protests were undoubtedly made behind the scenes. The Independent Broadcasting Authority which controls commercial television banned the advertisements on the grounds of bad taste, and 'Her Royal Highness?' died a quick death. Exploitation had, in this case, gone a little too far.

In real life, the Princess of Wales' 'media claustrophobia' set in a year or so after her marriage, when she had to cope not only with adjustment to the stuffiness and rigidity of a Royal existence, but also with an almost immediate pregnancy. After the birth of her child, she became alarmingly thin; and the headlines in the popular press at once cried 'Anorexia!' Persistent gossip said that she could not reconcile herself to the rituals of Royalty, and in particular the long holidays at Royal residences at Sandringham and Balmoral, with their archaic routines of slaughtering animals by day and playing charades and party games at night.

The Fleet Street diarists claimed that the young Princess was so wilful and temperamental that she was making her husband very unhappy. Better substantiated reports said that she had become a shopaholic and was spending a fortune on clothes.

The climax came during a winter skiing holiday when the Princess, pursued even on the *piste* by photographers on skis, and by others hanging out of helicopters buzzing above the slopes, showed openly her anger and resentment and reverted to an old habit of trying to hide her face.

Later in 1983, however the Prince and Princess of Wales made a very successful tour of Australia, and it is suggested in Britain that this was a turning point for the Princess. British journalists travelling with the Royal party commented openly on the fact that the 'anorexic' Princess was putting on a little weight, gaining a sun tan, and showing more confidence day by day as the obvious friendliness of the crowds lessened her nervousness. One columnist suggested that the fact that her ever-watchful in-laws were thousands of miles away also helped the Princess to relax. He said that as far as the new recruit was concerned, the Royal Family was 'caring but inhibiting'.

Interestingly enough, the British press also saw the tour, and in particular the popularity of the Princess, as a powerful factor in saving Australia from becoming a Republic. This idea is taken far more seriously in Britain than it ever has been in Australia, and the Royalist faction gave cries of dismay when the 'socialist' government of Bob Hawke came to power.

One scenario which was being discussed in London at the time of the Royal tour was that the Prime Minister (supposing it was still Hawke) would declare a Republic in 1988 as part of Australia's bicentenary celebrations and that former Prime Minister Gough Whitlam (now in Paris as Ambassador to UNESCO) would become the first president. An alternative theory was that despite all official denials, the Prince of Wales (who went to school in Australia) would be appointed as the last Australian Governor General. He would preside over the separation of Australia from the British Crown in the same way that his great uncle, Earl Mountbatten, did for India in the last days of the Raj.

The repeated love-ins between the crowds and the Princess of Wales on the 1983 tour were seen in Britain as averting these assorted dangers. And much was made of the supposition that Bob Hawke, who is known to be appreciative of women, was caught by the young Princess' charms. 'Hawke softens his public line on the monarchy', cried the headlines, enthusiastically if erroneously.

* * * * * *

The Eighties have, therefore, been a very mixed time for the Royal Family. The Royal Wedding, which the organizers had the wit to turn into a lavish musical, was enormously successful. Anybody who walked up and down the Mall the night before the ceremony (as I did) to watch the crowds build up for their overnight vigil could have no doubts about the genuine popularity of this Royal super-spectacle.

As well as boosting the ratings of the Royal Family, the wedding was a godsend for the Thatcher government. At that time—pre-Falklands—it was in the middle of a summer of discontent, with unemployment rising with terrifying speed to 2.8 million, and with the centres of cities going up in flames as urban rioting spread. But for weeks leading up to the wedding, and even for a little while afterwards, all that was forgotten. The nation was drunk with old-fashioned sentimentality.

The brilliant organization of the ceremony, with guests

coming from all over the world (thereby providing major problems for both protocol officers and security men) was also consoling to national pride. It proved that Britain still could carry out a complex operation with supreme efficiency, even if its industrial under-structure was crumbling.

The wedding did not do as much as had been hoped for Britain's overseas trade balance. The reports of urban rioting kept many American visitors away, and overall, the number of tourists was ten per cent down on the year before. Still, an estimated 700 million people watched the ceremony on television right around the globe, making it the most public wedding in the history of the human race.

The Royal jewellery collection benefited greatly from the event. On the day I walked round the display of wedding presents in the throne room of St James' Palace, press photographers were holding pieces of cardboard over display cases because they were having trouble with reflections bouncing off the priceless jewels and sumptuous gold and silver plate.

The presents were an extraordinary lot. They ranged from knitted tea cosies and a first-aid kit (with components labelled 'His', 'Hers' and 'Horse') to a boar's tusk from Vanuatu, two cowrie shells from Fiji, and a rush suitcase containing a quilt from Tonga—the quilt having been made by Queen Halaevalu Mata'aho herself.

All were conscientiously displayed, but the Arabs were the clear winners with a collection of presents which could be described, for once with absolute truth, as 'dazzling'. The Emir of Qatar and his Heir Apparent gave ornate gold and silver tableware, plus watches, jewels, and earrings. The Crown Prince of Saudi Arabia gave a huge malachite box which looked like something out of the Arabian Nights, and a glittering array of jewellery set with diamonds, rubies and pearls. The Emir of Bahrain gave a solid gold dhow, and the United Arab Emirates a diamond watch. The only competitors to the Arabs were the King and Queen of Thailand, who sent a remarkable jewelled necklace, and a gold box decorated with diamonds. It was hard not to speculate on how much the Royal Family must be worth in jewels and gold and silver plate alone. (Two years later, a journalist covering the Queen's tour of India was to comment sardonically on the amount of jewellery that she was wearing when she awarded the Order of Merit to Mother Teresa, who works among the world's poorest people.)

The Royal wedding also illustrated very clearly how times have changed since the Queen herself was married in 1947. In those days coverage of any Royal event remained respectful, and the satirists appeared to be taking a holiday. In even earlier times, when the Queen's uncle Edward, the Prince of Wales, was receiving what was then saturation coverage from the media, the popular song of the day was plaintive and adulatory:

> I've danced with a man
> Who danced with a girl
> Who danced with the Prince of Wales...

But in 1981, BBC radio listeners, asked to vote on songs connected with the Royal wedding, put into top place a highly satirical entry from Australia called 'The Ballad of Lady Di' sung to a raucous beat:

> And Di, Di Di
> Said 'Stick it in your eye,'
> The only man I'll marry
> Is Prince Charl-eye!

The 'Not The Nine O'Clock News' team, to whom nothing is sacred, starred in a glossy publication called 'Not The Royal Wedding', with the Australian actress Pamela Stephenson as Lady Diana, wearing a copy of her blue engagement suit, her watch and her ring. 'Not The Royal Wedding' looked remarkably like the wedding souvenir booklet, but anyone who bought it in innocence found inside such truly terrible jokes as 'A Di In The Loife...' and 'The Shape of Kings to Come'.

Punch, a publication still found in eminently respectable dentists' waiting rooms, went even further than *Private Eye*—which is usually guaranteed to produce the ultimate in gleeful bad taste on these occasions. A *Punch* cover at wedding time showed Lady Diana Spencer again in her blue engagement suit and displaying her ring—but the hands coming over her shoulder were not those of Prince Charles, but of Idi Amin. Inside *Punch* published an 'open letter' from the deposed dictator to Lady Diana about the loves of previous Princes of Wales. (The text was racist, tasteless, but very funny: 'Take de case o' de notorious Lily Langtry: she was known as de Jersey Lily on account of her habit o' givin' it away free to goalkeepers...')

To what extent the Royal Family is aware of this strongly irreverent undercurrent is a subject of endless speculation among the Royal watchers. It is highly likely that the Queen, at least, shuts her mind to it—in the same way that by ignoring it she was able to come to terms with the fact her Surveyor of Pictures was a retired KGB agent.

The pregnancy of the young Princess of Wales went very well, however, with only the bikini incident to mar it. The Princess had the baby in hospital, thus taking the Royal Family a further step into the twentieth century, and Prince Charles broke all precedent by being photographed outside St Mary's Hospital, Paddington, awkwardly carrying his new born son in his arms. Usually the first that is ever seen of a Royal baby is in the set-piece photographs taken at Buckingham Palace, with the Royal women wearing hats indoors (an inexplicable piece of English folklore), sitting stiffly on couches, and the rest of the family grouped around.

These occasions apart, Royalty did not like what happened to its image in the first few years of the decade. With Prince Charles safely married and about to become a father, the media turned its attention to Prince Andrew, who even as a teenager had shown signs of becoming much more relaxed in his attentions to women than his discreet elder brother.

The popular press was entranced when it discovered that not only was Andrew involved with an older American actress, but one who had starred in a number of soft-porn films. Koo Stark, austerely referred to as Miss Kathleen Stark by the more established newspapers, was a gift from heaven for papers engaged in a bitter circulation war—as indeed she was to cinemas in the dirty raincoat belt, which re-ran all her old movies.

The Palace bore with what dignity it could speculation on whether the Queen would give her permission for Andrew to marry his actress; and both the Prince and Koo Stark tolerated without protest, even if they did not actually enjoy, the round-the-clock watch which was kept on their movements.

Nevertheless, it was the Koo Stark affair which in 1983 brought the angry ill-feeling between the Palace and the press to a head. In the community generally this resulted in calls for a new statutory body to discipline the media. Rupert Murdoch's *Sun* newspaper—which, with its potent mixture of cheerful vulgarity, unapologetic right-wing sentiment and boobs-and-bum pinups is one of the main-stays of the Murdoch world-wide empire—at last went too far and provoked the Queen into taking, for the first time, legal action against a newspaper.

The Palace had for years made all Royal employees sign an 'undertaking of confidence' in an attempt to guard the privacy of the Royal Family, and this had worked, on the whole, very well. There have been no more betrayals of inner secrets on the scale of that of *The Little Princesses*, the book about the childhood of Princess Elizabeth and Princess Margaret by their former governess Marion Crawford.

But the *Sun* managed to find someone who was willing to

talk despite the undertaking which he had signed. This was a former Palace stores officer, Kieran Kenny, so low in the hierarchy and so modest in his demands that it was rumoured that the *Sun* paid him less than £2,000 for his story.

For a stores officer, however, Kenny seemed to have had a remarkable insight into life on the upper floors of the Palace. In the first instalment of his revelations, he said that Koo Stark stayed so often overnight that the Royal quarters were almost her second home. She made herself unpopular by giving staff orders, raiding the Royal pantry at all hours of the night, and helping herself to boxes of the Queen's own chocolates. After Royal parties, hungover guests could be seen staggering along the corridors at eight o'clock in the morning.

This was too much for the Queen, especially as the following day's episode in the *Sun* was previewed as 'When barefoot Di buttered my toast'. Alas, the world was never to hear the full story of this intriguing moment in history, for the Royal Household went immediately to the High Court and won an injunction halting the Kenny series. The *Sun*, nothing if not resourceful, turned its quarrel with the Palace into a page-one story: 'Queen Gags the *Sun*' it cried, boasting of the fact that it was the first British newspaper ever to have received such Royal attention.

(There was, however, some precedent. In 1981, the Palace won an injunction against a freelance journalist. He was trying to sell what he claimed were tapes of conversations between Prince Charles and Lady Diana Spencer, who was then staying in Australia.)

The *Sun* attempted to fight the Royal injunction, but it had no chance of winning. As the Queen's deputy press secretary Victor Chapman said: 'The servant has breached an undertaking of confidence which all Palace employees sign. In this declaration they agree not to make any disclosures about their work at the Palace. It is a legally binding document under civil law.'

The Queen had every reason to be angry about the Kieran Kenny affair. It came as the latest in the long line of incidents which had threatened the dignity of the monarchy. The one which must have distressed her above all others was the ease with which an unemployed and eccentric 31-year-old man called Michael Fagan managed to breach Palace security and find his way to her bedroom.

The unfortunate aspect of the whole thing for the Royal Family was its comic overtones, once it was seen that the Queen was not harmed and had probably never been in any danger. Hardly surprisingly, the Palace tried to hush the incident up; and the nation might never have heard anything about it had someone not leaked the story to the *Daily Express*. The satirists found something irresistibly funny about the idea of Fagan sitting on the edge of the Royal bed chatting up the Queen and asking for a cigarette, while the Royal bodyguards took their time about answering telephoned calls for help on the grounds that the Queen did not sound agitated. In the end, it was largely left to a footman, a chambermaid, and the Royal corgies, fresh and frisky from their morning walk, to deal with the intruder. Ironically enough, in the end Fagan was charged with no more than stealing half a bottle of Palace wine.

Hardly had the Palace recovered from that blow when there was another. A male prostitute approached the *Sun* newspaper, and offered to sell the story of his long association with the Queen's personal police officer, Commander Michael Trestrail. He had, he said, originally met Trestrail when the latter was a metropolitan police sergeant, and they had been lovers for many years.

The *Sun* virtuously refused to buy the story, but it went to the police with its information. The Home Secretary, William Whitelaw, was already under savage criticism over the fact that Fagan's intrusion into the Queen's bedroom had been announced to the nation not by him but by the *Daily Express*. He had no option but to tell the House of

Commons that Commander Trestrail had resigned, and the reasons for it.

Homosexuality is no longer illegal in Britain, and no one would have objected to Trestrail having a discreet liaison. It has been hinted at by Fleet Street diarists from time to time that homosexuals are rather valued as Royal servants as they are not distracted by family problems, are attentive and willing to work long hours, and offer no threat to the virtue of Royal ladies. However, there were two alarming things about the Trestrail case. The first was that he had been having a liaison with a male prostitute, with the obvious possibilities of blackmail which that offered. The second was that, like Geoffrey Prime in the GCHQ spy case, he had been positively vetted on more than one occasion, and it had not been discovered that he was homosexual.

The Trestrail affair had some echoes of that of Anthony Blunt. Like Blunt, Trestrail had received Royal honours, having been made a member of the Royal Victorian Order in 1978; and Blunt was also a homosexual.

Trestrail vanished from the Royal scene as quickly and discreetly as Blunt had done, but the scandal rumbled on for long afterwards, with calls (unheeded) for the resignations of William Whitelaw and the Metropolitan Police Commissioner. The main result of the Fagan and Trestrail affairs was a tightening up of Palace security, and a 'moving on' of a number of the lower-rank police officers involved.

One consolation which the Queen has had in the Eighties is that, as the spotlight switches to the younger Royals, her sister Princess Margaret becomes yearly less newsworthy.

For nearly three decades, from her love affair with Captain Peter Townsend to her liaison with Roddy Llewellyn, Princess Margaret had the same sort of explosive news quality as her uncle King Edward VIII had as Prince of Wales. Even during her marriage to Anthony Armstrong-Jones, now Lord Snowdon, no one quite knew what would happen next.

The last time that Princess Margaret was on full public view was in 1981, when the gossip columnist Nigel Dempster brought out a biography *HRH The Princess Margaret: A Life Unfulfilled*. Dempster, who moves in some elevated circles, is (or was) a friend of the Princess; and when the book was being written it was strongly rumoured in Fleet Street that she had given it her unofficial blessing, as she wanted to allow the full story of her marriage break-up to be known.

If this was so, she can hardly have been pleased with the result. The book shows her as a lonely, passionate, dissatisfied woman, spoiled but vulnerable, who only married the photographer Tony Armstrong-Jones because she had heard that Peter Townsend was about to marry again and there was no one else immediately available.

Dempster shows a woman given to indiscreet friendships. One which ended in tragedy was with the pianist Robin Douglas-Home who seems to have had some idea of marrying her, and who committed suicide after an assortment of the Princess's letters to him turned up in an auction in New York.

The most famous was with the young dilettante Roddy Llewellyn who was, according to Dempster, provided to divert her by another old friend, Colin Tennant, at a time when she was deeply depressed. Tennant told Dempster: 'She was taken with him immediately, and devoured him through luncheon.'

In fact, Llewellyn was a bad choice. He was a shy young man who (Dempster said) had already tried to commit suicide twice before he met the Princess, because of his doubts about his own sexuality. At one stage of their relationship, he fled the country because he could not cope with the situation; and it was then (once again, according to Dempster) that Princess Margaret took a small quantity of sleeping pills, more as a *cri de coeur* than as a serious attempt to commit suicide.

The ups-and-downs of the Llewellyn-Margaret affair and

the passionate attention paid to it by the media benefited Lord Snowdon who had had a long and stable affair with his present wife Lucy Lindsay-Hogg and wanted to marry her. Without the Princess's indiscretions, he would have found it very hard to persuade the Royal Family to tolerate the idea of divorce.

In her fifties, the Princess is now a middle-aged and sedate figure, her friendship with Roddy Llewellyn long over. She has retreated back into the safe world of royal obligations and rituals, and though there are occasional rumours that she intends to marry one of the equally middle-aged men who act as her escorts, she no longer excites or titillates Fleet Street. There are too many of the younger generation around now for that to happen.

The press had hopes for a while that the glamorous divorcee, the Princess Michael of Kent, would provide them with a Margaret-substitute. But the lady, though a little too dashing for a Royal, seems determined to thwart the gossip columnists by staying within the prescribed rules. Only *Private Eye* keeps up a lonely vendetta against her, insisting that her origins are by no means as aristocratic as she claims. But she is beautiful and stylish, and nobody cares.

Princess Anne, with her habit of telling the press to naff off and the rumoured rift in her marriage to Captain Mark Phillips, used to be a minor difficulty for the Palace. But her marriage, despite all the gossip, seems to be stable enough; and she is settling down into the kind of horsy county lady with a rather dim spouse that nature clearly intended her to be.

The Queen herself is showing signs of strain. After thirty years on the throne, she is now older than her father when he died. Unlike the Queen Mother (who remains, in her eighties, the star turn of any Royal occasion) she has never learned to relax when she is on duty. Her Christmas television appearances remain an obvious ordeal, and the pretty young Princess Elizabeth is disappearing inside a stiff and frumpish middle-aged woman who increasingly conjures up an image of Queen Victoria. The cameras these days often catch the uptight, anxious expression which her staff (according to her press secretary) call her 'Miss Piggy' look.

Barbara Castle, the former Labour Cabinet minister now a Euro-MP, complained of it in her diaries on an occasion when she and her husband were invited to Windsor for dinner with the Queen. When the Royal party arrived in the drawing room, the Queen shook hands seriously all round, then stood talking to Princess Anne 'with an air of almost glum indifference'. It was only later that 'her face relaxed into what can be her very charming smile. I can only conclude that she is either naturally shy or has inherited Queen Mary's glower without knowing it,' Mrs Castle said.

Those who have watched the Queen on more intimate occasions say that she is, however, politically very shrewd, having seen six Prime Ministers come and go. Gossip says that the two whom she has found least congenial are Ted Heath and her seventh, Margaret Thatcher; and the regular Tuesday evening audience between Monarch and Prime Minister are rumoured to be something less than cosy these days.

More than one commentator has pointed out that Thatcher, who is taller, more regal, and apparently much more sure of herself, rather tends to upstage the Queen. During the Falklands campaign in particular, Thatcher gave at times quite a reasonable impersonation of the first Queen Elizabeth (whom she has quoted on other occasions) at Tilbury.

The Queen is known to believe fervently in her role as Head of the Commonwealth, and she insists on attending the biennial meetings of Commonwealth Prime Ministers and Presidents. She takes no part in the actual conference, but she sees each of the heads of state individually and plays, where necessary, the role of tactful conciliator. It is the Queen who is usually given the credit for creating the relaxed atmosphere at Lusaka in 1979 which allowed the Rhodesian peace negotiations to get under way.

Oddly enough, this internationalism brought down upon her, early in 1984, the wrath of the supernationalist Enoch Powell. Criticizing her 1983 Christmas broadcast, he said in a speech in Leicester that the British people might turn against the monarchy if the Queen continued to show more interest in 'foreigners' than her own subjects. 'She has the interests and affairs of other countries in other continents as much, or more, at heart, than those of her own people,' Powell said. 'Even here in the United Kingdom, she is more concerned for the susceptibilities and prejudices of a minority of newcomers than for her British subjects.' Powell blamed her advisers: 'They seem afraid for her to speak as a Christian monarch to a Christian people, or as the British monarch to the British nation.'

* * * * * *

To the outside observer, it seem obvious that the Queen, if she was not bound by her Royal obligations, would be much happier doing something else.

She is at heart a countrywoman, devoted to dogs and horses, and never more at ease than when sloshing about in muddy fields in wellingtons and tweeds and a headscarf. The question has already been asked—and will continue to be asked with greater urgency—as to whether it would not be better for her to retire when she is sixty or sixty-five, and allow Prince Charles to take over her job. This is not without precedent, as Queen Wilhelmina of the Netherlands retired at sixty-eight, but the Dutch Royal Family does not see itself as quite in the same mystical light as its British counterpart. No one really knows what the Queen's feelings are; but she probably regards the monarchy, without much pleasure, as a lifetime, God-given task.

This presents obvious difficulties for the Prince of Wales,

who has the unhappy example always before him of another Prince of Wales, later King Edward VII, who had to wait until he was fifty-nine and a grandfather before he acceded to the throne. The Queen is a strong and healthy woman and may imitate Queen Victoria in more ways than one by living into her eighties. This will leave Prince Charles only semi-employed for a long time, and as he enters middle age he will no longer be able to continue with the strenuous physical activities which have won him his Action Man title. The idea persists in Britain that he wanted very much to become Governor-General of Australia, and might even have been installed by now at Yarralumla had it not been for the ill-fated events of 1975. The sacking of Prime Minister Gough Whitlam by the then Governor-General, Sir John Kerr, has ruled out any controversial appointment to the job for years to come.

Apart from the Queen's retirement, the question most often raised about the Royal Family is whether it provides a service worth the money spent on it. In the early Seventies, a select committee was set up by the Parliament to look into complaints from the Royal Household that it was going into the red because of rising inflation. The Queen's civil list is now adjusted according to the inflation rate, and the taxpayer meets the cost of the Royal residences, the Royal yacht and the Queen's Flight.

The cost of the monarchy has been estimated at about £20 million a year, which is less than what the government is spending on its new Trident weapons system. Most of this goes on financing the households. Personal expenses come from the civil list, which in 1983 was raised to a total of £4.9 million. The Queen received £3.7 million and the rest went to the Duke of Edinburgh, the Queen Mother, Princess Margaret, Princess Anne, Prince Andrew and Prince Edward. The Prince and Princess of Wales receive nothing from the civil list, as they have an income of about £400,000 a year from the Duchy of Cornwall.

The taxpayers get something back, however, for in 1983

341

the government received £15 million in revenue from the Crown Estates which the Queen (like other monarchs since George III in 1760) handed over to the state at the beginning of her reign. These are highly lucrative, ranging from property in the West End of London to exclusive salmon fishing rights.

Nevertheless hardened republicans still regularly ask questions in the House of Commons about Royal costs, pointing out that though the personal wealth of the Royal Family remains a well-guarded secret yet the Queen is obviously enormously wealthy. For this reason, the Palace equally regularly announces that an economy campaign is under way. In 1983 the campaign involved, among other things, using old newspapers for bedding down horses in the Royal Mews, and selling mushrooms from the Royal garden at Windsor.

Whether the Royal Family earns its money opening factories or shaking thousands of hands at Palace garden parties is a matter for debate. But no one has ever doubted the universal appeal of the magical illusion of lost grandeurs that Britain can still summon up on great occasions, and which cannot be equalled anywhere in the world.

Even the most ardent republican finds it hard to jeer at the spectacle of the Queen riding down the Mall at the head of her Household Cavalry on her way to the Trooping of the Colour ceremony. The flash of breastplates in the sun, the nodding of plumes, the jingling of harness, the rich smell of horseflesh is irresistible. As a spectacle, it is outdone only by that great indoor event, the State Opening of Parliament. No one but the British could carry off an event so intrinsically ridiculous: a monarch in full evening dress at eleven o'clock in the morning, wearing incongruous half-moon glasses with her crown, and so many jewels that she glitters like a magic idol; a consort wearing dress uniform and a sword; a Lord Chancellor who used to totter down the stairs backwards after presenting the Queen with the

Speech From The Throne until Lord Hailsham's age and infirmity made this remarkable feat too dangerous; peers and peeresses in velvet and ermine and diamonds, jewels flashing everywhere like stars in the glare of the television lights. As a theatrical performance, it has no equal anywhere in the world. Even Hollywood in its most extravagent days could not match it, and it never fails to take the breath away.

*   *   *   *   *   *

When Lord Copper, the proprietor of the *Daily Beast* in Evelyn Waugh's *Scoop*, sent his reluctant war correspondent William Boot (formerly the *Beast*'s country affairs writer) to the conflict in Ishmaelia he gave him explicit instructions:

> Remember that the Patriots are in the right and are going to win. The Beast stands by them four square. But they must win quickly. The British public has no interest in a war which drags on indecisively. A few sharp victories, some conspicuous acts of personal bravery on the Patriot side, and a colourful entry into the capital. That is the Beast's policy for the war.

It was also the Thatcher Government's policy for the war, and it was greatly helped in carrying it out by the more vociferously patriotic section of Fleet Street.

Mrs Thatcher was unable to understand, from beginning to end, while the whole of the media did not feel the same way, and she publicly attacked the BBC for talking of 'British troops' instead of 'our boys'.

When the managing director of BBC Radio, Richard Francis, said in a speech to the International Press Institute in Madrid—apropos of BBC reporting of reaction from Argentina—that 'the widow of Portsmouth is no different from the widow of Buenos Aires', there was talk on the Right of the Tory Party of outright treachery.

A BBC Panorama program on the Falklands brought

charges of 'despicable Argie bias', and when BBC chieftains met the Tory Media Committee to answer their critics there was, in the words of one MP who was present, 'blood and entrails all over the place'.

The Ministry of Defence was even surprised when some of the journalists with the South Atlantic Task Force rebelled against censorship. Michael Nicholson of ITN, who sailed on *Hermes*, was told by an MoD spokesman: 'You must have known you couldn't report bad news before you left. You knew when you came you were expected to do a 1940 propaganda job.'

But when we are considering the way in which the media covered the Falklands, it would be unwise to draw any general conclusions. The winter war in the South Atlantic was a freakish one-off event, bizarre from beginning to end.

I first heard of it in the unlikiest of places—the Syrian city of Aleppo. Someone brought to the hotel a little English-language newsheet put out by the Syrian Government, and in it was a brief report from Tass that Mrs Thatcher had sent a 'war armada' to the South Atlantic. The English group I was with fell about laughing, refusing to take it seriously; and it was not until considerably later, when we were back in Jordan and could buy some British papers that we found that a task force had indeed sailed for the Falklands. This somewhat lunatic beginning gave the whole episode, in the early summer of 1982, an air of unreality.

One of the Thatcher Government's many shrewd moves was to make sure that not a single foreign journalist sailed with the task force. The war was reported exclusively by British correspondents, most of whom became so intimately involved with the young men who were fighting and dying in that freezing landscape that they were unable to retain their objectivity.

The rest of us, the foreign press and the defence correspondents who had not been able to sail with the task force, had to make do with the 'Whitehall Follies', the daily briefings at the Ministry of Defence, which were held in a large room dominated by a portrait of Lord Nelson.

The MoD added to the amenities as time went on, providing a mobile canteen, an outside Portaloo, and a bank of visual display units (VDUs) which spewed out reams of computerized information about the ships in the task force.

What was lacking most of the time, was news and pictures. Robert Harris, in *Gotcha! The Media, the Government and the Falklands Crisis*, wrote:

> The Falklands campaign came to be called 'the worst reported war since the Crimea.' Newspaper correspondents' dispatches from the task force often arrived in London too late to be used; some never arrived at all. The first still picture from the South Atlantic did not come through until 18 May, over three weeks late, and even then it turned out to be an embarrassingly naked propagandist photograph of the Union Jack being unfurled over South Georgia. Newspapers were forced to rely on artists' impression of what was happening...
>
> For television, the situation was, on occasion, marginally worse than it had been during the Crimea. In 1854 the Charge of the Light Brigade was graphically described in *The Times* twenty days after it took place. In 1982 some TV film took as long as twenty-three days to get back to London, and the average delay for the whole war, from filming to transmission, was seventeen days.

What obviously terrified the British Government from the beginning was that television coverage of the Falklands could prove as counter-productive to official policy, as was the case during the Vietnam war. (I was in Britain in 1968 when the BBC was running nightly film on the Tet offensive, and I remember vividly the shock that it caused, even in a country which was not directly involved in Vietnam.)

It was lucky for Thatcher and her War Cabinet that the situation in the South Atlantic could be controlled in a way which had rarely happened before, and is unlikely to happen again. The government ensured that all copy, all film, had to be transmitted by task force facilities, and these were very limited. Telex reports and voice transmissions were constantly subject to delays because the Ministry of Defence was able to say, with perfect truth, that the media was over-loading the circuits and interfering with vital military and naval transmissions.

Television crews found to their rage that all attempts to use satellite facilities were blocked and that the only way they could get their film out was to put it on a ship sailing in a leisurely way to Ascension Island. From there, it was flown to London; hence the average delay of seventeen days from filming to screening.

The lack of film added another sinisterly comic element to the war. Not only were the newspapers dragging old pen-and-ink artists out of retirement, but television was forced to illustrate what was happening with animated diagrams, in the style of Space Invaders.

Fascinated viewers sat before their screens night after night, as toy ships and aircraft darted busily about. It was a time of great glory for retired generals and admirals and military strategists, who stood in front of models with pointers, or held earnest armchair discussions with each other on what might (or might not) be about to happen in the next phase of the war. (This came to deeply irritate the Thatcher Government, especially when the guesses were too shrewd. Some of Britain's former top brass, the government pointed out irritably, were signalling to the enemy what the task force commander's next move might be.)

The lack of picture cover contributed to the feeling that Britain was fighting a clean, almost bloodless, Boys'-Own-Annual-type war. Even the task force commander, Rear Admiral Sandy Woodward, looked like every boy's ideal naval officer, clear-eyed and gung-ho. No wonder a reader wrote to the *London Standard*: 'My wife and I haven't enjoyed the news so much since 1945.'

(The Falklands even cropped up in advertising. Stan Laurel, on a poster in a liquor off-licence window: 'I'm off to the Falklands, Ollie.' Oliver Hardy: 'Port Stanley?' Laurel: 'Just a little, thanks, Ollie.')

It was not until television film arrived showing the sinking ships, the carnage at Goose Green, the men with ghastly burns stumbling ashore after the landing ships *Sir Galahad* and *Sir Tristram* were hit at Bluff Cove, that the British public realized at last that the country was involved in a real and bloody war. When the viewers saw the rows of bodies wrapped in plastic lying at the bottom of muddy mass graves, or the scenes in field hospitals with surgeons thrusting their hands into gaping wounds in men's bodies, enthusiasm began noticeably to wane.

In the early days of the war, however, it was undoubtedly the more jingoistic section of the press which generated an explosion of nineteenth-century patriotism. The most famous headline of the war was 'GOTCHA!' in Rupert Murdoch's *Sun*, celebrating the sinking of the Argentine cruiser *General Belgrano*. Even the *Sun* editor had second thoughts, however, and in later editions the headline was changed to 'DID 1200 ARGIES DIE?'

The *Sun* brought out a 'STICK IT UP YOUR JUNTA' tee-shirt, and ran headings like 'THE SUN SAYS KNICKERS TO ARGENTINA' and 'GARTERS TO THE TARTARS'. Pinup girls in the tabloids wore knickers embroidered with the names of ships in the task force, or indecently enhanced their nudity with steel helmets and toy rifles.

More soberly, the *Daily Mail* compared Mrs Thatcher to Winston Churchill. 'The time of trial has brought forward the leader of the hour,' it said.

All the papers were excited by the fact that the Queen's son, Prince Andrew, was serving with the task force, and was as much in danger as any other non-Royal pilot. 'Go and get 'em, Andy,' cried the *News of the World*.

Even the *Times* (admittedly by now another part of Murdoch's empire) jumped on the patriotic bandwagon. 'WE ARE ALL FALKLANDERS NOW', it proclaimed in a leader, pointing out that the British were an island race, and—somewhat inconsistently—quoting John Donne: 'No man is an island...'

The main dissenting voices raised were those of the *Guardian* and of the *Daily Mirror*. The *Guardian* ran a cartoon reproducing the famous Zec drawing of World War II which showed a sailor clinging to a raft in a storm-tossed sea. The original Zec caption had been 'The price of petrol has been increased by one penny', and was a reference to the high cost in lives of bringing fuel to beleaguered Britain. The *Guardian*'s 1982 caption read: 'The price of sovereignty has been increased—Official'.

The *Daily Mirror* also questioned the cost of the war in terms of lives, and this brought down on both papers the patriotic wrath of the *Sun*. The title of *its* leader was 'DARE TO CALL IT TREASON'.

There are traitors in our midst... What is it but treason for the *Guardian* to print a cartoon showing a British seaman clinging to a raft, above the caption 'The price of sovereignty has been increased—Official'? Isn't that exactly calculated to weaken Britain's resolve at a time when lives have been lost, whatever the justice of her cause?

Imagine a cartoonist who produced a drawing like that in Buenos Aires. Before he could mutter: 'Forgive me, Senors,' he would be put in front of a wall and shot.

The *Guardian*, with its pigmy circulation and absurd posturing, is perhaps not worth attention.

The *Daily Mirror*, however, has pretensions as a mass-sale newspaper.

What is it but treason for this timorous, whining publication to plead day after day for appeasing the Argentine dictators because they do not believe the British people have the stomach for a fight and are instead prepared to trade peace for honour?

We are truly sorry for the *Daily Mirror*'s readers. They are buying a newspaper which again and again demonstrates it has no faith in its country and no respect for her people.

This was a tactical mistake on the *Sun*'s part, for the *Daily*

Mirror struck back with a force which reverberated in The Street of Shame for months afterwards.

In a leader entitled 'THE HARLOT OF FLEET STREET', it called the *Sun* 'a coarse and demented newspaper'. Since the Falklands crisis began, the *Mirror* said, the *Sun* had fallen 'from the gutter to the sewer... The *Sun* today is to journalism what Dr Josef Goebbels was to truth. Even Pravda would blush to be bracketed with it.'

Over a year later, in August, 1983, the *Mirror* was able to publish the findings of the Press Council that the *Sun* had fabricated an interview with Mrs Marica McKay, widow of the Falklands VC winner Sergeant Ian McKay.

The *Sun*, said the Press Council, had practised 'a deplorable and insensitive deception on the public'.

'Lies, damned lies, and *Sun* Exclusives,' the *Mirror* cried gleefully, changing its previous metaphor to suggest that the *Sun* was to truth 'what the Borgias were to chastity,' having 'forgotten what it is'.

The *Sun* is a thick-skinned newspaper. Its editor, Kelvin MacKenzie, once refused an invitation from the Queen to discuss press coverage of the Princess of Wales over drinks at Buckingham Palace on the grounds that he was too busy.

It survived the row over its Falkland coverage and has steadfastly refused to apologize for it. In the election of 1983, it played an important part in returning Thatcher to power by its unequivocal support. 'More than any other leader since Churchill was baying defiance at the Nazis, she has captured the hearts, the minds and the imagination of this nation,' the *Sun* said in its election day editorial.

At a time when newspapers are declining in circulation and influence, and even the *Times*, the mighty Thunderer, is only an echo of its former self, it fascinates observers of the British media that the *Sun*, with its open vulgarity and its evocation of old-fashioned sentiments, still manages to touch a popular nerve. It is the same nerve which Thatcher touched so successfully, despite the jeers of the sophisticates, and which won her her early successes.

CHAPTER SEVENTEEN

BLOOD SPORTS AND OTHER BRITISH PASTIMES

The Eighties in Britain may very well go down as the Decade of the Mole. Red moles were burrowing away in the industrial heartland, Muscovite moles were hard at work in the espionage Establishment, and even the hunting field, the sacred preserve of Britain's blood sports brotherhood, was not safe from subterranean undermining.

One of the most famous moles of 1983 was a man called Michael Huskisson, an undercover agent of the League Against Cruel Sports, who, as Michael Wright—a blood sports enthusiast in flat cap and plus fours—followed the hounds on foot and took high-quality photographs which members of the hunt were pleased to have as souvenirs of a good day out. What they did not know was that Michael Wright, in his other persona, was a veteran member of the Hunt Saboteurs' Association, a man with a criminal record for releasing beagles from a laboratory, and for desecrating John Peel's grave.

When Wright/Huskisson's other photographs—not the ones he had presented to hunt members—were published, and some live and bloody segments were shown on television, the outcry against blood sports grew. They showed huntsmen dangling a living mink high in the air while

350

slavering hounds jumped for it, and another hunter holding the heart of a pregnant hind while the hounds tore at the carcase. Huskisson said that the hind had a calf at foot which was slaughtered with its mother. By hunting tradition, the heart was ripped out to give as a memento to the man on whose land the kill was made.

Hunting is becoming increasingly popular as a spectator sport in Britain; and hundreds of people who have no ambition to ride to hounds follow the huntsmen on foot or by car. Michael Huskisson said in an interview after his pictures were published that while some hunters simply wanted the excuse to ride in the countryside without looking too closely at what went on, there was now an element of what he called out-and-out hooligan animal thugs.

There have been accusations for years that living animals were being thrown to the hounds to excite them, and that foxes were trapped and taken to other parts of the country to provide a day's sport.

These charges have always been denied with some passion by the hunts, which claim that field sports in Britain have strict codes of conduct, and that anyone who breaches them is disciplined. But the hunting Establishment was shaken by the Huskisson pictures, especially those which show, on the faces under the flat caps, an unmistakeable excitement at the sight of blood.

The popularity of hunting as a spectator sport is being matched, in the Eighties, by the growth of organized opposition to blood sports. The League Against Cruel Sports now has the Labour Party firmly on its side, for it has pledged in its manifesto that the next Labour Government will abolish hunting. The Conservatives are also by no means as solid as they were, and in 1983, the Conservative Anti-Hunt Council was formed. The Tory move away from blood sports will be helped by the fact that the Prime Minister could probably think of no more time-wasting way of passing a day, and most of the New Tories in her

351

Cabinet would be of the same mind. Blood sports are an Old Tory pastime, at least in their more active form. (Spectators are another matter.)

The British attitude to animals traditionally puzzles less complex nationalities. A passion for slaughtering animals is nothing out of the way, though it is rare to carry it to such lengths as the British do. (A recent biography of King George V showed that he had had only two real interests in life: killing living creatures and collecting stamps. He kept a double-barrelled shotgun beside his bed so that he could exercise with it and improve his gun arm musculature. George VI, the Queen's father, spent the last day of his life—February 5 1952—shooting at Sandringham, and as the beaters drove the game towards the Royal party 280 hares were slaughtered. The King did not have time to record the 'bag' because he died that night, and the page in the Sandringham game book has been left vacant.)

What baffles foreigners is how the British can reconcile this liking for killing, usually carried out in a highly ritualistic manner, with a sentimentality about animals unmatched in the world. Dogs and cats and budgies dominate British interiors, and the horse reigns in the county world.

This solicitude extends far beyond the creatures normally thought of as the companions of man. A favourite cause of the early Eighties was the safety of hedgehogs, which were found to be having trouble negotiating cattle grids. A retired military officer in the Midlands, Major Adrian Coles, founded the British Hedgehog Preservation Society, dedicated not only to research into the animals but also to campaigning for built-in escape routes on cattle grids. In other countries, this might be taken for a joke, but not in Britain. The Greater London Council, which at that time was founding the Gay Teenagers Group and the English Collective of Prostitutes (but threatening to cut off funds from the Boy Scouts on the grounds that they were too militaristic), announced that it intended to help one more minority group by fitting the cattle grids in its area with hedgehog escape ladders. The arts and recreation committee was given the job of overseeing their installation.

Bat preservation laws were also brought in in the early Eighties, though these had a mixed reception. Most people like hedgehogs; not everybody cares for bats. Nevertheless, it is now illegal in Britain to disturb a bat in its roost (even in domestic attics or church belfries) or to handle one without a licence from the Nature Conservancy Council. Anyone breaking the bat preservation law is subject to a fine of £1,000 *per bat*. 'An Englishman's home is no longer his castle in relation to bats,' one of Britain's leading bat experts, Dr Robert Stebbings, said warningly. Nor his church either, according to some clergymen who wrote bitter letters to the *Times*, complaining that the present nuisance of bat droppings on altars was likely to get out of hand now that the creatures had been declared sacred.

Where else but in Britain would a beer firm take a whole page advertisement in the national dailies to wish good luck and good mating to a male panda from London Zoo who was setting out by air to woo a possible wife in Washington?

Where else would the uncooperative mate which he left behind him, London's female panda Ching Ching, be taken to the private wing of a leading hospital for a check-up when she lost her appetite?

The Tower of London has ravens on its payroll. They are there, according to tradition, to keep the Tower from crumbling away; and with their glossy black bodies and malevolent eyes, they add a touch of the macabre to give tourists a *frisson*. In 1981, the corps of ravens fell below strength, and a new recruit called Jason was brought from Cornwall. He travelled first class by rail, and was formally received at the Tower by the Deputy Warder, the Master of the Ravens, and an Army brigadier. It was the nicest animal story to surface since the one about President Carter being attacked by a giant swimming rabbit.

The British passion for animals even extends to stuffed

ones, as in the famous national cult of the teddy bear. Incredulous foreigners watch each year as middle-aged men and women hold teddy bears' picnics in parks, and a shabby bear still sits on many a cupboard top in an adult bedroom, watching marriage-bed proceedings with his beady eyes. The Iron Lady herself, Mrs Thatcher, has a bear called Humphrey and in the summer of 1983, she sent him to a rather posh teddy bear's picnic at Belvoir Castle, the seat of the Duke of Rutland. He travelled by train, and British Rail (which for years has been trying without success to lure the Prime Minister into making a railway journey) made a booking for him in the name of H. Bear and party. It is hard to imagine (say) President Mitterrand, or Chancellor Kohl, or Mrs Gandhi, or even President Reagan sending a bear off to a picnic.

The British have a strong liking for whimsy, possibly because it appears to provide an agreeable contrast to the violent passions of more volatile races. In 1983, the garden gnomes of Britain picketed the Chelsea Flower Show, in protest against the Royal Horticultural Society's 'no gnomes' prohibition. The RHS is an elitist body and considers garden gnomes vulgar, though why these cheerful little creatures with their fishing rods and lanterns should be out of place in a show which relies heavily on commercialism and which even allows, as one scandalized commentator pointed out, plastic herons, remains obscure.

The gnome-making industry of Britain organized the gnome protest, and it imported life-size specimens in concrete from Germany to head it. The outsize gnomes were supported by as many of the small, red-coated variety as could crowd at the railings, but the Royal Horticultural Society remained unmoved.

Intense sentimentality about animals is probably the reason why the animal liberation movements in Britain have proved unusually militant. And, in their turn, the genuine movements have thrown up fringe groups which engage in guerilla action damaging to the liberation cause.

The more respectable bodies have even suggested that some of the activities of the early Eighties were not the work of genuine liberationists, but of *agents provocateurs*.

In December 1982, a group calling itself the Animal Rights Militia sent letter bombs to the Prime Minister, and to the Leaders of the three opposition parties. A caller claiming to represent the Animal Rights Activists announced in the same month that turkeys and chickens on sale at Harrods and Woolworths had been injected with the weedkiller Paraquat. No trace was found of any toxic substance, but the single telephone call did its work. Hundreds of birds destined for the Christmas market were withdrawn from the stores, and forensic laboratories had to work overtime to test every one. None of the reputable groups had ever heard of either the Animal Rights Militia or the Animal Rights Activists, and the executive director of the League Against Cruel Sports called them 'crackpot loonies' who were damaging the very cause which they pretended to support.

After the letter bombs, it was feared that there would be an attack on some member of the Royal Family, royalty being traditionally addicted to blood sports. Even the young Princess of Wales has been induced to slaughter a stag; and there was a small scandal early in January 1984 when it was reported that five-year-old Peter Phillips, son of Princess Anne, had been seen playing with a freshly killed pheasant during a shoot at Sandringham. According to those who saw it, the boy's father, Captain Mark Phillips, took the still warm bird from his retriever's mouth and tossed it to his son who swung it round his head.

The animal guerillas have, so far, left the Royals prudently alone, though there are continual protests from the older animal welfare bodies about the bad example being set to the nation. One small irony is that Prince Philip, Duke of Edinburgh, is President of the World Wildlife Fund.

Militancy, however, continues to grow. In 1984, an anti-angling lobby has gone into action, and is working on the difficult problem of how to sabotage trout streams without harming the fish.

Even the Vegetarian Society has become militant. In the early Eighties, members picketed the Royal Smithfield meat markets' show at Earls Court, and exhibitors had to run the gauntlet of shouting protesters holding placards which proclaimed 'Meat is Murder'.

*   *   *   *   *   *

Militancy broke out in some other curious places in the Early Eighties. One of the most bizarre examples was a new terrorist group which emerged early in 1982, specializing in threats to university dons. It called itself the Organization for the Preservation of Freedom, and used an IBM golfball typewriter to send out its messages instead of the old-fashioned method of pasting up words from newspapers on sheets of paper.

The Organization for the Preservation of Freedom surfaced in Wales, which already has a number of protest organizations. But the OPF turned out to have nothing to do with nationalism, the use of the Welsh language, or burning down British holiday homes. Its members appeared to be something much more rare. They are defenders of Charles Darwin or, as one of the dons threatened, Professor Chandra Wickramasinghe of University College, Cardiff, put it, 'a perverted group of extreme right wing neo-Darwinists'.

Professor Wickramasinghe had a series of threatening phone calls from OPF, and he received an elegantly typed letter which said: 'Our previous warnings to you were merely to scare you, and you no doubt dismissed them as jokes. But jokes they were not. Now we mean business. You have three weeks to get out of Cardiff, or you and your family will regret the consequences.'

Professor Fred Hoyle, astronomer, academic, media

personality, science-fiction writer and black hole expert, also received threats; and the police and Special Branch took them seriously enough to provide protection for both men while the scare was on.

The appearance of this highly selective hit group was irresistible to connoisseurs of quirkiness, for most attacks before have come from the other side of the debate—from furious deists who see Darwin's theory of evolution as a threat to established religion.

Hoyle and Wickramasinghe seem to have upset the Darwinists with their book *A New Theory on the Origins of Life*, and with Wickramasinghe's public contention (as a witness in the so-called 'monkey trial' case in Little Rock, Arkansas in late 1981) that the Darwinist case is weak and non-factual. The random occurrence of life on earth was extremely unlikely, Wickramasinghe said during his evidence, and evolution should not be taught in schools as fact.

Hoyle went even further, claiming that life arose in outer space and came to Earth in the form of cometary material, or cosmic spores. He saw an intelligence behind this—not that of God, Architect of the Universe, but, more likely, that of a highly developed civilization which was threatened with extinction and which sought to preserve itself by sending off seminal material into the cosmos so that a derivative civilization might spring up.

Thus Hoyle and Wickramasinghe managed the neat trick of offending not only conventional Christians, but also the Darwinists, who saw these theories as attempting to destroy one of the most sacred tenets of twentieth-century thought, the concept of natural selection.

This story, however, has a happy ending. The sight of stalwart policemen guarding the two heretics was, presumably, too much for the OPF; and it passed away without much struggle into the limbo of lost protest movements.

The British have, in any case, a passion for lost causes.

The flourishing Fellowship of the White Boar, which has 2,500 members throughout Britain and abroad, is dedicated to rehabilitating Richard III—who for five hundred years has been given, so its members say, an undeservedly bad press. In 1983 (the five hundredth anniversary of Richard's accession) the present Duke of Gloucester gave the Fellowship the respectability which it had been craving for decades and became its president.

Riccardians are teachers, doctors, librarians, clergymen—anyone, in fact, who believes that Richard III was maligned, and that he was a virtuous man and a true king. They wear the Fellowship badge, which displays the White Boar (Richard's personal armorial sign); and, in extreme cases, male members adopt the hairstyle of the period.

Richard, in the Fellowship view, was the victim of Tudor propaganda, put out to justify his murder at Bosworth Field and to legitimize the slender right of his successors to the throne. Riccardians say that even the stories of his deformities are untrue. The portrait of the King at Windsor Castle showing one shoulder higher than the other has been X-rayed, and the uneven line is shown to have been added by a later hand.

The Fellowship, in the Eighties, has set out physically to refurbish Richard's image. A statue paying tribute to him as a soldier has been put up in Leicester, at a cost of £20,000. There is a new memorial to him in Leicester Cathedral; and Sutton Cheney Church, the nearest church to Bosworth Field, is kept permanently decorated in his honour with the white roses of York entwined with laurels.

The present Duke of Gloucester, also Prince Richard, has no doubt about his namesake's claim to rehabilitation. During his two-year reign, he says, Richard III was an enlightened king, who pushed through social legislation to benefit the poor and who founded ten colleges of education. He questions whether Richard of Gloucester murdered the little Princes in the Tower, as he does not think that it is in character. Richard was forgiving to his real enemies, and so was unlikely to slaughter children whose only crime was their existence. The Duke thinks that the little Princes either died naturally, or were given new identities to hide their origins. The stories of murder, deformity and degeneracy were probably written into history at the time of Henry VIII.

Ironically, a donation towards the Fellowship's funds has come from Lord Olivier—whose crookbacked, snarling Richard has done as much as anything to blacken his image in modern minds. The Riccardians are now working towards having the bones which are alleged to be those of the little Princes and which were found in the Tower exhumed and reexamined, in the hope of establishing their date and the cause of death.

During the early Eighties, other bones—nearly as old as those of the (presumed) little Princes in the Tower—presented a problem when Henry VIII's flagship, the *Mary Rose*, was raised from the floor of the sea. During the diving operations, skeletons of about 200 of her crew and/or of the fighting men who were on board when she sank four centuries ago were recovered, and the bones were brought on land. What then emerged was a nice little theological puzzle. When the *Mary Rose* went down in 1545, King Henry had already broken with the Pope over his divorce from Katherine of Aragon, but he had not yet reformed the liturgy. The Book of Common Prayer in English had not yet been published; and the Church of England, in its present-day form, had not emerged.

All the men on board the *Mary Rose* would have undoubtedly been baptized in the Church of Rome, but were on their way, whether they realized it or not, to becoming Anglicans. Should they be buried, therefore, when the time came (and after the forensic scientists had finished with their bones) as Roman Catholics or as Protestants?

There was also an argument, of course, about *how* the skeletons should be disposed of: on land, on sea, or in the crematorium ovens. Cremation was ruled out, as it was not customary in Tudor times; and so was sea burial, on the grounds that 200 skeletons in shrouds might foul the propellors of passing ships. It was finally decided that the sailors and fighting men should be buried on land, overlooking Spithead where the *Mary Rose* capsized and went down, with the loss of all on board. The ceremony will be a mixture of Roman Catholic and Anglican ritual. It will be a sung requiem, with the Ordinary of the Mass in Latin, but the Lessons and Lord's Prayer in English, with anthems by English composers. The actual interment, however, will be late twentieth century, using the Alternative Service Book.

Funeral rites have their own attraction in Britain—for just as the English garden excels all others, so does, in its own way, the English cemetery. Some European cemeteries may be grander; but for elegaic charm, there is nothing to equal the English churchyard, with its overgrown, mossy graves and its mournful willows. My favourite cemetery is Highgate in London. It is world famous as the burial place of Karl Marx, but it has many more attractions than that. I had never been to Highgate, even to make the obligatory visit to Karl Marx's grave, until 1981, when I saw by a discreet advertisement that the Friends of Highgate Cemetery were having an open day. This turned out to be a remarkable occasion. The Friends, most of them bearded men in corduroys or women with untidy hair and Shirley Williams accents, handed out leaflets pinpointing the most rewarding graves or dispensed teas at trestle tables.

I learned that Marx is not buried in the 'old' section of the cemetery but across the road in the 'new' section. He is incongruously interred among the Christian crosses and the marble angels. Because of Marx, the 'new' section is a place of pilgrimage. Russians come in busloads, Chinese in marching squads.

The Marx grave is dominated by the massive bearded head on top of a pedestal, above the legend, which says 'ALL PHILOSOPHIES HAVE ONLY INTERPRETED

THE WORLD IN VARIOUS WAYS. THE POINT HOWEVER IS TO CHANGE IT.' On the day I was there, fourteen identical bunches of florists' flowers were at the base of the pedestal. Whoever delivered them had not even bothered to take off the wrappings, and they lay in a rain-sodden heap.

The 'old' side of the cemetery is far more interesting. It was originally a private enterprise, opened in 1839 in the grounds of what was previously an old manor house on the outskirts of London. The cemeteries in London itself were overcrowded, and there were vague fears of an epidemic because of corpses poisoning the water supply. In 1975, the owners, United Cemeteries Ltd, closed down the 'old' part as it too had no more room for burials—and, not knowing what else to do with an unwanted property, passed the rights to Camden Council. Faced with a repairs bill of £1 million to preserve the graves, and annual upkeep, of £50,000, the Council rapidly backed off. So, with the competence that the English can display when their passions are engaged, the Friends of Highgate Cemetery came into being and bought the land—thirty-seven acres of prime real estate with splendid views—for £50. They hope the Council will eventually take over the upkeep, but in the meantime, parties of volunteers are chopping back the foliage which is smothering the graves, though in fact its overgrown condition is part of its charm.

It is one of the most beautiful places in London, studded with famous names, and with a stunning collection of Victorian funereal architecture. The centrepiece is the Egyptian-inspired Catacombs: long, mysterious avenues of above-ground vaults, with chained, creaking doors, and sinister apertures through which the brave may squint. It is said that a witches' coven uses it after dark, and that necrophiliacs haunt it. Before the Friends took over, film companies used to make horror movies there, but this is now strongly discouraged. The movies drew after them undesirable visitors. 'They started by stealing lead from the coffins, then they started stealing people,' our guide said ominously.

Dante Gabriel Rosetti buried his young wife Elizabeth Siddal in the Highgate cemetery (though not in the Catacombs) when she died of tuberculosis. He also buried some of his poems with her. And then, regretting it, he was moved some years later to dig up the corpse and recover the poems. The exhumation was after dark, and when the coffin lid was taken off, Lizzie's long red hair (famous in pre-Raphaelite paintings) had grown and filled the entire coffin. It glowed in the lantern light like a fire—or so our guide said, adding with a disarming smile that we did not have to believe it if we did not want to.

*   *   *   *   *   *

Balancing this charm and whimsy is the darker side of the British character. Britain, a nation which spends an enormous amount of sentiment on animals (when it is not killing them), is notorious for its ill-treatment of children. Apart from the atrocious cases of domestic cruelty, which are dealt with by the courts or the National Society for the Prevention of Cruelty to Children, the ritual beating of children in schools (particularly public schools) remains a source of amazement to foreigners.

Flagellation is, of course, *le vice anglais*, and, as the *New Statesman* said in a leader on the subject in 1983, flagellomania is embedded in the British psyche.

The pressure group STOPP (Society of Teachers Opposed to Physical Punishment) published a report called 'A Quarter of a Million Beatings' in 1981, and followed it up in 1983 with another called 'Once Every 19 Seconds'. It says that there are now 1,256 beatings a day in British schools, or about 238,688 a year. STOPP has published a table of the 'Top Twenty Beating Schools' which includes, among others, a Roman Catholic boys school in Manchester which averages 176 beatings for every 100 boys.

STOPP says children there are caned for relatively minor offences including unpunctuality and poor work, and many are beaten over and over again.

The European Court of Human Rights wants Britain to come into line with most of the other European countries which do not permit school children to be beaten, but so far it has not had much success in applying pressure.

In 1983, the Court awarded compensation to two Scottish families whose children had been penalized over flogging. One was a Fife boy who was barred from school for two terms for refusing to submit to being beaten with the 'tawse', the leather strap which is the Scottish equivalent of the cane. The boy, then 21, appealed to the Court on the grounds that his educational prospects had been affected. He was awarded £3,000, with £8,800 in costs to his mother. The other boy was threatened with the cane but he was not actually beaten, and his mother was awarded £940 costs to cover her appeal to the Court. Announcing its verdict, the Court said that it was a violation of human rights for children to be physically punished without the parents' permission. All this failed to impress the British educational authorities, which saw it as another example of interference from across the Channel in Britain's sovereign right to conduct its own affairs as it chooses.

However, the Thatcher Government at last reluctantly agreed that it should perhaps take some notice of the Court's ruling. In future, there will be two types of school children: those who can still be flogged, and those who cannot because their parents disapprove of corporal punishment. This solution found favour with nobody and the leader writers called it a preposterous and unworkable solution. The public schools will undoubtedly be reluctant to outlaw beatings, especially in those where the task of flogging is largely handed over to the older boys. It is interesting that flagellation is, on the whole, an upper-class taste.

The taste for murder is more universal. 'Britain has the

best murders in the world,' says the playwright John Mortimer, who in his other persona is a criminal lawyer. I have heard news editors describe ordinary murders (domestic upsets, crimes of passion, drunken assaults and so on) as 'fish-and-chippy'. Britain may have its share of fish-and-chip murders, but it also has an unusual number of the caviar kind.

A fascinating aspect of the British character is the national penchant for multiple murder. The ability of the murderers to get away with it for so long may also be linked with other British characteristics: the secretiveness, the ability to wear masks, the dislike of nosy-parkering.

Two truly spectacular mass murderers kept the tabloid headline writers in business in the early Eighties. Both of them broke the previous record which was held by John Christie, the necrophiliac killer of whores, who turned Number 10 Rillington Place, London, into a charnel house in the late Sixties. (The house itself became such a magnet for ghouls that it was eventually demolished, and the street renamed. Look for Rillington Place in the London street directory and you will not find it.)

Peter Sutcliffe, better known as the Yorkshire Ripper, also had a mission to kill prostitutes; but by the time the police caught him, he had reached the stage where he regarded any woman alone on the streets at night as a legitimate target. His last three victims were a girl walking home at night after visiting her family, and two university students. He attacked four more women, but these survived.

There was a touch of necrophilia about some of the killings, an echo of the Christie murders. In one case, Sutcliffe returned to a woman's body ten days after her death to mutilate it, and in another, he came back a month after the killing to put a newspaper under his victim's arm.

The breast of one of his victims had been bitten, giving the police one of their few clues: the man they wanted had a gap between his front teeth. Only one woman was sexually assaulted, so it was quite likely that the killer was not seeking sexual gratification. Using a hammer and a screwdriver, he mutilated his victims, and also carried out a three-part ritual (police never disclosed what it was, for fear of emulators) after their deaths.

The Sutcliffe case raised all sorts of fascinating side-issues, from women's rights to press ethics. Feminists were angry about the distinction made between Sutcliffe's 'respectable' victims and the women he killed earlier, and there were suggestions that society takes the deaths of prostitutes lightly, considering they are in a high-risk occupation. 'Respectable' girls are a different matter. They have relatives and friends who can lobby MPs and demand more police action. After the death of the thirteenth victim, radical feminists went out on the streets of Leeds demonstrating against the apparent inability of the police to catch the Ripper, and the organization 'Women Against Violence Against Women' called (unsuccessfully) for a curfew for men in the Ripper's territory unless they were accompanied by women.

The Sutcliffe case also put into question the general competence of the British police. The hunt for the Ripper stretched over five years, and cost yearly £4 million. Despite the expensive manhunt, which strained the resources of the West Yorkshire force, Sutcliffe in the end was caught by pure accident, by a couple of vice squad police patrolling an area of Sheffield where prostitutes were known to take their clients. When they checked the number plates of a car in which Sutcliffe had been sitting with a woman, they found they had been stolen, and it was on that charge that he was originally arrested. It was later found that Sutcliffe had been interviewed at least nine times by detectives in their general check-up on men in the Ripper's area, and that his car was logged forty-six times in red light districts. Some of the Identikit pictures clearly fitted his face, so much so that his workmates made jokes about him being the Ripper; and one of his acquaintances went to the police and said bluntly that he was suspicious of Sutcliffe. But the police ignored all these leads.

When Sutcliffe came to trial at the Old Bailey the nagging question arose, not for the first time, as to whether a man who has killed and mutilated thirteen women can be considered sane. Sutcliffe and his counsel did their best to prove that he was not, claiming that voices which he had heard in a graveyard had given him instructions to seek out and murder prostitutes. At the same time, he had continued to live an ordinary suburban life. He worked as a lorry driver and lived in a comfortable two-storey house in a village near Bradford with his wife, Sonia, performing all the usual rituals of Sunday visits to his own family and to his in-laws. His relatives and most of his friends remain incredulous to this day that behind the mask of the dutiful husband they knew there could be a multiple murderer.

The jury at the Old Bailey refused to accept the plea of insanity, and Sutcliffe was found guilty of murder and sentenced to life. This immediately caused problems for the State, for murderers who prey on women and child molesters are difficult to fit into the routine of an ordinary prison. In the past, prisoners with records far less frightful than Sutcliffe have had to be kept in separate sections with their own special guards.

In fact, two years after he was sentenced, Peter Sutcliffe appeared in Newport Magistrates' Court with a badly scarred face. He had been slashed by another prisoner with a piece of broken glass, and the three wounds had needed eighty-four stitches to close them. In his court appearance, he displayed the pious self-righteousness that seems not uncommon in murderers. The other prisoners did not understand him, he said, and called him nasty names, but he did not bear them any grudges. 'There is a lot wrong with society today,' he said confidingly to the Bench. 'It's depraved. All they think about is money and finances. There are no moral values.' He was still hearing his 'voices', Sutcliffe said. They gave him advice when he was depressed.

In 1984, Sutcliffe was moved from Parkhurst prison to Broadmoor, an asylum for the criminally insane. Despite the verdict of the jury at his trial, he has now been diagnosed as suffering from paranoid schizophrenia, and was claimed by Parkhurst prison officers to be a danger to staff and inmates.

The Sutcliffe case also brought up the question of press responsibility and ethics (or otherwise) of cheque-book journalism. Sutcliffe was tried, convicted, and (metaphorically) hanged before he ever stood in the dock at the Old Bailey. While Sutcliffe was being questioned, and before he was sent for trial, the nation's television screens were full of pictures of police officers congratulating themselves on the fact that the search for the Ripper was over, and interviews with Sutcliffe's neighbours and family. Two scared and skinny prostitutes who had been approached by Sutcliffe before his arrest were also interviewed, even though they were likely to be witnesses at his trial.

Legal experts were scandalized by the media coverage of the case, saying that there were a number of instances of clear contempt. Not only had witnesses been interviewed, but a photograph of the accused man had been published. Almost all newspapers linked Sutcliffe with the whole Ripper series of murders, though no legal connection had been established. A specimen of Sutcliffe's handwriting had been published, though handwriting could be a link in the prosecution case.

The contempt was so clearly established that it was believed the Sutcliffe case would become a watershed, and the government would take the opportunity to move against the offending editors and television producers. It was indeed a watershed, but mainly because the media got away with it, showing up the contempt laws as weak and ineffective. The Sutcliffe case pushed the boundaries of what is permissible a good deal further out, with possible future consequences for the traditional British concept of an accused person being considered innocent until proved guilty. The coverage of the Ripper murders was much more in the American style of 'anything goes'.

During the period Sutcliffe was awaiting trial, every person remotely connected with him was offered staggering sums for their 'exclusive' stories. The prize target was Sonia Sutcliffe, the accused man's wife, who turned down all offers, though she could have named her own figure. It was a vintage year for cheque-book journalism; and a number of complaints were made to the Press Council, which delivered its usual rap over the knuckles and pious cries of dismay. This achieved very little, and cheque-book journalism flourishes as part of the British way of life.

One consequence, however, has been a stiffening in the demand for reform of the Press Council itself. Since late 1983 it has had a new chairman, the former Australian Governor-General Sir Zelman Cowen, but what it wants is some new teeth.

The other spectacular murder case of the Eighties had echoes of the Christie affair too, in that it featured the disposal of bodies in a suburban house—or, to be exact, two houses: one in the North London suburb of Cricklewood, and one in Hornsey not far away.

At 195 Melrose Avenue, Cricklewood, and in a flat at Cranley Gardens, Hornsey, a 37-year-old civil servant and former policeman, Dennis Andrew Nilsen, killed fifteen men and dissected, boiled and burned their bodies, flushing chunks of human flesh down the lavatory.

The Nilsen case pointed up two things: one was the extraordinarily isolated nature of the British household, when a solitary murderer can turn a domestic interior into a slaughterhouse without anyone noticing. Until a plumber was called to unblock a drain (he found lumps of human flesh in it), the neighbours had remained unaware of what was happening, though there had been some complaints about the number of bonfires which Nilsen lit in his back garden. The other revealing aspect of the case was the illumination which it threw into the shadowy world of the 'missing persons', the young drifters who leave their homes and families in the provinces and disappear into the great maw of London. In 1983, when the Nilsen case was being heard, there were 6,683 people reported missing in London. Of these, 2,000 were boys and girls between fourteen and seventeen. Many thousands more are never reported to police.

It was in this world that Nilsen found his victims. He picked them up in pubs, usually using his dog Bleep who accompanied him everywhere as an excuse to strike up a conversation. He took them home with him for drinking sessions, and in his statement to police he said that if they listened to him and were willing to enter into discussions on politics or any other subject which currently interested him, he let them live. If they fell into a drunken sleep, he strangled them, usually with one of his own ties. That was how he kept count. 'I started with fifteen ties, at the end I had only one left, a clip-on,' he told police.

Like Sutcliffe, Nilsen was something of a ritualist. When his victims were dead, he washed and powdered their bodies, and compared them with his own in a mirror. Then he butchered them, using skills which he had mastered in the Army catering corps. Apart from pieces of flesh in the drains, police found two severed heads in the flat at Cranley Gardens.

Nilsen was described at his trial by psychiatrists as a man drowning in his own nightmares. There was one ghastly story of how, when he went with his dog Bleep for a walk, he took with him a carrier bag full of human organs, which he left on the footpath. A passer-by found it and took it to a police station. What the police said when they opened it remained unrecorded.

Nilsen was basically homosexual, though he had had relations with women; but he told police that after the first killing he was no longer able to have sexual relations. He described himself as 'a creative psychopath who lapses into a destructive psychopathic condition induced by rapid and heavy ingestion of alcohol'.

His counsel, asking the jury to return a verdict of manslaughter on the grounds of diminished responsibility, put it more simply. Anybody capable of such horrific acts as boiling heads and parts of bodies on the kitchen stove must, he said, be out of his mind. The jury, however, did not agree. As in the case of Peter Sutcliffe, they refused to accept insanity as an excuse, and in November 1983 Nilsen was sentenced by a judge at the Old Bailey to life for murder, with a recommended minimum sentence of twenty-five years.

Police were able to discover the identity of only some of his victims. Families in the provinces with missing children may still be wondering if their sons are among the vanished ones.

Nilsen said that he came in the end to care only for his dog which must, one can only assume, have been a silent witness to what was happening in those grisly interiors. When Nilsen was arrested, Bleep was taken to the Battersea Dogs' Home where, in the classic tradition of faithful dogs, he lay down and died within three weeks.

This sad little story undoubtedly moved the readers of both the tabloids and the glossies more than the fate of Nilsen's unknown victims.

CHAPTER EIGHTEEN

WHAT SORT OF BRITAIN?

The past is another country: so is the future.

What happens to Britain in the late Eighties and in the Nineties depends to a large extent on the state of the world economy, into which it is inextricably enmeshed. But futurologists are already hard at work sketching out predictions for the next two decades, and into the next century.

The guessing game started at the beginning of the Eighties, when the two favoured scenarios were the Ruritanian Solution and the Eastern European Outline.

In 1981, the *Times* ran a piece called 'Ruritania, Here We Come', advancing the theory that Britain would eventually become a vast museum, staging, with the aid of the Royal Family, archaic and splendid spectacles for tourists to gawk at. This view was echoed by a businessman who said to me at about that time that Britain would shortly be kept afloat 'only by North Sea Oil and tourism'.

The Eastern European scenario arose out of what seemed to be the likelihood of a hard Left takeover of the Labour Party. The Bennites, the Right said, were intent on turning Britain into some sort of grey version of an Eastern European bloc state, dominated by an all-powerful Party.

At that time, I talked to the former editor of the *Times*, Sir William Rees-Mogg, who pushed the idea even further and suggested a new concept: the Chilean Solution. He agreed with the idea that a hard Left government might come to power in Britain, and said that this would upset so many people (he cited the readers of the *Daily Telegraph*, who are a bulwark of British conservatism) that there would be a right-wing coup.

This would draw in groups like skinheads and the fascist Right 'There are more potential Blackshirts about in the early Eighties than I have seen before in my lifetime,' Rees-Mogg said.

The decline of the hard Left and the resurgence of Thatcherism had, within a couple of years, taken the edge off these dramatic predictions. Futurologists still believe, however, that until there is a marked upturn in the British economy, the nation is walking along a dangerous path.

The continuing division of Britain into two nations, North and South, is in itself an ominous sign. James Bellini forecasts a future of high tech centres in the South, surrounded by low tech villages, from which skilled workers commute by steam train. Their leisure will be spent in traditional craft work, and the villages will also include non-commuters who will earn a living as craftsmen, professional rather than amateur. These, Bellini says, will be the lucky ones in the employment zones of the future, about 2010 AD.

But to the North, there will be vast regions of desolation, with ruined factories and rusting machinery. (There are areas like this already; I have seen them.) Activity will be congregated round the agri-centres, and around data-base, high tech complexes, rearing like mediaeval castles among the relics of industrial Britain. 'Outside the privileged villages and the centres of real economic influence, unemployment is of epidemic proportions, ravaging the illiterate population in true Black Death style, says Bellini in *Rule Britannia*.

Dr John Eatwell, a Fellow in Economics at Trinity College, Cambridge, is only marginally less alarmist. In a BBC program called 'Beyond 1984', he forecast the destruction of large sectors of Britain's manufacturing industry over the next decade, and unemployment rising to five million by 1993.

Britain, Dr Eatwell says, is in the grip of de-industralization. Between 1979-81, 1.6 million jobs disappeared in Britain, and 80 per cent of them were in manufacturing.

As conditions worsen, the Army will be called in 'as Britain's social fabric is consumed in the flames of economic despair'.

A more sober warning has come from a source which frightened the Conservatives, because the prophet of doom was not a radical, but an unassailable figure of the Establishment. Sir John Hoskyns has been in turn a professional soldier, a successful businessman, and, from 1979 to 1982, head of the Prime Minister's own policy unit at Number 10 Downing Street.

At the annual dinner of the Institute of Directors in September 1983, Hoskyns outraged his audience by predicting that unless new blood was brought into government and the civil service, Britain would slowly drop out of the industrialized western world:

> Over the past 30 years, we have suffered the consequences of a massive failure of intelligence and nerve on the part of an inbred political establishment... For the purposes of government, a country of 55 million people is forced to depend on a talent pool which could not sustain a single multi-national company. Indeed, it is extraordinary that such a systems seems, nevertheless, regularly to produce quite remarkable individuals. But there are rarely enough of them to build a remarkable government. And, these days, we need remarkable governements...
>
> I do not believe that the antique conventions, culture and machinery which failed us between 1950 and 1980 will somehow succeed between 1980 and 2000.

Hoskyns urged that the Prime Minister should bring

talented outsiders into government and the civil service, and spoke scathingly of professional politicans who became amateur ministers, burdened with impossible workloads and moving from one unfamiliar brief to another. The government would have to find a solution to its problems quickly, he said, as North Sea oil would begin to run out, leaving it sitting on a series of economic time bombs.

There is also, of course, the theory that Britain will be taken over by the Japanese. There is already a small but bright galaxy of Japanese firms blazing away in Britain, pioneering new methods of industrial relations and setting new production records.

A survey in 1983 identified twenty-five Japanese companies in the United Kingdom, most of them set up in areas of high unemployment, where they are providing badly needed new jobs. (They are also taking advantage of the government's grant of 22 per cent towards the cost of new buildings, plants and equipment, which is available to firms establishing themselves in what are euphemistically called 'Special Development Areas'.)

Using Japanese management techniques and advanced technology, they are revolutionizing lagging British productivity, though overall it is still about 10 per cent lower than in Japan. The first of the Japanese firms, YKK Fasteners, was set up in Cheshire in 1972 to manufacture zips. Now the emphasis is on colour television, videos, and hi-fi equipment, but Japanese-run firms are also making anything from fine worsted to fishing tackle.

The 'Japanese phenomenon' is increasingly being mentioned with envy in British boardrooms; and in 1983, Durham University Business School ran a seminar on the Art of Japanese Management for fifty British middle managers.

The unions have proved surprisingly amenable to the Japanese management's refusal to tolerate a number of unions in a plant. The Japanese believe, probably rightly, that rigid demarcation practices and the consequent lack of flexibility is a symptom if not a cause of the British disease.

The Sanyo Industries (UK) Ltd plant at Lowestoft in Suffolk provides a classic example of Japanese tactics. When Sanyo took over from Phillips, there were seven recognized unions and two or three unofficial ones.

Now there is only one, the Electrical Electronic Telecommunications and Plumbing Union, which has signed a no-strike agreement with management. As well as incorporating all the workers into one union, Sanyo has also introduced 'status harmonization', which means that everyone from the managing director to the office workers and apprentices wears the same specially designed uniform and eats in the same canteen.

Sanyo claims that it used to take British workers 6.1 hours to assemble a television set, compared to 1.9 hours in Japan. The process now takes less than one hour, the exact number of minutes being a trade secret.

The rest of British industry is not sure yet whether to be critical or envious. But it looks as though the Japanese presence is firmly embedded in Britain, and anxieties over a possible Japanese takeover are stirring in the national psyche. When Dunlop sold off 25 per cent of its tyre division to Sumitomo Rubber Industries in 1983, the company felt obliged to put full page ads in the national press, explaining plaintively that the deal was a comparatively small one, and that the British should not run away with the idea that 'Dunlop has been sold to the Japanese, lock, stock and tennis racquet'.

* * * * * *

The Ruritarian Solution still has its defenders. Tourism is a massive foreign currency earner for Britain, though the sheer volume of visitors is now becoming an embarrassment. London in the summer is now so crowded that during the early Eighties, groups of irate Londoners started pursuing the idea of an anti-tourist organization.

Ingenious ideas for luring tourists to areas which have so far missed out on the boom are being floated.

We have already seen that Glasgow is running a hard-sell promotion, as is Ulster. Liverpool has a continuing bonanza with Beatles tours; and in 1984, any place remotely connected with George Orwell can be sure of a steady flow of pilgrims. Most unlikely of all, the town which Orwell made infamous in *The Road to Wigan Pier* is cashing in on the Orwell boom.

Orwell wrote of 'monstrous scenery of slag-heaps, chimneys, piled scrap iron, foul canals, paths of cindery mud criss-crossed by the print of clogs'. And of domestic interiors: '...labyrinthine slums and dark black kitchens with sickly, ageing people creeping round them like black-beetles'.

Undeterred by all this, Wigan council announced plans in late 1983 to spend well over £2 million redeveloping the Wigan pier area to attract business, industry, and tourists with Orwellian tastes. Ironically enough, though, there has never been an actual pier at Wigan. What the locals referred to as a pier was simply a wharf stretching out into the Leeds and Liverpool canal.

If Britain is to become one vast museum, its main attraction will be (apart from the Royals and their arcane ceremonials) its great houses. Probably no other European country has such a diversity of magnificent country houses so easily accessible within a comparatively small area.

The recession of the early Eighties caused dismay in the stately home business, as the number of visitors dropped sharply away. This was especially so in the period when Americans were staying away in large numbers because of the unreal exchange rate between sterling and the dollar.

However, business picked up as the world recession eased, and more and more houses are being opened to visitors. Unfortunately for good taste, it seems that a beautiful and historic house is not itself a sufficient magnet, and some of the most remarkable examples of country house architecture in Britain are now surrounded by fun fairs, motor museums and safari parks.

House ownership has become a new form of show business. Knights in armour on horseback can be enountered in parks which once were roamed only by deer; and archery contests, concerts and fetes take place all through the summer. Madame Tussauds waxworks has taken over Warwick Castle, one of the most famous castles in Britain, and has staged an 'Edwardian country house weekend' there, with the aid of cunning examples of the wax modeller's art. Every country house has a gift shop filled with mass produced 'country craft' objects, each shop an exact copy of the one before.

The delicate minded wince when they see this widespread evidence of vulgarization, but the owners of country houses claim that they are making heroic efforts to save Britain's architectural legacy against enormous odds. (The Duke of Bedford, most famous of the showmen-aristos, had to pay off the then equivalent of US dollars 8 million in estate duties when his father, the old Duke, died.)

A report in 1982 by the conservation group 'Save Britain's Heritage' showed that owners are not always winning the struggle. Between the end of World War I and the end of World War II, 459 country houses were knocked down. Those who assumed that this could not happen again in the present super-sensitive climate were staggered by the report, which showed that another 595 historic houses have been lost since 1945, some of them dating from the thirteenth century. 'Save Britain's Heritage' has published a photographic record of 'the tragic progression' of the vanishing houses of England in an attempt to save any more falling to the wrecker's ball.

* * * * * *

Britain has more problems looming up in the next two decades, however, than the economy or vanishing country houses. It must face up to three major dilemmas, each affecting both domestic and foreign policies. Each concerns a territory outside mainland Britain.

The first is the closest and most urgent: Ulster. Although at first glance it is a domestic problem, it has strong foreign policy elements because it affects Britain's relations with the Republic of Ireland, the United States and NATO.

In the short term, there are two obvious possibilities. One is that the European Community may interfere more than it has done so far, and bring pressure on Britain to make concessions to Sinn Fein and to the government in Dublin. The other is that an incoming Labour or coalition government might hand over the problem to the United Nations, which would send in a peace-keeping force. This 'solution' to the Ulster problem has already been floated, but the prospect sends both Unionists and Republicans into a frenzy.

The second dilemma for Britain in the mid-to late Eighties is the future of the Falkland Islands, though this could be more easily dealt with if Margaret Thatcher is overthrown by her Party or if she leaves office. It is Thatcher who is strongly wedded to the concept of Fortress Falklands, not the bulk of the Conservative Party. It was she who told a crowd in Downing Street when she announced the Argentine surrender: 'Today has put the Great back into Britain,' and there is no reason to believe that she has so far changed her mind.

The Falklands have immense personal significance for Thatcher. Politically, the war in the South Atlantic halted the reverse in her fortunes and sent her soaring upwards in the polls. They turned her into a war leader, brought her the admiration of Britain's allies, and gave her a dream of restoring Britain's stature in the world.

The concept of Fortress Falklands is far more difficult to sustain, however, now that the military junta in Argentina has left the stage and been replaced by a civilian government which is adopting a much softer and more conciliatory line. Even if Thatcher's dislike of any form of negotiation continues to gain domestic support, Britain is likely to be seen as being intransigeant by the rest of the world (including its most important ally, the United States) unless it moderates its position.

The cost of keeping the Falklands British is being increasingly questioned. In 1983, garrisoning the islands cost £400 million. Over three years, the total cost is expected to be £1 billion, and this does not take into account replacing the ships and planes and equipment lost by the armed services.

The official figures in any case, have been queried— notably by the School of Peace Studies at Bradford University. Dr Paul Rogers, a senior lecturer at Bradford, has said that the government is downplaying the statistics, and that the actual cost is now close to £1 billion a year.

Late in 1983, the anti-Fortress Falklands lobby had an unexpected convert: the former Secretary of State for Defence, John Nott (now Sir John), himself a member of Thatcher's War Cabinet, the man who stood beside her in Downing Street when she cried 'Rejoice!' over the first British victory.

Maintaining a large garrison in the Falklands was 'a nonsense', and the policy horrified him, Nott said in an interview. Ideally, Britain's presence should be limited to a small base on South Georgia, which could also serve its economic interests in Antarctica. 'What I deplore so much is that we simply cannot afford another peripheral defence commitment,' Nott said, adding gloomily that he could not, however, see a way out of the present impasse.

The ironic thing about the whole Falklands episode is that though the war was fought, according to Thatcher, to defend the islanders' way of life, yet the aftermath of the conflict is in fact destroying it.

Most Falklanders live in these lonely and uncomfortable islands because they prefer solitude, isolation and rural simplicity. Now they find themselves a part of a garrisoned

British base in the South Atlantic, the site for a strategic airport due to open in the mid-to late Eighties, and overrun by lonely and potentially lascivious soldiery and tough, hard-drinking construction workers.

The Falklands Development Corporation is paying a chief executive £33,000 a year to encourage immigration. There is talk of developing a major fishing industry round the islands, and speculation about oil exploration against the day when the North Sea fields run dry. Small entrepreneurs of the sort beloved of the Thatcher government are flying in to set up enterprises ranging from fish-and-chip shops to woollen mills. There are even reports of union disputes on the islands, with local shepherds and the construction workers on the £215 million airport threatening to strike for more pay.

Thatcher and her War Cabinet may have saved the Falklanders from becoming Argentinian, but the South Atlantic operation has shattered their way of life forever.

* * * * * *

Britain's third problem is Hong Kong. At the beginning of the Eighties, this looked conveniently far away both geographically and in the time scale. No need to worry, anybody thought, until nearer 1997, when Britain must hand over the colony to China.

The Thatcher government did make one careful move. By passing the Nationality Act, it has ensured that there will be no great flood of Hong Kong Chinese into Britain, however unhappy these former British citizens may be about becoming involuntary citizens of a communist republic. Britain does not want them, and will keep them out.

But Britain is responsible for Hong Kong until 1997, and it is already seeing the colony's prosperity eroded by lack of confidence in the future, and endangered by a flight of capital.

A veteran Asia-watching journalist, Murray Sayle, forecast early in 1984 that the wealthy (numbering about 40,000) will be gone from Hong Kong before 1997.

The majority of Hong Kong Chinese will have to stay and hope for the best, but Sayle says that there are about half a million western-educated Chinese in all the professions who are likely to emigrate if they can find somewhere to go. These people will start moving out as soon as they can.

Another obvious problem arises with Hong Kong. The present regime in Peking, under the master pragmatist Deng Xiaoping, is obviously willing to make concessions and to allow the colony to retain many of the more useful features of capitalism when it becomes part of China.

But Deng cannot live forever, and as he moves into his eighties, he may not continue to keep his tight grip on the radicals. Another Cultural Revolution in China would mean, as the last one did, violent upheavals in Hong Kong—but this time with much more serious consequences.

It is hard at this stage to predict what the popular reaction in Britain would be to any serious challenge to the nation's sovereignty in any of its remaining outposts. When I left London at the end of 1983, the mood of national exultation over victory in the Falklands had faded, but echoes of it were still unmistakeably there.

Even in the Labour Party, a hankering after the old days of imperial grandeur lingers on. Those who call for withdrawal from the EEC unconsciously express it, wanting Britain to be an independent sovereign nation again instead of part of the European economic jigsaw. 'We are a world power and a world influence, or we are nothing,' Harold Wilson said when Labour came back to office in 1964; and two decades after, this concept still runs through much political thinking on the Left and on the Right.

It has been left to a few lonely voices to call on Britain, as the left-wing historian E. P. Thompson did in 1983, to 'happily resign ourselves to leaving behind forever the pretensions of a great power, leaving the world to say of our imperial past, as Malcolm said of the old Thane of Cawdor, "nothing in his life became him like the leaving of it"'.

Another historian, A. J. P. Taylor, whom I interviewed in the early Eighties, agreed. It was a mistake, he said, for Britain to pretend any longer to be a great power. A retreat from greatness was inevitable, and it was wise for the country to make peace with necessity.

* * * * * *

But is Britain's future really so frightful as the futurologists suggest?

During the years I lived in London in the early Eighties, overseas visitors were always complaining that Britain was not what it used to be.

So it is not. I think in many ways it is better.

If the class system still exists, it is slowly breaking down, and this process will accelerate in an era of high social mobility.

Britain is becoming a multi-cultural society; and despite the fears engendered by the riots of 1981, the generally high level of tolerance in the British character will, with luck, allow such a new society to be born without too many bloody birth pangs.

When I talked to that ancient sage A. J. P. Taylor in his summer home in an old mill on the Isle of Wight, he was unimpressed by the summer riots of that year. The eighteenth century in Britain, he said, plucking one example from history, was a very violent era. The sports of the time were cockfighting and bullbaiting, and at public executions, the mobs fought with medical students for the bodies of hanged men. (The students wanted the bodies for dissection, the crowd wanted to amuse themselves by tearing them to pieces.) That doesn't happen in the Eighties.

In 1831, Taylor said, rioters burned down the Bristol

Town Hall, the courts of justice, and the Judge's residence, because they were fed up with the slow progress of the Reform Bill. In 1887, socialists and trade unionists fought a pitched battle in Trafalgar Square with police over the right of free assembly. In Liverpool in 1911, troops shot dead two demonstrators during a railway strike. There were street riots all through the nineteenth century, and violent religious clashes over ritualism in the Church of England.

Dr Taylor was also unimpressed by the so-called threat from the Left. The minutes of a meeting of the World War I Cabinet in 1919, he said, showed the ministers of the day complaining about the dangers of a coming communist revolution, and one Cabinet member was concerned over having only a sporting shotgun to defend himself.

Even Dr Eatwell, one of the prophets of disaster whom I have quoted earlier, sees some positive aspects. In his book *Whatever Happened to Britain*, he said:

> Manufacturing is not the most pleasant of pastimes, and economics isn't everything after all. Surely in many intangible ways Britain offers a quality of life which is the envy of the world. The pageantry of royalty, the elegance of Henley, Wimbledon and Ascot, the unarmed police, the cosy pubs, the civility of everyday communication—all these are part of a way of life which seems to transcend economic decline.[2]

(It is true that he then goes on to even gloomier prophecies, but the concession is made).

Eatwell did not mention one of Britain's greatest glories: the achievement in the arts, which—particularly in the theatre—is hard to match in the English-speaking world.

The subtlety and deviousness of the British character continues to seduce Anglophiles. The British countryside remains as ravishing as ever, and no capital city in the world is as rewarding to live in as London. It is incomparably and prodigally rich, a city whose charms are impossible to exhaust, and, despite its overcrowding, it is still graceful, gracious and calm.

New York is, of course, more stimulating, but living in New York is like being high on psychedelics all the time. To return to London is to feel the peace and familiarity of an old friendship.

As the barrister-playwright John Mortimer pointed out in a spirited defence of Britain late in 1983, the annual homicide rate for the whole of the British Isles is less than one-third of that for New York City alone. He went on:

> There can really be no doubt that we live in the most beautiful, the most tolerant, the most politically mature, and for all the enormous strains put upon it by unemployment, by increasing poverty and the decline in social services, the most peaceful of countries. We really must stop telling ourselves that we should all be like Americans, who in my experience work no harder and take far longer to express the simplest of thought than we do, or like the Germans with their exaggerated respect for authority, or like the Japanese who rush out and practise playing golf for the company.

If the Thatcher experiment fails, and the patient is not improved by the bitter medicine, Britain probably will sink quite rapidly to the status of a second-rate power.

There seems to me nothing wrong with that. Second-rate powers are often, in their own way, prosperous enough, and very comfortable places to live in. Britain's difficulty at the moment is that it is living above its station, spending millions on defending the undefendable, and billions more on a deterrent which would be irrelevant in the event of a war between the superpowers.

A Britain remodelled as a small power, concentrating on service industries and high tech, exercising moral suasion rather than military might, displaying its wealth of intellectual and physical treasures to the world, and cultivating its national genius, would be a very agreeable thing to see indeed.

INDEX

385